Critical Indigenous Rights Studies

The field of 'critical indigenous rights studies' is a complex one that benefits from an interdisciplinary perspective and a realist (as opposed to an idealised) approach to indigenous peoples. This book draws on sociology of law, anthropology, political sciences and legal sciences in order to address emerging issues in the study of indigenous rights and identify directions for future research.

The first part of the volume investigates how changing identities and cultures impact rights protection, analysing how policies on development and land, and processes such as migration, interrelate with the mobilisation of identities and the realisation of rights. In the second part, new approaches related to indigenous peoples' rights are scrutinised as to their potential and relevance. They include addressing legal tensions from an indigenous peoples' rights perspective, creating space for counter-narratives on international law and designing new instruments.

Throughout the text, case studies with wide geographical scope are presented, ranging from Latin America (the book's focus) to Egypt, Rwanda and Scandinavia.

Giselle Corradi is senior researcher at the Human Rights Centre of Ghent University.

Koen De Feyter is professor of public international law at the University of Antwerp.

Ellen Desmet is assistant professor of migration law at the Faculty of Law and Criminology of Ghent University, Belgium.

Katrijn Vanhees is a PhD researcher (2014–2018) at the Human Rights Centre of Ghent University.

Routledge Research in Human Rights Law

Available titles in this series include:

The Positive Obligations of the State under the European Convention of Human Rights
Dimitris Xenos

International Human Rights Law and Domestic Violence
The effectiveness of international human rights law
Ronagh McQuigg

The Right to Religious Freedom in International Law
Between group rights and individual rights
Anat Scolnicov

The Right to Development in International Law
The Case of Pakistan
Khurshid Iqbal

Global Health and Human Rights
Legal and Philosophical Perspectives
John Harrington and Maria Stuttaford

Human Rights, Constitutional law and Belonging
The Right to Equal Belonging in Democratic Society
Elena Drymiotou

Dignity, Degrading Treatment and Torture in Human Rights Law
The Ends of Article 3 of the European Convention on Human Rights
Elaine Webster

The Right to Housing in Law and Society
Nico Moons

https://www.routledge.com/Routledge-Research-in-Human-Rights-Law/book-series/HUMRIGHTSLAW

Critical Indigenous Rights Studies

Edited by Giselle Corradi,
Koen De Feyter, Ellen Desmet
and Katrijn Vanhees

Routledge
Taylor & Francis Group
LONDON AND NEW YORK

First published 2019
by Routledge

2 Park Square, Milton Park, Abingdon, Oxfordshire OX14 4RN
52 Vanderbilt Avenue, New York, NY 10017

Routledge is an imprint of the Taylor & Francis Group, an informa business

First issued in paperback 2019

British Library Cataloguing-in-Publication Data
A catalogue record for this book is available from the British Library

Library of Congress Cataloging-in-Publication Data
Names: Corradi, Giselle, editor. | Feyter, K. de (Koen), editor. | Desmet, Ellen, editor. | Vanhees, Katrijn, editor.
Title: Critical indigenous rights studies / edited by Giselle Corradi, Koen de Feyter, Ellen Desmet, and Katrijn Vanhees.
Description: Abingdon, Oxon [UK] ; New York, NY : Routledge, 2018. | Includes bibliographical references and index.
Identifiers: LCCN 2018009977| ISBN 9781138729339 (hbk) | ISBN 9781351747561 (web pdf) | ISBN 9781351747554 (epub) | ISBN 9781351747547 (mobipocket)
Subjects: LCSH: Indigenous peoples–Civil rights. | Indigenous peoples–Legal status, laws, etc.
Classification: LCC K3247 .C75 2018 | DDC 342.08/72–dc23
LC record available at https://lccn.loc.gov/2018009977

ISBN: 978-1-138-72933-9 (hbk)
ISBN: 978-0-367-48135-3 (pbk)

Typeset in Galliard
by Swales & Willis Ltd, Exeter, Devon, UK

Contents

Contributors

J.M. (Kelly) Breemen is a PhD candidate at the Institute for Information Law (IViR, University of Amsterdam). She graduated from the Institute for Information Law's Research master's programme in Information Law (cum laude, 2012). She was nominated for the UvA Thesis Award for her master's thesis on sui generis rules for the protection of traditional cultural expressions (TCEs). Her PhD thesis concerns the protection of TCEs from three legal perspectives. Her research interests lie in the sphere of culture and law, copyright law and freedom of expression. She aims to bring together topics at the intersection of the legal domains of copyright law, cultural heritage law and human rights law.

Dorothée Cambou is a post-doctoral researcher at the University of Helsinki, formerly also a post-doctoral researcher at the Northern Institute for Environmental and Minority Law (NIEM) at the Arctic Centre in the University of Lapland. Currently, the focus of her research lies in human rights law, in particular concerning the rights of local communities and indigenous peoples. She has also developed an expertise in the field of sustainable development and Arctic governance. She holds a PhD of Laws from the Vrije Universiteit Brussel where she defended a thesis on the legal significance of the right of indigenous peoples to self-determination and its implications for the Sámi people.

Fons Coomans is professor of human rights at the Faculty of Law, Maastricht University. He holds the UNESCO Chair in Human Rights and Peace at the Department of International and European Law. He is the Director of the Maastricht Centre for Human Rights and a member of the Netherlands Network for Human Rights Research. His fields of research include the international protection of economic, social and cultural rights, the right to education, health and food in particular, the extraterritorial scope of human rights law, and international supervisory mechanisms in the field of human rights. He teaches master's courses on international human rights law and on human development and human rights at the Faculty of Law of Maastricht University. He is a founding member of the Consortium on Extraterritorial Human Rights Obligations and member of the Dutch Section of the International

Commission of Jurists (NJCM). He is also a visiting professor at the University of Cape Town.

Giselle Corradi is senior researcher at the Human Rights Centre of Ghent University. She holds a PhD in Law (2012), a master's degree in Comparative Studies of Culture (2005) and a bachelor's degree in Law (2002). Her research focuses on the relationship between legal pluralism and human rights from a legal anthropological point of view. She has conducted and supervised qualitative studies of law and society in several countries and regions, including Mozambique, Bolivia, Sierra Leone, Greece and Belgium.

Koen De Feyter is professor of public international law at the University of Antwerp, where he founded the research group on law and development. He acted as one of the founding fathers of the Law and Development Research Network (LDRn). He publishes in the area of international sustainable development law and human rights. He has conducted socio-legal fieldwork in Asia and Africa and currently contributes to a long-term research project on indigenous rights in Bolivia.

Ellen Desmet is assistant professor of migration law at the Faculty of Law and Criminology of Ghent University, Belgium. She is a member of the Human Rights Centre and of the Centre for the Social Study of Migration and Refugees (CESSMIR). Her PhD research concerned indigenous peoples' rights in the context of nature conservation, with a case study on Peru (KU Leuven, 2010). Her current research focuses on asylum and migration law, paying particular attention to human rights and legal anthropological perspectives.

Guillermo Fernández-Maldonado holds a doctorate in Law and a master's degree in Public Administration (Alcala de Henares University, Spain) and a Juris Doctor degree (Catholic University, Peru). He is the Deputy Representative of the Office of the UN High Commissioner for Human Rights (OHCHR) in Colombia. He was the Human Rights Adviser to the UN System in Ecuador (2007–2014) and the Deputy of the Human Rights Unit in the UN Mission for Afghanistan (2004–2007). Between 1994 and 2004, he worked in various capacities in the UN Mission for Guatemala. He worked at the UN Truth Commission for El Salvador (1992) and later was the Head of the Central Verification Unit for Human Rights of the UN Mission for El Salvador (1993–1994). Previously, he worked at the Peruvian Senate as legal adviser and as a Lecturer at Catholic University Law School. He has wide experience in human rights and indigenous peoples' rights.

Salvador Herencia Carrasco is a PhD candidate in Law, University of Ottawa. He is a former Legal Adviser to the Andean Commission of Jurists, a Senior Counsel to the Constitutional Court of Peru and the Chief Human Rights Legal Adviser to the Peruvian Department of Justice and Human Rights. Currently, Salvador is the Director of the Human Rights Clinic of the Human Rights Research and Education Centre, University of Ottawa and coordinator of the project "Business & Human Rights in the Americas". The project focuses on the impact of extractive industries on indigenous peoples in Latin America and the responsibility of Home States. As part of the project, he has presented before the Inter-American Commission on Human Rights and submitted amici curaie to national courts and the Inter-American Court of Human Rights on cases regarding the right to consultation, self-identification, territory as well as environmental safeguards on behalf of indigenous peoples.

Maja Janmyr is professor of International Migration Law at the University of Oslo. She is also an affiliated scholar at the American University of Beirut and has been an affiliated researcher at the American University in Cairo. Janmyr has published widely on a range of refugee law issues, including a monograph on the human rights responsibilities of the United Nations High Commissioner for Refugees (UNHCR). Her research interests are broadly in the fields of international migration law and socio-legal approaches to international law.

Liliana Lozano is a PhD researcher at the Division of Geography in the University of Leuven (KUL) in Belgium. She received a bachelor's degree in Business Administration at the Universidad del Pacifico (Peru) and a master of science degree in Culture and Development Studies at the University of Leuven. She has been a practitioner for more than ten years, leading projects related to forest, climate change and natural resource management in the Peruvian Amazon, working closely with indigenous peoples, state actors and civil society organisations. She has conducted research on the politics of climate change, focusing on the areas of multi-level governance, indigenous social movements, forest tenure reforms and conservation policy instruments, such as payment for environmental services (PES) and reducing emissions from deforestation and forest degradation (REDD+).

Asier Martínez de Bringas is assistant professor in Constitutional Law (University of Deusto) and member and researcher at the Institute of Human Rights Pedro Arrupe. Vice Dean in Research, Faculty of Law (University of Deusto: 2015–2017). His research has focused on theory of human rights, rights of indigenous peoples, multiculturalism, interculturalism, postcolonialism, critical legal studies and human rights, and so on. He has published numerous books and scientific articles on these topics. He has developed his work in Latin America with indigenous peoples and social movements.

Katrijn Vanhees is a PhD researcher (2014–2018) at the Human Rights Centre of Ghent University. She holds master's degrees in History and Law, both obtained at Ghent University. She is an affiliated researcher of the Centre for Gender Studies, University of Rwanda. Her PhD focuses on improving land rights for women in Rwanda. The research investigates the underlying causes of women's restricted access to land in Rwanda by studying the gender-based division of socio-economic power and resources in the household and the local community as a whole.

Lieselotte Viaene is a Belgian anthropologist, with a PhD in Law (2011, Ghent University, Belgium), specialising in indigenous peoples' rights, legal anthropology, transitional justice and indigenous ontologies with extensive academic and policy research experience in Guatemala, Ecuador, Colombia and Peru. She is currently (2016–2018) a Marie Skłodowska-Curie research fellow at the Centre for Social Studies (CES), University of Coimbra (Portugal) with the project GROUNDHR, which focusses on the challenges of grounding indigenous human rights epistemologies and the construction of intercultural dialogue in consultation processes on natural resources in Guatemala and Colombia. Lieselotte is also an associate post-doctoral researcher at the Centre for Human Rights of Ghent University (Belgium). She also worked, amongst others, at the Office of the United Nations High Commissioner for Human Rights (OHCHR) in Ecuador (2010–2013) where she coordinated the activities regarding indigenous and afro-descendent collective rights and transitional justice.

1 The contours of a field of critical indigenous rights studies

Giselle Corradi, Koen De Feyter, Ellen Desmet and Katrijn Vanhees

1. Setting the scene

The identification, conceptualisation and realisation of indigenous peoples' rights give rise to a variety of – often unexpected or unforeseen – challenges.[1] Some of these are related to the interplay between diverging cosmologies and subjectivities, marked by the colonial encounter. Others may be caused by the fact that not all issues relevant for indigenous peoples today are extensively or appropriately covered by existing legal frameworks and/or in academic research. Questions arise as to the normative content of indigenous peoples' rights, the transformative potential of rights discourse, and the limits of law to realise human dignity.

This volume proposes to move towards a field of 'critical indigenous rights studies'.[2] During the past decades, indigenous scholars have given shape to the emerging discipline of 'critical indigenous studies',[3] characterised as "a knowledge/power domain whereby scholars operationalize Indigenous knowledges to develop theories, build academic infrastructure, and inform our cultural and ethical practices".[4] In this context, the term 'critical' is used to distinguish between indigenous and non-indigenous epistemologies and analytics. The field of critical indigenous studies, then, aims to "challenge the power/knowledge structures and discourses through which Indigenous peoples have been framed and known".[5]

1 Most chapters in this volume are based on papers that were presented and discussed at the *Sixth Multidisciplinary Meeting on Indigenous Peoples (EMPI)*, which was co-organised by the editors at Ghent University on 10–11 June 2015.

2 Compare E Desmet and others, 'Conclusions: Towards a Field of Critical Children's Rights Studies' in W Vandenhole and others (eds), *Routledge International Handbook of Children's Rights Studies* (Routledge 2015).

3 See, for instance, the journals *Wicazo Sa Review*, the *International Journal of Critical Indigenous Studies*, the *Native American and Indigenous Studies Journal*, the *Journal of Māori and Pacific Development*, and the book series *Critical Issues in Indigenous Studies*.

4 A Moreton-Robinson, 'Introduction: Locations of Engagement in the First World' in A Moreton-Robinson (ed), *Critical Indigenous Studies: Engagements in First World Locations* (The University of Arizona Press 2016) 5.

5 ibid. It encompasses Native American studies/Indian studies, Native studies, Native Hawaiian studies, Māori Studies, and Aboriginal studies. ibid. 8.

When suggesting to engage in 'critical indigenous *rights* studies', the editors of this volume – being non-indigenous lawyers and legal anthropologists – have a different, and more modest, ambition. The research focus is more specific, pertaining to the rights of indigenous peoples. The terms 'indigenous peoples' rights' and 'indigenous rights' are used interchangeably in the book. It should be noted, however, that the meaning of either term may vary according to the context the authors are dealing with. The terms can either refer to rights of indigenous peoples as recognised in international law or to indigenous rights as understood by indigenous peoples themselves. There is a degree of overlap between these two ways of perceiving of indigenous rights. Indigenous peoples participated in the drafting of the United Nations Declaration on the Rights of Indigenous Peoples (UNDRIP), for instance, and the document thus reflects many of indigenous peoples' own understandings of their rights. Indigenous peoples also regularly invoke the rights attributed to them by international or domestic law as their rights. But it is also very well possible that elements of an indigenous people's own conception of rights are not reflected in the law, or that an indigenous people contests the authority of others to legislate on certain matters relating to their internal and local affairs, including on the determination of rights that they should have or not have.

In this volume, the term 'critical' refers to an attitude of questioning the content, functioning and potential of law: how, why and by whom are indigenous peoples' rights given shape? Which tensions arise in these struggles relating to the identification, conceptualisation and realisation of indigenous peoples' rights, and where do opportunities lie for the realisation of their rights? How do indigenous rights interrelate with other human rights, other branches of the law and other strategies of social action?

A critical approach to indigenous rights studies aims to go beyond a mere ascertainment of 'implementation gaps', the latter presupposing rights the content of which is set and not called into question any more, but which 'only' have to be implemented in order to realise their transformative potential. Although we do not underestimate how serious these gaps are, we believe that in order to understand the role of indigenous peoples' rights in social change, it is fundamental to examine the actors and factors that interplay with the formulation of rights and influence how they acquire meaning and impact in concrete contexts.

As we explain in more detail on page 15, a critical approach to indigenous rights benefits from an interdisciplinary outlook. Various chapters in this book therefore draw on several disciplinary perspectives, including sociology of law, (legal) anthropology and political sciences. In addition, a critical approach to indigenous peoples' rights does not equal a detached or neutral stance. Most chapters in (especially the second part of) this book seem – at least implicitly – to aim to contribute to a more effective realisation of indigenous peoples' rights through their analysis.

It is submitted that a critical approach towards *indigenous peoples' rights* benefits from adopting a realist (as opposed to an idealised) approach towards *indigenous peoples*. The 'otherness' of indigenous peoples, combined with their historically marginalised position in society, have injected a flavour of glorification and idealisation into much academic research. Regarding the relationship with the natural environment, for instance, the Romantic image of Indians as noble savages, expressed in the writings of Locke and Rousseau, was taken up again in the twentieth century to refer to the supposedly balanced relationship of indigenous peoples with their surroundings.[6] Such idealised constructions and stereotypes limit the possibility to adopt a critical perspective in indigenous rights research. Moreover, if such romantic images of indigenous peoples turn out to be not supported by reality, this may have detrimental consequences for the recognition of and respect for the rights of these groups.[7] As such, the assumption of a harmonious relationship of indigenous peoples with nature has had the contradictory consequence that higher expectations have been attached to the attitudes and actions of these peoples towards the environment.[8] Similarly, discussions on indigenous justice have tended to either idealise it as an expression of communal harmony or demonise it as barbaric and inherently incompatible with human rights.[9]

The book is divided into two parts. The first part investigates how changing identities and cultures impact rights protection. In the second part, new approaches related to indigenous peoples' rights are scrutinised as to their potential and relevance. They include addressing legal tensions from an indigenous peoples' rights perspective, creating space for counter-narratives on international law, and designing new instruments. The case studies cover a wide geographical scope, with a focus on Latin America, but including studies on Egypt, Rwanda and Scandinavia, as well. After briefly presenting the various contributions, this introduction reflects on what the chapters teach us regarding the critical indigenous rights approach, and identifies directions for future research.

2. Presenting the chapters

2.1. Changing identities and cultures

The definition of indigenous peoples has always been a thorny issue, not least in international law. The main risk associated with the adoption of a legal definition is that it may allow states to interpret it in a restrictive manner in order to exclude from rights protection entire groups with legitimate claims. But although international law does not define indigenous peoples, the following elements have been associated with the identification of indigenous peoples: self-identification, their

6 KH Redford, 'The Ecologically Noble Savage' (1991) 15 *Cultural Survival Quarterly*, 1.

7 R Niezen, *The Origins of Indigenism: Human Rights and the Politics of Identity* (1 edn, University of California Press 2003), 182.

8 E Desmet, *Indigenous Rights Entwined with Nature Conservation* (Intersentia 2011), 49.

9 For example, see the treatment of indigenous justice in the constitutional case *La Cocha 2* in Ecuador, as discussed by L Viaene and G Fernández-Maldonado in Chapter 10 of this volume.

existence as a group prior to colonisation, their non-dominant position in society, their multidimensional relationship to their lands, territories and resources, and their intention to maintain a distinctive way of life. The chapters in the first part of this book remind us that the fluid and hybrid nature of identity calls for a critical examination of these elements and how they are mobilised in concrete cases.

Today's increasingly interconnected world poses challenges for indigenous peoples' identities. Indigenous peoples' responses to these challenges can be situated on a spectrum that ranges from assimilation strategies to the essentialisation of their distinctiveness. Against this backdrop, Part I of the book focuses on identification processes and mobilising indigeneity strategies. Dominant societies are characterised by hegemonic identity discourses that do not tolerate the coexistence of other identities. These discourses are enforced through various strategies, such as framing any attempt to recognise an aberrant identity as a threat to national security. Chapters 2 and 3 by Janmyr and Vanhees, respectively, argue that there is a need for indigenous peoples to address and discuss issues that arise from these contentious situations. Chapter 4 by Martínez de Bringas identifies the legal challenges entailed by the fluid and dynamic nature of identity in contexts of migration. How do indigenous identities evolve in contexts where these identities are often a priori delineated? This question constitutes a common denominator of the three chapters of the first part of the book. In addition, these chapters move beyond the ideal image of indigenous peoples as a homogeneous and harmonious group.

In Chapter 2, Janmyr focuses on the struggle of the Nubian people for the return to ancestral land in Egypt. She identifies the tension between preserving the hegemonic narrative of a unified, national Egyptian identity and the challenges of the Nubians to be recognised as a group with a particular identity. Throughout the years, Nubians have employed different frameworks to advocate for a return to their ancestral lands, each with varying success. She explains how the Nubians have endeavoured to frame themselves as indigenous, as a strategical manoeuvre to claim back their ancestral lands. However, framing their cause as indigenous has meant a setback for their advocacy efforts because their claim was considered as a hostile threat to national unity by the Egyptian government. Changes in political power and the wave of Arab nationalism further complicated their struggle for a return to their ancestral lands. By explaining how the Nubians attempt to mobilise different frames to negotiate a return to their ancestral lands, Janmyr sheds light on how these discourses may coexist and how they are flexibly employable. She discusses how both the minority rights discourse and the indigenous rights framework can be relevant for the Nubians' struggle. Furthermore, Janmyr draws our attention to the fact that actors with opposite interests can appropriate exactly the same discourses. To illustrate this point, she describes how the Egyptian government enforced a resettlement programme for the Nubians under the guise of 'development' policies. This political move instigated the Nubians to reappropriate the development discourse to lobby for a return.

Interestingly, Janmyr questions the relevance of land ownership for the construction of Nubian identity in present-day Egypt. Does the loss of ancestral lands imply an impoverishment of their collective identity? Besides mapping mobilisation strategies from an heterogenous identity perspective, she utilises a realistic approach to highlight intragroup tensions. By de-essentialising the Nubian identity, she diversifies Nubians' advocacy tactics along generational lines. No consensus is reached when it comes to deciding which strategic path should be chosen to support their cause. The old generation prefers to handle the issue through domestic frameworks, such as the development frame. Yet, the younger generation prefers to take the matter up to the regional level by filing a complaint against the Egyptian government with the African Commission on Human and Peoples' Rights.

The next chapter by Vanhees explores the struggles of Twa people to position themselves within the Rwandan discourse on identity at the political level and highlights two possible pitfalls when choosing 'indigenousness' as a category of analysis and advocacy work. Twa people of Rwanda claim to be descendants of the Pygmy communities of Eastern Africa. Often forgotten or ignored in accounts on Rwanda, Twa people are the third group identity in Rwanda, besides Hutu and Tutsi. Research has estimated that nowadays, 25,000 to 30,000 Twa people live in Rwanda, which is an estimated 0.41% of the entire population. Prior to the rezoning of the forests and the rise of green politics, Twa used to live in the forestry areas of Rwanda as hunter–gatherers. However, their way of living was threatened due to the increasing loss of forests. Nowadays, their socio-economic situation is characterised by poverty, a low education level, discrimination and landlessness. In its efforts to improve Twa's living conditions, civil society denounces the ongoing structural discrimination and their impoverishment. During the process by civil society of exploring different advocacy pathways, the notion of indigenousness has come to the fore. In her chapter, Vanhees points out different challenges when mobilising this framework. To begin with, explicitly emphasising a particular identity that deviates from the Rwandan notion of 'oneness' constitutes a threat to national security. The political discourse of unified identity in Rwanda does not allow for any identity diversification, given the country's horrendous past with hegemonic identity politics.

In the second part of her chapter Vanhees elaborates on how identifying as indigenous entails a risk of essentialising Twa's lifestyle. Their socio-economic situation is often too easily causally linked to the fact that they are part of a discriminated or historically marginalised group. Their current land situation is indeed significantly worse than that of other groups in Rwandan society; however, the reason behind this cannot be entirely based upon their identification as a marginalised group. Consequently, this chapter explores how Twa's socio-economic identity has changed because of different survival strategies in order to adapt to an ever-changing society. It touches upon three main themes concerning land: the genocide of 1994, the formalisation of the land market and land scarcity.

The final part of the chapter draws attention to the intragroup dynamics within Twa communities that create opposing interests and claims to land. It focuses specifically on Twa women's struggle to gain access to land and how they articulate certain land claims within their community. By highlighting women's experiences, this part intends to shed light on the intersectional features of Twa's socio-economic situation that need to be taken into account during the identification process. In her conclusion, Vanhees states that exploring the challenges of Twa communities when advocating for their specific needs reveals the complexities of manoeuvring in a society that is characterised by dominant identity discourses. Moreover, her chapter points out the need to accommodate transformative and intersectional (gender) features of group identity in the identification debate in order to avoid reification of their destitute socio-economic status.

In Chapter 4, Martínez de Bringas analyses how migration processes affect the identities and rights of indigenous peoples, drawing on insights from, among others, international human rights law and the sociology of law. The growing international recognition of indigenous rights has not been matched by a comparable enthusiasm of states for migrant rights in general or indigenous migrant rights in particular. From a methodological point of view, Martínez de Bringas points out that both the lack of sociological data on indigenous migratory processes and the absence of a conceptual framework on the relationship between indigenous peoples and migration pose specific challenges for this type of research. Mapping indigenous migratory processes, he distinguishes between 'indigenous ancestral mobility' and 'transnational indigenous migration' and takes the rural world/urban world dialectic into account. To analyse the sociological complexity of indigenous migration, he suggests to study both the causes of migration (i.e. voluntary and forced migration) and its consequences, distinguishing between the impact of indigenous migration on the indigenous communities of origin and the impact of non-indigenous migration on indigenous communities.

Martínez de Bringas argues that indigenous migratory processes are mainly triggered by the violation of their individual and collective human rights, for instance, concerning the ancestral territory. He identifies various tensions relating to indigenous migration, for instance, between how indigenous peoples are constructed in human rights instruments, on the one hand, and in a migration context, on the other, as well as between the experiences of indigenous identity in the host and home countries, for instance, relating to the degree of politicisation. In his conclusion, he calls for more research on the role of cultural identities in migratory processes from the perspective of indigenous migrants themselves. The challenges arising from the fact that indigenous migrants need protection of their human rights, both as migrants and as indigenous peoples, also require more in-depth study. A particular issue of attention constitutes the extraterritorial application of human rights that were conceived to be applied only in ancestral indigenous territories.

As these chapters illustrate, identities are not only changing because of external influences. Internal dynamics may change a group's identity from within. Both Janmyr and Vanhees explore intragroup tensions with regard to claiming group rights. Janmyr has found opposing views on rights mobilisation strategies between different generations. In the chapter of Vanhees, intergenerational tensions concerning attitudes towards land are identified, as well. Other tensions can be situated along gender lines. For instance, Vanhees argues that, even though

Twa people are generally known for their underprivileged socio-economic situation, Twa women are victim of intersectional discrimination. Their position as a woman within a marginalised community causes additional challenges to secure their livelihood. The chapter by Martínez de Bringas deals with intragroup differences in terms of mobile vs. non-mobile indigenous sub-groups and the implications of these distinctions in terms of rights enjoyment. As his chapter demonstrates, a third challenge of changing identities is the impact of increased migration and the de-territorialisation of indigenous peoples. These developments question the so-called intrinsic link between land and indigeneity, not only in definitional debates but also with regard to rights claims. With these reflections, the first part of this book underscores the need to ground indigenous peoples' rights on a dynamic interpretation of indigenous peoples' identity.

2.2. Innovating the law

The second part of the book explores new lines of thinking and recent initiatives related to indigenous peoples' rights along three thematic axes: legal tensions existing between indigenous peoples' rights and other branches of law, the development of counter-hegemonic narratives of international law and the emergence of new legal instruments on indigenous peoples.

2.2.1. Dealing with legal tensions in light of indigenous peoples' rights

The first section of the second part focuses on the protection of immaterial goods of indigenous peoples, namely, traditional non-western knowledge (chapter of Coomans) and traditional cultural expressions (chapter of Breemen). The chapters analyse how existing legal constructions could be interpreted and applied as to better account for the specific rights of indigenous peoples concerning the protection of their knowledge and culture. These constructions specifically concern a human right (the human right to enjoy the benefits of scientific progress, chapter of Coomans) and a legal branch (intellectual property law, with a focus on copyrights law, chapter of Breemen).

In Chapter 5, Coomans aims to make the human right to enjoy the benefits of scientific progress (REBSP) more concrete and thus more relevant. There is an increased need to discuss this right, as knowledge production continues to be legally defined on the basis of an underlying rationale of monetary output in a globalised economy. Often this definitional process takes places in the global North, where progress and the benefits of scientific production are centralised. This situation disregards the value and importance of traditional non-western knowledge that has different definitional features, such as knowledge guardianship, instead of patent ownership of knowledge based on market-driven logics.

In today's globalised world, Coomans therefore proposes a dual perspective on the REBSP. Such a perspective recognises that scientific progress may result from both industrialised societies *and* traditional non-western knowledge systems. Adopting an analytical and normative approach, he discusses the legal basis of the REBSP as well as its normative content and scope. After clarifying the concepts of 'science', 'progress' and 'benefits', which are used in various human rights instruments, Coomans zooms in on questions surrounding the identification of the rights holders and duty bearers of the REBSP. Whereas it is, for instance, generally accepted that the state is the main duty bearer of the REBSP, there is less agreement with regard to the role of private corporations. He then discusses the substance of the REBSP in various specific situations, as well as the nature and scope of the obligations flowing from the REBSP, paying particular attention to extraterritorial obligations.

In order to enhance the significance of the REBSP from a dual perspective, Coomans identifies various challenges. To begin with, several questions arise as to the operationalisation of the REBSP in a world of growing inequality between "'have' and 'have-not' countries in science and capacity to apply scientific advances". Other challenges include possible conflicts of interest between human rights and intellectual property rights, as well as the development of a human rights-based approach to the implementation of the REBSP. In order to ensure full participation of indigenous and local communities, 'Community Protocols', in which communities lay down rules regarding the access to and use of traditional knowledge on their genetic resources by third parties, may be an inspiring practice. Given the initial phase of the conceptual development of the REBSP, Coomans suggests drafting a manual within the framework of the Convention on Biological Diversity in order to identify different approaches to the RESBP, list good practices and provide guidelines for implementation.

Chapter 6 by Breemen explores the interrelation between copyright law and human rights law in the context of the protection of traditional cultural expressions (TCEs). These two legal domains are assessed for tensions – for instance, between indigenous and non-indigenous views on creative production and protection – and opportunities for protecting TCEs.

Breemen starts with contextualising the emergence of TCEs within the wider debate on indigenous peoples' rights. Moreover, she points out the need to discuss the protection of TCEs on a global level due to an increasingly interconnected world. Consequently, there are various views on what exactly TCEs encompass and how they should be protected. Defining TCEs proves to be problematic because indigenous knowledge systems and intellectual property law have different interpretations of traditional cultural expressions. Indigenous peoples regard it as collectively owned knowledge that is integrated in their way of living. From an intellectual property rights perspective, on the other hand, TCE is interpreted as a static concept that can be defined in a clear-cut way. Following a realistic approach to the definitional debate, Breemen seeks to answer the question of who has the power to define the concept of TCEs.

Furthermore, the chapter highlights the contrasting views between the copyright law approach and indigenous peoples concerning the aim of TCE protection. The former perspective desires to protect a monopoly on TCEs, whereas the latter's interpretation of protection shifts the focus towards a user regulation of the communally shared knowledge.

In the final part, Breemen explains how a human rights perspective could be capable of transcending these copyrights tensions, by discussing four human rights concepts in the context of TCE protection: dignity, equality and non-discrimination, self-determination and participation. She concludes that the human rights framework creates the opportunity to move beyond the ill-fitting copyrights rationale and to create a comprehensive answer to TCE protection issues that does justice to indigenous views. She points out the limitations of a human rights approach, as well, warning for the consequences for individuals of a collective identity approach and indicating possible implementation challenges.

Both chapters focus on tensions within the law and the inappropriateness of the current design of these legal constructions – which were not conceived to deal with the (collective) concerns of indigenous peoples. Even though the two authors have a different starting point and a different way of engaging with intellectual property rights law, they both ground their analysis in a human rights perspective as a way to deal with legal tensions in light of indigenous peoples' rights. Coomans starts from a human right (the REBSP) and points to its complex and strained relationship with the intellectual property rights regime. His analysis mostly stays within human rights law, suggesting a dual approach to the REBSP, which considers both western and non-western knowledge. Breemen starts from an intellectual property approach and points to its limited possibilities to adequately protect TCEs. She proposes that a human rights perspective could offer a way out of at least some of these tensions. Finally, both authors point to the drawbacks inherent in a human rights approach, for instance, regarding implementation.

2.2.2. Creating space for counter-narratives of international law

Historically, public international law is a product of negotiations between states, from which indigenous peoples have been largely excluded. Two chapters in our book discuss experiences of indigenous peoples that have consciously decided to engage with public international law. In doing so, however, they are also challenging statist understandings of the law. They are using avenues offered by international legal instruments to insert into the legal system indigenous understandings of, respectively, responsible environmental management and human rights – concepts that were in the past defined by states only.

Chapter 7 by Lozano focuses on agency and reclaiming decision-making power by the indigenous Amazonian peoples. It pays specific attention to environmental regulations in the context of climate change. Even though mapping the issue of climate change is science based, the solution is mostly inspired by neoliberal objectives. For instance, emissions trading is a cap-and-trade policy intended to reduce pollution by offering economic incentives to achieve this goal. This climate change apparatus, which is mostly inspired by market-oriented approaches, does not respond to the reality of indigenous Amazonian peoples. One of these regulations is the Reducing Emissions from Deforestation and Degradation (REDD+) mechanism. REDD+ is designed to stabilise greenhouse gas emissions in the atmosphere by imposing regulatory frameworks to accomplish this objective. This initiative was created at international level but relies on countries' commitment to design and implement the core ideas of REDD+ in a national instrument.

Lozano analyses the responses of the Coordinator of the Indigenous Organizations of the Amazon Basin (COICA) to the REDD+ mechanism. REDD+ has been criticised for destabilising land relations and enforcing forest management schemes that negatively affect indigenous peoples' livelihoods. However, it also enables local communities to participate in the designing process at the national level. By customising the discourse on environmental conservation, COICA has gained the status of a valuable actor within the wider debate on REDD+. Inter-institutional activist strategies consist of different tools such as networking, diplomacy and constructing alliances.

As a result of their discontent with REDD+, COICA has successfully constructed a counter-narrative, the so-called Amazon Indigenous REDD+ (AIR) that uses indigenous concepts of responsible nature management as a basis. Indigenous leaders have mastered to speak on behalf of their peoples in both a global and local setting. The process of norm socialisation enables them to translate local realities on a global level and vice versa. Using indigenous peoples' own language and concepts, the counter-narrative is more responsive to the lived realities of the Amazonian peoples. By analysing this counter-narrative, the chapter deconstructs the role of indigenous peoples with regard to climate change. Lozano warns for an idealised description of indigenous peoples as environmental agents, but at the same time emphasises the benefits of this image for advocacy efforts. Their efforts have resulted in an alternative framing of the REDD+ debate and have successfully engaged the international community in their discourse.

Chapter 8 by Herencia Carrasco approaches the case law on indigenous rights in the inter-American human rights system from 'third world approaches to international law' (TWAIL) perspective. He argues that there is a need to adopt such a perspective due to the inherent limitations of the inter-American system that work against economic and social rights, and collective rights.

After decolonisation, TWAIL scholars argued that international law should become less state centred and should open up to social movements and indigenous peoples. These actors should participate in international lawmaking and in international organisations. Third world states should act as facilitators and thus discontinue practices of marginalisation inherited from the former colonial powers. Human rights law lends itself in particular to this further 'decolonisation': the direct participation of indigenous peoples in the reconstitution of the human rights paradigm would contribute to its inclusiveness. The implication would be that their collective concerns, over issues regarding their identity, autonomy, territory and culture, would be at the forefront of new human rights discourse.

Herencia Carrasco perceives new opportunities for adopting a TWAIL perspective within the inter-American human rights system due to the 2016 adoption of the American Declaration on the Rights of Indigenous Peoples and recent decisions acknowledging that indigenous peoples are collective subjects under international law. He also recognises, however, that a TWAIL approach to the inter-American human rights system remains to be elaborated fully and merits further study.

Retrospectively, at the heart of both efforts is a battle for the recognition of indigenous peoples as authors of international law and, more broadly, for the recognition of their normative conceptions as a source of law.

2.2.3. Designing new instruments

The third section of the second part of the book deals with two recent initiatives to design legal instruments on indigenous peoples. The first one is situated at the transnational level, that is, the case of the draft Nordic Sámi Convention (chapter by Cambou), whereas the second one concerns the national level, that is, the case of the law on the coordination and cooperation between indigenous and ordinary jurisdictions in Ecuador (chapter by Viaene and Fernández-Maldonado). Although these initiatives involve very different political contexts, both chapters show that the integration of international standards on indigenous peoples into new legal tools that emerge within other scales of governance is far from automatic. Indigenous peoples continue to fight long struggles for the incorporation of their human rights into national and transnational legal arenas.

Chapter 9 by Cambou discusses the relevance of the 2005 draft Nordic Sámi Convention and how the right to self-determination is delineated in it. Originally proposed by the Sámi Council, a non-governmental organisation, as an instrument that would include the Sámi in Russia, the 2005 draft Convention applies to the Sámi peoples of Finland, Norway and Sweden. The final goal is to adopt a binding treaty that first needs to be approved by all three Sámi parliaments and is subsequently subject to ratification by the three states. The depository (Norway) will in due course notify not only the three governments, but also the three Sámi parliaments of the entry into force of the Convention. The 2005 draft Convention therefore offers a novel approach to treaty making in contemporary international law on indigenous peoples. However, at the time of writing, uncertainty remains about the ultimate outcome of the drafting process.

Cambou's contribution focuses on how the draft Convention deals with the vexed issue of the right to self-determination. Since this right is recognised in the draft Convention, Cambou analyses its concrete scope along political, resource and transnational dimensions. The draft Convention reflects a "sliding scale model of self-determination", according to which the more significant the issue is to the Sámi peoples, the more influence they have over the matter, including a limited right to veto certain decisions that could have a damaging impact on vulnerable Sámi areas. In addition, the draft Convention requires that national governments undertake measures to clarify and secure the property rights of the Sámi at the local level. According to Cambou, while the provisions of the draft Convention do not follow the letter of international legal instruments on indigenous peoples, it constitutes an adequate model to implement the right to self-determination in the Nordic context.

As Cambou demonstrates, a consequence of perceiving of the Sámi as a people is the recognition of their 'transnational' right to maintain and develop contacts, relations and cooperation across the borders of the states where they live. If the ratification process were successful, the entry into force of the Convention would demonstrate to governments around the world, so Cambou argues, that inclusion of the right to self-determination of indigenous peoples does not necessarily threaten state territorial integrity. Nevertheless, it will require the signatory parties to undertake significant legal and institutional reforms, and the provisions on the use of land and water – typically representing a compromise between the negotiating parties – may prove to be contentious in their practical implementation.

In Chapter 10, Viaene and Fernández-Maldonado analyse the dynamics at play in Ecuador during the drafting processes of secondary legislation to regulate legal pluralism; that is, the articulation between indigenous and ordinary jurisdictions. The adoption of such a law is envisaged in the 2008 Constitution, which is among the most progressive in the world regarding indigenous rights as it aligns with international standards enshrined in ILO Convention 169 and the UNDRIP. But even though various bills have been drafted, no law has been enacted so far. Adopting an 'implementation gap perspective', the authors of this chapter aim to identify the causes of this gap between the state's obligation to respect indigenous peoples' rights to administer justice and the effective realisation of this right.

As privileged observers of, and participants to, the drafting processes of this coordination and cooperation law given their functions at the Office of the United Nations High Commissioner for Human Rights at the time, the authors provide a detailed account of the socio-political dynamics surrounding these processes – within both the Executive and the larger political arena. Obstacles to approving such a bill included racist and colonial attitudes permeating dominant Ecuadorian society, the lack of a grounded understanding of indigenous justice and a gradual drifting away of the Correa government's policies and practices from the principles that had been enshrined – by the same political movement – in the Constitution. They also argue that some political actors were concerned about the negative impact the implementation of indigenous peoples' right to administer justice would have on the prevalent extractivist development model, due to the entwinement of indigenous peoples' rights to administer justice and to their lands, territories and resources. In the *La Cocha 2* judgement, concerning a homicide case, the Constitutional Court aligned itself with the restrictive approach that the Correa government had been developing towards indigenous justice, attributing material jurisdiction to the ordinary justice system.

Viaene and Fernández-Maldonado stress the role of historical and current unequal power relations between the dominant society and indigenous peoples to explain the unfulfilled potential of the 2008 Constitution regarding indigenous peoples' rights to administer justice. The Ecuadorian case shows that international and constitutional law's recognition of indigenous rights is not necessarily matched by changing power relationships on the ground. They conclude with some reservations as to whether a coordination and cooperation law, if adopted, would succeed in realising indigenous peoples' rights to administer justice.

Taken together, these two chapters indicate that the coherent consolidation of indigenous peoples' rights at different levels of governance constitutes a major pre-requisite for these rights to contribute to reshaping power relations between indigenous and dominant groups. As the chapter by Cambou argues, strengthening indigenous peoples' political rights by securing their participation in decision-making processes in different spheres (internally, nationally and internationally) is key. But the actual realisation of these rights presupposes a redistribution of power that privileged sectors typically resist. This is all the more the case in view of indigenous peoples' interests and claims over land and natural resources. With this in mind, the chapter by Viaene and Fernández-Maldonado shows that the implementation of indigenous political rights may easily come to be under threat, even in contexts where strong constitutional protections are in place. In a way, these realities remind us of the importance of scrutinising the role of law in social change from an empirical point of view. As the case of Ecuador teaches us, although the legal developments in the case of the Sámi seem to be positive, it remains to be seen what concrete effects they will have.

3. Moving towards a field of critical indigenous rights studies

3.1. The limits of the law

Our authors have no difficulty in acknowledging the limitations of law in dealing with indigenous issues. For the sake of clarity, these limitations can be grouped as limitations inherent in the law itself, limitations flowing from the ambivalent attitude of indigenous peoples towards using non-indigenous law and the limited impact of law on social change.

The inherent limitations of international law in general, and of human rights law specifically, are well known. They are definitely prevalent also in the area of indigenous rights, so it may be worth going through them here once again. States are the dominant norm entrepreneurs in public international law. The adoption of international instruments requires gaining the support of a sufficient number of relevant states. This often results in the use of vague language even in provisions that touch upon the object and purpose of the instrument. Vague language leaves room for various interpretations, and there is no guarantee that the interpretation favoured by indigenous peoples will prove to be the dominant one in international or domestic practice (Coomans, Herencia Carrasco).

Public international law is a fragmented system. There are many different lawmakers. This may create opportunities at fora that are sympathetic to indigenous rights, but it also leads to tensions between international instruments that are based on very different premises (Breemen, Coomans).

Numerous international instruments that are referenced throughout the book as potentially beneficial to indigenous peoples are not legally binding.

The UNDRIP, a key legal instrument for the protection of indigenous rights, was adopted as a non-binding declaration. Difference of opinion remains on the extent to which provisions of the Declaration have passed the customary law test.

Treaties are only binding on states upon their consent. States remain free to ratify a treaty or not. ILO Convention 169, another crucial instrument on indigenous rights, has only been ratified by a 'fairly small' (Breemen) number of states.

International enforcement mechanisms in the area of human and indigenous rights tend to have little means to ensure implementation. Avenues for access to these mechanisms for individuals, and particularly for peoples, remain limited and, when available, are often subject to separate state consent. Human rights mechanisms may give more or less attention to certain rights within their brief (Coomans). They may be conservative in allowing indigenous peoples to contribute to the interpretation of rights (Herencia Carrasco). They may be influenced by political considerations (see Janmyr on the limited impact of the Universal Periodic Review process and Martínez de Bringas on paper indigenous rights in a migration context).

Broadening the perspective, it is clear that 'the law' on indigenous rights consists of regulation at multiple levels, ranging from the global over the regional to the national and the indigenous. The legal system is complex and, even with the necessary political will, technically difficult to manage. In any case, its operationalisation requires further (legal, judicial) intervention by actors that have been vested with the necessary authority. Once again, very often those actors will be state institutions rather than indigenous peoples; representation of indigenous peoples within those institutions may be very limited or non-existent (Janmyr, Vanhees). State institutions decide on the effect of international law within the domestic legal system and, within domestic law on how to deal with indigenous jurisdiction (which may include denying that any indigenous peoples exist on the territory altogether (Janmyr)), and in cases of endorsement of legal pluralism, with the coordination between the ordinary and the indigenous jurisdiction. Indigenous law may not be part of legal education, and judicial operators may not recognise the validity of indigenous jurisdiction and persist in colonial or racist attitudes (Viaene and Fernández-Maldonado).

The characteristics outlined here above may contribute to the hesitation of indigenous peoples to rely on internationally recognised indigenous rights. Clearly, they do not own such rights, and thus, strategic considerations will determine whether use is made of them. Many factors may impact such a decision, most prominently a pragmatic assessment of the effects the claim and its potential outcome will have on the living conditions of the relevant group (compare Janmyr on factors explaining the move towards the framing of Nubian demands within the international indigenous rights framework).

Indigenous peoples are not internally homogeneous: there may also be significant divisions within the community. This may explain why in some instances rights claims are made, while in other instances where human or indigenous rights could be equally relevant, no claims are forthcoming (Vanhees on women's rights).

In a migration context, the fracture between the migrant group and their community of origin (Martínez de Bringas) may be irreparable.

The alternative to using indigenous rights recognised in (international) public law is to reject the existing law as a law of others that is unable to adequately respond to indigenous needs and instead to assert sovereign lawmaking. This may be expressed through an insistence on self-determination and self-identification or through the production of international indigenous instruments that offer an alternative to international law. In its most radical form, this may mean giving up any protection offered by the existing law (Breemen).

Finally, the book offers several examples of state failures to implement indigenous rights recognised in international and/or domestic law. Clearly, the law is not enough, particularly when the exercise of rights by indigenous peoples contradicts the economic policies of state institutions (Herencia Carrasco). The law grounds action, and indigenous rights offer opportunities for legal mobilisation by indigenous groups (Janmyr), but social change triggered by law "is determined by the interaction between power, political struggles, and the instrumental interests of the main stakeholders" (Viaene and Fernández-Maldonado). In their case study on Ecuador, Viaene and Fernández-Maldonado discover a process of 'deconstitutionalisation' following the introduction of legal pluralism, leading to a limitation of the application of indigenous jurisdiction. They express doubts about whether a law properly regulating the relationship between indigenous jurisdiction and ordinary jurisdiction would suffice to enable the exercise of indigenous justice by indigenous authorities. The assignment of state financial resources to strengthen the indigenous jurisdiction may be of primary importance.

3.2. Thinking beyond the legal discipline

Given the limits of the law discussed in the previous section, there is a need to study the position of indigenous peoples within and beyond the law from different disciplinary perspectives. The chapters in this book demonstrate different ways of interdisciplinary engagement. A first observation is that the level of explicitness regarding disciplinary positionality diverges. Some authors clearly indicate the disciplines or fields they draw upon. Examples include Martínez de Bringas (sociology of law and international human rights law), Janmyr (legal mobilisation studies), Coomans (legal sciences) and Carrasco (TWAIL scholarship and international human rights law). Whereas an explicit disciplinary 'attribution' is not always necessary, this may help in interpreting how certain concepts and frameworks are used. In other chapters, pinpointing the (inter)disciplinary position of the authors appears more difficult (e.g. Lozano, Vanhees, Viaene and Fernández-Maldonado). This may testify to the growing interconnectedness and cross-fertilisation between (inter)disciplines such as the anthropology of law, the sociology of law and the political sciences. It may also suggest an impossibility or reluctance of identifying oneself with one or more disciplinary perspectives.

Secondly, the degree of interdisciplinary interaction[10] differs. Whereas some chapters aim to 'combine' various perspectives, other chapters take in their own analysis a predominantly legal approach. Yet, the way they do so is inspired by insights from outside the legal sciences, as regarding, for instance, the contribution of non-western knowledge to scientific progress (Coomans), the significance of TCEs (Breemen) and the multidimensionality of the right of self-determination in the eyes of indigenous peoples (Cambou). These insights contribute to the formulation of more adequate responses within the law.

As research methodology is concerned, about half of the chapters are based on empirical research, mostly semi-structured interviews, sometimes also participant observation (Janmyr, Lozano, Martínez de Bringas, Vanhees, Viaene and Fernández-Maldonado). The other chapters draw more on analytical and/or normative methods (Breemen, Cambou, Coomans and Herencia Carrasco). This demonstrates that critical indigenous rights studies can be developed both as desk studies and on the basis of fieldwork.

Various chapters point to the *inadequacy of prevailing conceptual, theoretical and normative frameworks* to address the realities and rights of indigenous peoples within both the legal sciences and the social sciences. Breemen highlights the frictions between the basic tenets of copyrights law and indigenous views. Martínez de Bringas points to the substantive contribution that an international sociology of migration processes could make regarding indigenous peoples. Other chapters focus more on the *operationalisation* of indigenous rights, for instance, through the adoption of a transnational convention (Cambou) or a coordination law between ordinary and indigenous jurisdictions (Viaene and Fernández-Maldonado).

Another observation is that 'human rights' are analysed from different points of view, which are embedded in different (inter)disciplinary perspectives. Human rights are understood in various ways, for instance, as 'law' (e.g. Breemen, Cambou, and Coomans) or as 'discourse' (e.g. Lozano, Janmyr, and Vanhees).[11] In some chapters on human rights law, the rights recognised to indigenous peoples in international human rights law constitute a *benchmark* against which to evaluate other developments (such as the adoption of a transnational convention on the right to self-determination, cf. Cambou, or a law coordinating ordinary and indigenous jurisdiction, cf. Viaene and Fernández-Maldonado). Human rights law may also be presented as a *solution* to address legal developments in other branches of the law that do not take indigenous peoples' specific rights into account (Breemen). In other chapters, human rights law itself is the *object of study and critique* in a less or more radical way. Coomans proposes a dual approach in order for the human right to enjoy the benefits of

10 See generally JT Klein, *Interdisciplinarity: History, Theory, and Practice* (Wayne State University Press 1990).

11 See M Goodale, 'Locating Rights, Envisioning Law Between the Global and the Local' in M Goodale and SE Merry (eds), *The Practice of Human Rights: Tracking Law between the Global and the Local* (Cambridge University Press 2007), 5–10.

scientific process to be locally relevant. Herencia Carrasco argues that the inter-American human rights system should be fundamentally transformed if it wants to offer real protection to the economic, social, cultural and collective rights of indigenous peoples. He holds that

> if we are to advance the field of human rights law within the [Inter-American human rights system], we must think beyond existing treaties and increasingly turn to socially-based evidence to expand our notions of law—to progress towards systems of law that have indigenous peoples at the forefront and not only at the receiving end.

Engaging with human rights *discourse* can be very fluctuating, as Janmyr shows in her chapter on Egypt. Whereas the constitutional enshrinement of the issue of Nubian return led to a declining interest in human rights discourse, recent decrees envisaging militarisation and agricultural development of Nubian lands triggered a revalorisation of human rights among the Nubians.

Another indication of the interdisciplinary perspective is the implicit and explicit attention paid to issues such as agency, intersectionality and framing that are well developed as analytical frameworks in the social sciences. Lozano, for instance, recounts how a transnational indigenous movement, faced with the inappropriate REDD+-framework, proposed its own alternative. Herencia Carrasco calls upon a fundamental transformation of international law, in which indigenous peoples can participate on an equal level as states. Vanhees warns that the agency of the Twa when dealing with their land has not been sufficiently highlighted. This leads to distorted explanations of their socio-economic disadvantaged situation, as being attributable to their "stereotypical identity". She also uses intersectionality to analyse intragroup dynamics with a specific focus on gender. Janmyr discusses the use of indigeneity as a frame for the Nubians to advance their claims.

Finally, every disciplinary perspective, or even combination of various (inter)disciplinary perspectives, inevitably only sheds a particular ray of light on a particular part of reality. This volume remains within the legal and social sciences. A truly holistic understanding of how indigenous peoples' rights, and in particular their rights to their lands, territories and resources, acquire meaning requires a more robust interdisciplinary approach, combining not only different conceptual and theoretical frameworks from within the legal and social sciences, but including insights from the exact sciences (such as conservation biology and ecology), as well.

4. New directions in indigenous rights research: breaking its isolation

Despite the advances in the recognition of the rights of indigenous peoples at international and regional levels, indigenous peoples continue to struggle to operationalise these rights in contexts that are deeply marked by discrimination and exclusion. Against this backdrop, the chapters of this book have analysed the challenges involved from different perspectives. In addition, some of these chapters have reflected on where opportunities may lie for the realisation of indigenous rights. The following lines of enquiry have transpired, in turn pointing towards new directions in indigenous rights research: first, heterogeneity, transformation and hybridity of indigenous identity; second, the relevance of indigenous rights for the common interest of society; third, the role of indigenous rights as a stepping stone towards the recognition of rights of non-indigenous groups; fourth, the effects of indigenous rights in social and cultural change; and fifth, indigenous peoples' counter-hegemonic strategies of resistance. What all these topics have in common is a concern with breaking the isolation of indigenous rights (research). We believe this would contribute to improving social justice for both indigenous peoples and societies at large.

4.1. Dealing with heterogeneity, transformation and hybridity of indigenous identity

The social construction of a group as indigenous entails a collective process of identification in which prominence is given to that which distinguishes an indigenous group from the rest of society. This logic of differentiation forms the basis upon which indigenous peoples are conferred specific rights.[12] While it is undeniable that indigenous peoples reflect characteristics that distinguish them from other groups, it is necessary to question how this differential logic works in practice. In her contribution on indigenous peoples' involvement in the REDD+ global debate, Lozano argues that indigenous peoples' strategic reliance on a different identity, tightly intertwined with the environment, proved useful. But as the chapters by Janmyr and Vanhees clearly illustrate, not all groups with potential claims to indigeneity see this logic as advantageous or even possible. This is strongly related with the particular colonial histories that affected different regions and with how dominant and marginalised groups were constituted in colonial and post-colonial periods. Although the cases discussed by these authors are located in Africa, a region where indigenousness is highly contested,[13] Chapters 2 and 3 raise issues that are equally applicable in contexts where the identification of indigenous groups may seem less problematic, namely, how to take account of transformation, intragroup diversity and hybrid identities.

In most parts of the globe, indigenous ways of living have been eroded or are under serious pressure, which tends to diminish group cohesion. This creates

12 This is not the exclusive case of indigenous peoples, but it applies to several groups and minorities in general. On this topic see D Cooper (2004) *Challenging Diversity, Rethinking Equality and the Value of Difference* (Cambridge University Press) and R Dhamoon, *Identity/Difference Politics: How Difference is Produced and Why it Matters* (UBC Press 2009).

13 FM Ndahinda, *Indigenousness in Africa. A Contested Legal Framework for Empowerment of 'Marginalised' Communities* (TMC Asser Press, 2009).

internal frictions and opens the door for well-known strategies to divide and rule. In addition, as the chapter by Martínez de Bringas shows, current realities of global interconnectedness and mobility may result in indigenous migration towards urban centres nationally and transnationally in search for a better life. In these contexts, indigenous peoples develop new forms of identity. At the same time, large segments of society are disenfranchised by the very same elites that benefit from the exploitation of indigenous peoples. Consequently, it becomes relevant to study how experiences of heterogeneity within indigenous groups, as well as experiences that members of indigenous groups share with members of other groups in society, may become appropriate platforms for claiming rights. This requires the use of nuanced analytical frameworks to explain the connections between identity (trans)formation and social action.

4.2. The relevance of indigenous rights for the common interest of society

International human rights law has made significant progress in the recognition of indigenous peoples' rights, and although the exact scope of some of these rights may remain contested, a variety of actors, including indigenous peoples themselves, have resorted to human rights law in order to advance indigenous claims. Several chapters in this book reflect the view that integrating international standards on indigenous peoples into other branches of law and levels of governance constitutes a pre-requisite for the realisation of indigenous peoples' rights. At the same time, attention is paid to the reasons why the concrete implementation of these standards remains difficult. As we argue below, additional research is needed on the consequences of implementing indigenous rights for the common interest of societies.

In their chapters, Coomans and Breemen examine what international standards on indigenous peoples imply for legal regimes that impinge upon traditional non-western forms of knowledge and cultural expressions. Both authors remark that international standards regard indigenous customary laws as potential vehicles for the implementation of state obligations. As a result, they point to the need to develop mechanisms to coordinate indigenous rules on the protection of indigenous knowledge and national intellectual property laws. Similarly, the chapter by Viaene and Fernández-Maldonado also rests on the premise that it is necessary to incorporate international standards into secondary legislation dealing with the coordination of state and indigenous institutions. In their analysis on how and why this became a battlefield in Ecuador, they identify two main reasons leading to considerable setbacks in the protection of indigenous rights to administer justice. One is of a cultural nature; that is, the widespread racist and colonial attitude towards indigenous peoples and their institutions. And the other is of a political nature; that is, the fear that empowering indigenous legal institutions may result in obstacles to the activities of extractive industries in view of the need to acknowledge indigenous laws on land and territory.

When reflecting on how these insights connect with other contributions in the book, a correlation can be made with the above-sketched analysis (pages 3 to 7) on the complex relationship between identities and rights. One could say that in the case of Ecuador, cultural elements that underlined difference between indigenous groups and the majority gained prominence over socio-political realities affecting societies at large, that is, the exclusions and rights violations generated by extractive industries, which could ground the construction of similarity and alliance between indigenous and non-indigenous groups. States often argue that they cannot implement indigenous peoples' rights in a manner that goes as far as to block projects that are of strategic importance to the entire country.[14] However, it is often elites who mainly benefit from such projects, not the 'general' population. Therefore, we need to critically examine how the construction of indigenous difference by the state and other powerful actors may undermine not only the implementation of indigenous rights, but also rights protection in general.

4.3. *Indigenous rights as a stepping stone towards the recognition of rights of non-indigenous groups*

Another interesting area for future research revolves around the question of whether rights currently granted to indigenous peoples should be available to non-indigenous communities, as well.[15] Perhaps not all rights. Perhaps not all communities. Perhaps not in all circumstances. This is precisely what future research should investigate. But clearly, there are non-indigenous communities that face threats that are very similar to those faced by indigenous peoples. Such communities would benefit greatly from (a measure of) the protection currently offered to indigenous peoples. In addition, research included in this book on the dynamic identity of indigenous peoples may in any case mean that the distinction between non-indigenous and indigenous identities is not necessarily cast in stone.

Some inspiration may be taken from the African Commission on Human and Peoples' Rights approach to peoples' rights. In the South Cameroon case, the government of Cameroon had argued that the South Cameroonians were not a people, because nothing differentiated them from the majority except their language that they had inherited from their erstwhile colonial masters. The African Commission held that the South Cameroonians were not indigenous, but that this did not mean they were not a people entitled to collective rights protection. The Commission agreed that ethno–anthropological attributes could be a characteristic of a people, but held that these attributes were necessary only when determining the 'indigenology' of a 'people'. They were not the only determinant factor to accord or deny the enjoyment or protection of peoples' rights. The

14 M Barelli, 'Free, Prior and Informed Consent in the Aftermath of the UN Declaration on the Rights of Indigenous Peoples: Developments and Challenges Ahead' (2012) 16 *International Journal of Human Rights* 1.

15 See also, as regards natural resource rights, E Desmet, 'Identifying Rights-Holders in Natural Resource Regimes: A Critical Assessment of the Peruvian Protected Areas Legislation' (2016) 8 *Hague Journal on the Rule of Law* 135.

people of South Cameroon were not an African indigenous community, but they were nevertheless a people because "they manifest numerous characteristics and affinities, which include a common history, linguistic tradition, territorial connection and political outlook. More importantly, they identify themselves as a people with a separate and distinct identity".[16]

Non-indigenous peoples are thus already entitled to protection under the African Charter on Human and Peoples' Rights. In the Endorois case, the African Commission crucially recognised that there was a need to protect "marginalized and vulnerable groups in Africa" who have not been accommodated by dominating development paradigms, leading to mainstream development policies that violated their human rights.[17]

Taking its cue from the African Commission's case law, future research could thus draw on indigenous rights instruments to further develop the law in such a way that it offers adequate protection to marginalised and vulnerable groups that have not been accommodated by dominant development paradigms.

4.4. The effects of indigenous rights in social and cultural change

As Cambou highlights, international human rights standards on indigenous peoples require an exercise in belated state building. The latter aims at reshaping how power is distributed among societal groups in order to create more egalitarian and respectful relationships. For this purpose, increasing the decision-making capacities of indigenous peoples is paramount, not only internally, by means of autonomy in the governance of communal affairs, but also nationally and internationally, with their participation in mainstream institutions. This presupposes a reconfiguration of the state, that is, to move from the logic 'indigenous vs state' towards the logic 'indigenous in state', which entails both inclusion and a transference of power towards indigenous groups.[18] It is therefore not surprising that the concrete implementation of such measures is met with strong resistance. But a lack of implementation should not be equated with a lack of effects.

As discussed on page 22, two main factors tend to combine in the poor implementation of indigenous rights: on the one hand, indigenous peoples' presence in lands and areas with natural resources on which they have claims that contradict the interests of powerful groups, and on the other hand, indigenous peoples' subaltern position in society, which often translates into low levels of political representation.[19]

16 African Commission on Human and Peoples' Rights, *Kevin Mgwanga Gunme et al. v. Cameroon*, communication 266/2003, par. 178.

17 African Commission on Human and Peoples' Rights, *Centre for Minority Rights Development (Kenya)* and Minority Rights Group on behalf of Endorois Welfare Council v. The Republic of Kenya, communication 276/2003, par. 148.

18 MA Wilhelmi, 'Derechos y Pueblos Indígenas: Avances Objetivos, Debilidades Subjetivas' (2015) 24 *Revista de Antropologia Social* 127–147.

19 ibid.

In their study of the reasons that explain compliance with judicial decisions on social rights, Langford et al. found that

> one underlying yet somewhat immutable factor is the public status of the litigants. Implementation of judgements that must overcome prejudices against ethnic minorities and other highly stigmatised groups represent a particular challenge. (. . .) when the litigants are poor, excluded from the political process, or otherwise less capable of exerting political pressure, we should expect a lower likelihood of compliance regardless of the cost of compliance, simply because these plaintiffs have less collective political capital.[20]

A parallel seems to exist between this particular factor accounting for compliance with social rights judgements and one of the principal causes for the lack of implementation of indigenous peoples' rights. As suggested by Wilhelmi, when subjects of rights hold a certain degree of power, that is, when they are not in a position of extreme exclusion or inequality, 'rights' may have a catalysing effect and serve as platforms for social mobilisation.[21] In other words, they may open spaces of exchange among social actors, reconfigure social imaginaries and reinforce or weaken certain social meanings, which may in turn derive in momentum for collective organisation and action. In the case of indigenous peoples, Wilhelmi finds a fundamental contradiction: the effectiveness of indigenous peoples' rights depends on these groups' actual power position in society, which is generally weak. But as Wilhelmi recognises, rights may have important social and cultural effects that go beyond their implementation. For example, indigenous rights discourses may influence positively or negatively popular representations of these groups. In other words, it is necessary to study further under which circumstances the mobilisation of indigenous rights opens and closes spaces to revisit social meanings and imaginaries on indigenous peoples, which may in turn affect their power position.

In the contribution by Lozano, we see these dynamics at play. Although her chapter does not directly address the mobilisation of indigenous rights, she shows how the indigenous peoples of the Amazon basin have profiled themselves as allies in nature conservation in order to enhance their participation and decision-making capacities on environmental issues. The contributions by Janmyr and Vanhees seem to suggest that resorting to indigenous rights discourses may be rather detrimental to the populations they study. Bearing this in mind, it is necessary to pay attention to how indigenous rights articulate with other strategies of action among different parallel approaches undertaken by indigenous groups in

20 M Langford, C Rodriguez-Garavito and J Rossi, 'Introduction: From Jurisprudence to Compliance' in M Langford, C Rodriguez-Garavito and J Rossi (eds), *Social Rights Judgements and the Politics of Compliance. Making it Stick* (Cambridge University Press 2017) 28.

21 Although the author does not make it explicit, 'rights' are understood here both as law and discourse. AM Wilhelmi (n 18) 127–147.

order to assert their rights. We need to delve deeper into how these combined strategies interplay with one another and whether they have mutually reinforcing or undermining effects on their realisation.

4.5. Indigenous peoples' counter-hegemonic strategies of resistance

When studying indigenous peoples' strategies of resistance and the role of indigenous rights therein, it is essential to continue to look critically at existing legal instruments, mechanisms and institutions. The chapter by Herencia Carrasco is particularly concerned with this point. He argues for the inclusion of indigenous voices in international law institutions, such as the inter-American human rights system. Interestingly, this is entirely in line with international law's standards concerning indigenous rights to participation. Although Cambou does not approach the subject from this point of view, the draft Nordic Sámi Convention can be said to appropriate the hegemonic language of international law in order to subvert colonial logics. The right to self-determination as delineated in this instrument should conduce to a dialogic relationship between the signatory states and the Sámi as a transnational community. The contributions by Breemen and Coomans also suggest that existing international human rights law on indigenous peoples should be mobilised as a valuable resource to deconstruct mainstream approaches to the protection of knowledge and TCEs from an indigenous point of view. Finally, the contribution by Lozano provides a rich example of how indigenous peoples actually appropriate and disrupt hegemonic legal instruments and discourses in order to advance their agendas. It would be worth exploring how these counter-hegemonic strategies may also serve other marginalised non-indigenous groups.

These five proposed research lines suggest to open up research on indigenous peoples' rights and their strategies of resistance in order to connect with and engage in research on other (marginalised) groups in society. Such a more holistic approach will lead to a deeper understanding of similarities and differences, potentials for synergies and needs for distinctiveness, which in turn may contribute to the realisation of human dignity for all.

Part I

Changing identities and cultures

2 Indigeneity vs development

Nubian rights mobilisation in Egypt

Maja Janmyr

1. Introduction

One of the most overlooked issues within the field of indigenous rights studies is arguably the concept of indigeneity in the Middle East and North Africa.[1] In these regions, many countries refuse to acknowledge the existence of indigenous peoples within their borders, let alone recognise their rights. This chapter seeks to explore the complexities regarding indigenous rights in the Middle East and North Africa through a discussion of Nubian indigeneity in Egypt.

For reasons such as government repression, lack of knowledge of indigenous issues, and a lack of international and academic activism, Nubians are arguably latecomers to the international process that has developed over the last 30 years concerning indigeneity. Today, it is not uncontroversial in Egypt to speak of Nubians as an indigenous people. Moreover, only few Nubian groups mobilise their rights by using the indigenous peoples' rights discourse. The Egyptian government has long attempted to homogenise the Egyptian population and enforce a single national identity. Consequently, it has as such persistently denied the existence of any indigenous people or ethnic minority groups in the country.

This chapter argues that any meaningful exploration of Nubian indigenous rights calls for the adoption of a historically informed analysis of the processes of rights mobilisation. While the literature on indigenous peoples and minority groups often sidesteps the question of legal mobilisation in authoritarian states – such as Egypt[2] – this chapter seeks to explain Nubian mobilisation and demands by using conceptual tools from legal mobilisation studies. The term "legal mobilisation" is broadly used to describe any type of process by which individual or collective actors invoke legal norms, discourse, or symbols to influence policy or behaviour. Legal mobilisation seeks social change through legal norms or discourse and extends beyond litigation to include activism.[3]

1 S Frantzman and others, 'Contested Indigeneity: The Development of an Indigenous Discourse on the Bedouin of the Negev, Israel' (2012) 17 *Israel Studies* 78.

2 For a detailed account of the history of authoritarianism in Egypt, see M Kassem, *Egyptian Politics: The Dynamics of Authoritarian Rule* (Lynne Rienner Publishers 2004).

3 M Bernstein, 'Gender, Queer Family Politics, and the Limits of Law,' in M Bernstein and R Reimann (eds), *Queer Families, Queer Politics: Challenging Culture and the State* (Columbia University Press 2001); K Bumiller, *The Civil Rights Society: The Social Construction of Victims*

This chapter argues that Nubian activists in the past decade have mobilised for recognition of indigeneity primarily to achieve a bigger goal – to return to ancestral lands. Indigeneity can therefore in the Nubian context be seen as a strategy or, in the legal mobilisation lingua, a frame to pursue other specific goals. Framing is generally seen as the process through which movements mobilise "symbols, claims and even identities in the pursuit of activism".[4] The application of indigeneity as a frame does not necessarily mean that Nubians do not consider themselves genuinely indigenous, but only that there is a recognition that being considered indigenous may be particularly strategic for Nubian land claims. As will be shown, however, it was the more localised frame of development that eventually led to a constitutional right of Nubian return.

In pursuing these aims, the chapter begins with a historical account of Nubian displacement and resettlement, followed by a section outlining Nubian marginalisation in the context of Egyptian Arab nationalism. It thereafter considers the growing Nubian rights mobilisation and explains how the question of returning to ancestral lands is the most important demand among Egypt's Nubians. It further details two primary competing frames: on the one hand, indigeneity and international human rights, and, on the other, development. Before concluding, the chapter explores the tensions that arise when it comes to Nubians' demands of returning to ancestral lands. These tensions are analysed on a global, local, and generational level.

This work is based on fieldwork and archival research in Cairo, Egypt, between March and May 2014, and in February 2015. Semi-structured interviews were conducted in Cairo and via Skype with a limited number of key Nubian activists. This chapter is furthermore based on an analysis of published and unpublished legal materials. These include petitions to the UN and draft laws concerning Nubian return, as well as Nubian-related news publications and Nubian groups on social networking sites.

2. Displacement and resettlement

At the turn of the twentieth century, Nubians "did not regard themselves as being members of one ethnic category" but rather identified themselves as "regionally-based ethnic sub groups".[5] Collectively known as "Nubian" only after their displacement, Nubians comprise three culturally ethnic and linguistically distinct groups: the Kenuz, Fadicha, and Arabs.[6] For thousands of years, the Nubian

(Johns Hopkins University Press 1988); P Burstein, 'Legal Mobilization as a Social Movement Tactic: The Struggle for Equal Employment Opportunity' (1991) 96 *American Journal of Sociology* 1201.

4 R Williams, 'The Cultural Contexts of Collective Action: Constraints, Opportunities and the Symbolic Life of Social Movements' in DA Snow and others, *The Blackwell Companion to Social Movements* (Blackwell 2004) 93.

5 R Poeschke, *Nubians in Egypt and Sudan: Constraints and Coping Strategies* (Saarbrücken Verlag für Entwicklungspolitik 1996) 27.

6 R Fernea and others, *Nubian Ehtnographies* (Waveland Press 1991) 187.

people lived in villages along the banks of the Nile, stretching from Aswan in southern Egypt and into northern Sudan.[7] They retained here their own distinct languages, customs, and cultures.[8]

In 1899, the boundary between Egypt and Sudan was solidified, and as a result, the Nubians were arbitrarily divided between the two countries. During the early twentieth century, Egypt's Nubians were again uprooted when a series of dams were built along the Nile river by the British colonial powers.[9] During a period of modernisation, former president Nasser initiated the Aswan High Dam project in the mid-1950s. While the project was intended to provide more land for agriculture and improve Egypt's electricity production, the dam soon became the very symbol of Egypt's sovereignty. Its construction constituted a critical moment for a revitalised nation that had been subject to decades of external control. However, the construction also caused the flooding of a large area along the Nile, including the lands that are known today as "Old Nubia" – generally considered as the land where Nubians used to live between the Nile's first cataract and the Egyptian border with Sudan.[10]

Not long after, Egyptian authorities began forcibly resettling Nubians to so-called resettlement communities in southern Egypt. In addition to those that either had been uprooted in the colonial era or had already migrated to other parts of Egypt, approximately 50,000 Nubians from some 45 villages were resettled to places such as Kom Ombo, located roughly 50 kilometres north of the city of Aswan. Individuals who were relocated to Kom Ombo faced many problems that have been well documented in the literature.[11]

Although President Nasser had promised that "the benefits that the Nubian people will enjoy are very great",[12] few Nubians were satisfied with the resettlement. The most pressing matter was the lack of adequate housing in the areas to which the Nubian people were relocated, which turned out to be either non-existent or of very poor quality. After relocation, the conditions for most Nubians worsened. Each family struggled to survive on a small plot of land and state subsidies.[13] That said, access to some services nevertheless improved after relocation, and women in relocated areas were able to benefit from increased access to education and better provision of facilities and services.

7 ibid. 187.

8 While one group of Nubians are Arabic speakers, the Nubian language can be divided into two dialects: Kanzi and Fadicca. See E Smith, 'Place, Class and Race in the Barabra Café: Nubian Urban Spaces and Media Identities' in D Singerman and P Amar, *Cairo Cosmopolitans* (American University in Cairo Press 2006).

9 Minority Rights, 'World Directory of Minorities and Indigenous Peoples, Nubians' <http://www.minorityrights.org/3932/egypt/nubians.html#sthash.AZOAEZgA.dpuf> accessed 27 May 2015.

10 S Allen, 'Nubians and Development: 1960–2014' (MA dissertation, American University in Cairo 2014) 6.

11 See, for example, Poeschke (n 5) or HM Fahim, *Egyptian Nubians: Resettlement and Years of Coping* (University of Utah Press 1983).

12 Poeschke (n 5) 36.

13 Fernea and others (n 6) 126.

While the Egyptian government developed a formula for distributing reclaimed land to Nubians based on their previous ownership in Old Nubia, there were significant delays in the distribution for some families. The long Nubian history of labour migration was thus exasperated, in which many families temporarily settled elsewhere while waiting for compensation and the construction of homes.[14] The adverse effects of Nubian displacement are still being felt more than four decades later. In 2010, the number of Nubian families who had not been compensated for their confiscated homes was estimated at 5,221.[15] In September 2004, it was furthermore revealed that the Ministry of Agriculture had planned to sell large tracts of land in historic Nubian sites such as Abu Simbel to non-Nubian, wealthy property developers.[16]

The effects of Nubian displacement have been described as far more profound than limited to physical and economic damage. Rather,

> Those successive waves of displacement and eviction represented an overwhelming threat to an indigenous group of people with unique cultural characteristics that distinguished them from the rest of the Egyptian society. The uniqueness in which the Nubians were endowed was essentially due to the geographic and economic environment that evolved through history along the Nile in a way in which we can say it modelled the features character of Nubian culture [sic]. Consequently, displacing this population away from this special environment, and removing them to other habitats in which those conditions were not available, has threatened the essence of their uniqueness.[17]

Indeed, while the United Nations Educational, Scientific, and Cultural Organization (UNESCO) had carefully relocated Pharaonic and Nubian ruins prior to the creation of Lake Nasser, little care was taken to safeguard the culture and tradition of the Nubian people. Nubians appear not to have been consulted about the location and the design of the new villages, and many claim that the new houses were not "culturally appropriate" for the Nubians.[18] In addition, the government insisted that the Nubian farmers become members of farming cooperatives and grow sugar cane, which was not one of their traditional crops.[19]

14 E Hughes, 'Displacement and Indigenous Rights: The Nubian Case' in S Venkateswar and E Hughes, *Politics of Indigeneity* (Zed Books 2011) 130.

15 ECHR, 'Individual NGO Submission to the Office of the High Commissioner for Human Rights on the Occasion of the Seventh Session of the Universal Periodic Review 2010 Egypt' <http://lib.ohchr.org/HRBodies/UPR/Documents/Session7/EG/ECHR_UPR_EGY_S07_2010_EgyptianCenterforHousingRights.pdf> accessed 2 March 2017, para 10.

16 G Nkrumah, 'No benighted Nubia' *Al-Ahram Weekly* (15 August 2013) <http://weekly.ahram.org.eg/News/3681/32/No-benighted-Nubia.aspx> accessed 2 March 2017.

17 ECHR (n 15) para 8.

18 ibid. para 16.

19 Allen (n 10); A Mossallam, 'Hikāyāt Sha'b: Stories of peoplehood, Nasserism, Popular Politics and Songs in Egypt 1956–1973' (PhD dissertation, London School of Economics and Political Science 2013) 50.

While the resettlement furthermore put family ties under stress and disregarded historical rivalries between the three Nubian groups,[20] as this next section will show, it was also followed by a process which activists have dubbed "de-Nubianisation".

3. Marginalisation and Egyptian Arab nationalism

The concept of *religious* minority has long been part of Egyptian legal traditions, and certain religious minorities – most notably the Copts – have been tolerated. Egypt was furthermore one of many Arab states that voted in the United Nations for the 1992 Declaration on Minority Rights, the 2007 Declaration on the Rights of Indigenous Peoples, and the 2001 UNESCO Declaration on Cultural Diversity. Government actions at home have nevertheless long focused on homogenising the Egyptian population and on consolidating a single national identity. This position has long been explicitly laid out in article 1 of the 1971 Constitution: "Egyptian people are part of the Arab Nation and work for the realisation of its comprehensive unity". Thus, ethnic, racial immigrant, and mode of production-based minorities and indigenous groups are not officially recognised in Egypt.[21]

At the heart of Egyptian nationalism thus lies the absence of formal boundaries between, for example, Nubians and other Egyptians. As a result of being incompatible with nation-building politics, census data effectively erase indigenous and minority presence. Therefore, it is almost impossible to estimate the current number of Nubians in Egypt.[22] Assessments vary greatly among Nubian activists – some put their community's population in Egypt at around 300,000, while others go so far as to suggest that the number is approximately three million.[23] It is nevertheless clear that Egypt's Nubians distinguish among themselves in a number of aspects. This is not the least because they are dispersed both abroad and across Egypt: in larger cities and in more than 50 different Nubian villages, most of which do not remain in their original locations. Some may not even identify themselves as Nubian, but rather as Egyptian, Egyptian–Nubian, or some other label of self-identification.

Rights have generally been contextually linked to *citizenship*. Kymlicka and Pföstl have argued that this may be historically explained in part by the Ottoman Empire's legacy of the millet system, under which minorities were understood as second-class citizens and not part of the larger society.[24] At UN

20 Committee on the Elimination of Racial Discrimination, Summary Record of 1048th Meeting, UN Doc. CERD/C/SR.1048 para 11.

21 S Zuhur, 'Claiming Space for Minorities in Egypt After the Arab Spring' in M Ennaji (ed), *Multiculturalism and Democracy in North Africa: Aftermath of the Arab Spring* (Routledge 2014).

22 ECHR (n 15).

23 ibid.

24 W Kymlicka and E Pföstl (eds), *Multiculturalism and Minority Rights in the Arab World* (Oxford University Press 2014).

level, Egypt has explained how all legislation is applied equally to all citizens without discrimination.[25] The Egyptian representative argued with regard to the Nubians in 1994 that

> there was no discrimination against them [the Nubians]; they could practise their own occupations and accede to very high positions in all walks of life. For instance, there were Nubian ministers, senior members of the judiciary and teachers at all levels.[26]

Such explanations have nevertheless met criticism by, among others, Rosalyn Higgins who in 1993 argued that Egypt had misapprehended the question of minorities:

> It was not correct to say that, if all a country's citizens were treated well and without discrimination, it therefore had no minorities. The existence of minorities - such as adherents of a religion other than that professed by the majority, or speakers of a language other than that spoken by the majority - was an objective factor. To deny the existence of the minorities referred to in article 27 [of the ICCPR], on the grounds that such persons enjoyed all the rights to which they were entitled, was to confuse two entirely separate issues.[27]

A key feature of Arab nationalism is thus the adoption of Arabisation policies in Egypt that privilege the Arabic language and stigmatise other local dialects and cultures as backward and divisive. Already in the early 1960s, anthropologists warned of a "cultural extinction" of the Nubians.[28] Nubian activists have furthermore explicitly referred to a "process of de-Nubianisation". This process is said to include the resettlement of Arab groups in the lands that Nubians wish to return to and renaming these sites with Arabic place names in addition to "pushing Nubians into Arabicisation through biased educational curricula at the expense of their own languages and culture".[29] An aggravating factor is, furthermore, that it has never been possible to study the Nubian languages within the Egyptian education system. After resettlement, the language of instruction in the newly built schools was exclusively Arabic, which was recognised by the 1971 Constitution as the only state language.

Egypt's nationalism moreover appears to have reinforced historical and racial structures of oppression, where prejudice against Nubians has been long

25 Statement by Representative of Egypt, UN Human Rights Committee, Summary Record of the 1247th Meeting, UN Doc CCPR/C/SR.1247 para 14.

26 Statement by Representative of Egypt, Committee on the Elimination of Racial Discrimination Summary of 1049th Meeting, UN Doc. CERD/C/SR.1049 para 8.

27 Statement by Higgins, UN Human Rights Committee, Summary Record of the 1247th Meeting, UN Doc CCPR/C/SR.1247 para 15.

28 Allen (n 10) 35.

29 ECHR (n 15).

prevalent.[30] Ever since their displacement, Nubians as a collective have been marginalised politically, socially, and economically. This marginalisation has led to widespread stereotyping and discrimination, and a considerable portion of Nubians, disproportionate to the larger Egyptian population, are employed in unskilled labour.[31] Stereotypes against Nubians are also prevalent in Egyptian media and films, which often portray Nubians as door attendants, servants, or drivers.[32]

In Egypt, as in other Arab states, minority politics is often subject to harsh forms of control and is highly securitised.[33] Any advocacy for the existence of a separate group with a distinct language and history has been perceived as constituting a threat to national security.[34] Nubians have been largely apolitical for the past half century *precisely* because such political organisation has been met with distrust or outrightly repressed.[35] This is particularly the case when they have reached out internationally to raise awareness of the Nubian plight. The "protection of minorities" was one justification for Egypt's colonial rule. This legacy has therefore raised suspicion that minorities collaborating with foreign powers seek to do so in order to weaken state rule.[36] This is also the main reason why Nubians in Egypt only rarely have joined causes with Nubians in Sudan.

Nubian political representation in government and national assembly has been considered very low, and Nubians have had few, if any, institutions to directly defend their rights or speak on their behalf on matters directly affecting them.[37] Emotional appeals for governmental sympathy for the Nubian situation therefore have for decades been vocalised primarily within the cultural sphere, through literature and arts. There has also been a "reluctant and very qualified recognition" for the promotion of Nubian culture in Egypt, which has been limited to mainly academic and archaeological curiosity. The Nubian Museum in Aswan, established to promote Nubian culture, is perhaps the clearest example of this, even though the Egyptian government made its best to delineate it as an essentially *Egyptian* project.[38]

30 F Abbas, 'Egypt, Arab Nationalism, and Nubian Diasporic Identity in Idris Ali's Dongola: A Novel of Nubia' (2014) 45 *Research in African Literatures* 147.
31 S Dersso, *Egypt: Constitutional, Legislative and Administrative Provisions Concerning Indigenous Peoples* (ILO and African Commission on Human & Peoples' Rights 2009); ECHR (n 15).
32 For an overview of media racialism, see E Smith, '"In His Heart and Soul He's Egyptian, the Nile Flows through His Veins": Bakkar as Egyptian and African' (2009) 5 *Critical Interventions* 123.
33 Kymlicka and Pföstl (n 24).
34 Dersso (n 31); Hughes (n 14).
35 Nkrumah (n 16).
36 Kymlicka and Pföstl (n 24).
37 Dersso (n 31) 21.
38 Hughes (n 14) 132.

4. Nubian rights mobilisation

Nubians as a collective have recently begun to mobilise for their rights on an unprecedented scale. This has been largely due to the emergence of a number of legal and political opportunities, which created the conviction that an organised challenge to the status quo would be successful.[39] The rise of a number of protest movements calling for the end of Egypt's one party rule beginning in 2004–2005, importantly functioned as a prelude for Nubian action.[40] The 2008 Bread Crisis, which erupted when a large general strike broke out in response to low wages and rising food costs, served as inspiration for a new generation of activists and created political momentum to mobilise and demand rights specifically to the Nubian people.[41] Not the least, the general emergence of grassroots youth movements during the Bread Crisis triggered the engagement of a new generation of Nubians. Many of these might have never visited Old Nubia but have arisen as the most vocal and politically engaged. One example is the Nubian Democratic Youth Union (NDYU), which was formed in 2009 by Nubian university students to "defend the rights of the Nubian people and minority groups in Egypt".[42]

Another important mobiliser of Nubian rights was the Egyptian Center for Housing Rights (ECHR). Established in 2004, the ECHR is a Cairo-based non-governmental organisation specialised in claiming for, and defending the right to, adequate housing. In 2010, the ECHR attempted to internationally shame the Egyptian government into strengthening Nubian rights by submitting a petition to the UN Office of the High Commissioner for Human Rights (UN OHCHR). This move was unprecedented and bold, and sought to raise support for the recognition of Egypt's Nubians as an indigenous people under international law.[43] I will discuss this matter in detail on pages 36–39.

Equally, instrumental for paving the way for a broader rights movement was the Egyptian–Nubian Association for Lawyers (ENAL). Despite being broadly framed as working with issues other than Nubian rights, ENAL has since (2009) filed several lawsuits concerning return to Nubian lands and/or for fair compensation for the loss of these. ENAL has even elaborated several draft laws concerning Nubian return. ENAL's draft laws proved highly significant in the Nubian post-revolutionary rights movement.

By far the most significant turning point for Nubian activism, however, was the Egyptian Revolution in 2011, during which Egyptian activists organised protests against, and eventually toppled, the Mubarak regime. Before this, Nubians

39 D McAdam, *Political Processes and the Development of Black Insurgency, 1930–1970* (University of Chicago Press 1999); D McAdam and others, *The Dynamics of Contention* (Cambridge University Press 2001).

40 R el-Mahdi, 'Enough! Egypt's Quest for Democracy' (2009) 42 *Comparative Political Studies* 1011.

41 Interview B, February 2015.

42 Humanity in Action, *Youth for Democracy: Learning from Non-Violent Struggle across the World* (HiA 2012).

43 Interview G, March 2015.

had never taken to the streets politically, but now, many participated in anti-government protests. While most participated as Egyptians *and* Nubians, not either/or, the Revolution offered an opportunity for many young Nubians to express their "organised anger" against the government for its failure to recognise Nubian rights.[44]

Nubian grievances were nevertheless exacerbated in 2012, when a new post-revolutionary parliament had been elected, bringing an Islamist-led coalition to power. Nubians as a group still lacked parliamentarian representation,[45] and, during the presidency of Mohamed Morsi of the Muslim Brotherhood, Nubians as a collective were effectively excluded from the constitutional assembly that was responsible for drafting the first post-revolutionary Constitution. For many, the Revolution was seen as a disappointment because the strategy of the Mubarak regime on containing the Nubians appeared to live on.[46]

Real change first came about in July 2013, when the military once again ousted an Egyptian president and suspended the heavily criticised and divisive 2012 Constitution.[47] By this time, many Nubian actors were mobilising for change, ranging from youth groups mobilising through social media and/or street protests, the emergence of an ostensibly armed movement, to the increased involvement of the largely European-based Nubian diaspora. This highly fragmented group was nevertheless largely unified when a new constitutional approach ensued. This time, Nubians as a collective were actively involved, and a new Constitution was adopted through a referendum in January 2014. The Constitution stipulates the preservation of cultural diversity and criminalises discrimination of all kinds, including discrimination between citizens on the basis of race or skin colour. As I will show below, this Constitution addressed a number of Nubian concerns when it comes to return to ancestral lands.

5. Demanding return to ancestral lands

Land struggle is a central issue in the Nubian collective identity, and when activists speak of Nubian rights, first and foremost is the question of return. Today, "Nubia" must be seen as a dynamic space of land, and the demand of return is therefore not homogenous among Egypt's Nubians. Many advocate for the right to return to the "closest point" to their original lands around Lake Nasser or to Old Nubia.[48] Some are more specific in their demands, articulating precise areas that they view as logistically feasible.[49] It is thus no surprise that, while Nubian activists generally agree that return to ancestral lands is the most

44 Interview A, February 2015.

45 Nkrumah (n 16).

46 ibid.

47 Amnesty International, *Egypt's New Constitution Limits Fundamental Freedoms and Ignores the Rights of Women* (2012).

48 ECHR (n 15).

49 Allen (n 10).

important demand, there is less agreement about the strategies and methods to be used to further this demand.

In the following section, I suggest that Nubian activists primarily employ two frames in mobilising for return to ancestral lands. The first frame is based upon international human rights and, most importantly, the indigenous peoples' rights framework. The second has its roots in the history and politics of Nubian displacement throughout the last century. These competing frames suggest tension between not only the global and the local, but also intergenerational tension.

5.1. Indigeneity and global human rights

Nubians in Egypt have only rarely been included in international listings of minority groups and indigenous peoples.[50] The Indigenous World, for example, listed the Amazigh-Berbers as the only indigenous groups in North Africa, while the 2008 edition of the *World Directory of Minorities and Indigenous Peoples* included the Copts in Egypt as an indigenous group in the Middle East.[51] A 2009 joint study by the ILO and the African Commission on Human and Peoples' Rights (ACHPR) nevertheless identified three groups in Egypt as indigenous: the Berbers, Bedouins, and Nubians.[52]

For reasons previously explained, the question of framing Nubian return to ancestral lands within the international indigenous rights framework was basically non-existent before Manal el-Tibi and the ECHR first raised the issue. Since then, the ECHR has been instrumental in framing Nubian demands within this discourse. The main argument goes that the recognition of Nubians as an indigenous people would force the Egyptian government into allowing Nubians to return to their traditional lands around the High Dam Lake.

This approach appears to have been triggered by at least two largely concurrent events in the mid-2000s. First, the ECHR received a large number of complaints concerning the housing rights of Nubians across Egypt following the increased media focus on Nubian issues.[53] This triggered the ECHR to focus much of its work precisely on the issue of Nubian land rights. Second, in 2007, the ECHR head el-Tibi was writing her Master of Laws thesis on Nubians as an indigenous people as part of the international human rights programme of the American University in Cairo.[54] As such, el-Tibi was highly influenced by the global aspects of human rights. She soon became instrumental in what Merry refers to as "translating" international human rights "down" into local systems and "translating" actors' local stories "up" by telling these stories using "global rights language" to achieve their objectives.[55]

50 Dersso (n 31).
51 Minority Rights (n 9).
52 Dersso (n 31) 16.
53 Interview C, February 2015.
54 LLM thesis on file with author.
55 SE Merry, *Human Rights and Gender Violence: Translating International Law into Local Justice* (University of Chicago Press 2006).

El-Tibi's relation with the American University in Cairo without doubt shaped ideas and understandings in the Nubian community. What she learned here in part constituted the basis for the 2007 conference "Nubia between Resettlement and Development", co-organised by the ECHR and a local Nubian group in Aswan. This appears to be the first known instance of the Nubian community engaging with the indigenous discourse.[56] By gathering 1,500 Nubians, it sought to secure community acceptance to bring the Nubian plight to the UN OHCHR as this body completed its Universal Periodic Review (UPR) of the status of human rights in Egypt.[57] As with many other similar initiatives, the conference stirred a media frenzy, focusing on potential Nubian secession from Egypt, and Egyptian security services allegedly attempted to prevent the conference from taking place.

In 2010, the ECHR submitted a petition to the UN OHCHR asking the UN to request that the Egyptian government grant Nubians "international legal status" as an indigenous people. It moreover requested that the Egyptian government adopt special measures for Nubians, for example, by providing amendments to the Egyptian Constitution to recognise the existence and the rights of indigenous peoples.[58] If supported by a considerable part of the Nubian community, a petition to the UN requesting international recognition as an indigenous people could arguably be seen as one of the most explicit "declarations" of indigeneity. However, the extent of Nubian support for this petition appears disputed and unclear.[59]

More than anything else, there was a clear strategic value of being indigenous for Nubian land claims. For el-Tibi, the ultimate goal of bringing the Nubian cause to the attention of the international community was to have Nubian complaints included in the UN's UPR of Egypt.[60] If the UN agreed with the ECHR's assertion that Nubians are indeed an indigenous people, many Nubians were hoping that they would enjoy the added force of international law behind their claims to their ancestral lands. More precisely, the recognition of Nubians as an indigenous people would, in the view of el-Tibi, entail that the Egyptian government would have to allow Nubians to return to the lands around the High Dam Lake where their traditional lands are located and under the same names of their traditional villages.

For the ECHR, the 2010 UPR process nevertheless turned into a disappointing setback. When the UN Working Group on the UPR published its final report, the plight of Nubians in Egypt was not mentioned. The ECHR's attempts to involve Nubian representatives in the UN Expert Mechanism on the Rights of Indigenous Peoples had also been stranded. Adding insult to injury, after the

56 Hughes (n 14).

57 Interview G, March 2015.

58 See also UN, 'Summary prepared by the Office of the High Commissioner for Human Rights, in accordance with paragraph 15 (c) of the annex to Human Rights Council resolution 5/1' UN Doc. A/HRC/WG.6/7/EGY/3 para 44.

59 Interviews C and D, February 2015.

60 M Bradley, 'People of the Nile Appeal for Greater Rights' *The National* (10 February 2010).

submission, el-Tibi also faced harsh accusations that she was calling for Nubian secession. This "very risky" political situation effectively prevented the ECHR from submitting a new petition prior to the next UPR on Egypt in 2014.[61]

For some activists, the failure of the ECHR's UN petition was a missed opportunity to highlight the status of Egypt's Nubian community.[62] Others are currently questioning whether it is actually beneficial to their cause to emphasise Nubian indigeneity – even arguing that the ECHR pushed the limits too far by using this discourse.[63] For many, the lessons learned from the UPR process were clear: "What happened after the declaration of indigeneity [the ECHR petition]? Nothing. We need more than recognition. More than papers".[64]

While not a single informant interviewed in 2015 was of the opinion that Nubians were not – at least "more or less" or "somehow" – indigenous, many appear to have entered into a silent agreement to refrain from confrontational strategies; that is, framing their claims in terms of indigeneity.[65] Some expressed their fear that categorically addressing these demands through the discourse of indigeneity might be interpreted by Egyptian Arabs as either an acknowledgement that Nubians are in fact different from Egyptians in general, thus not Egyptian, or as an accusation that Egyptian Arabs colonised Nubia.[66] While many Nubians consider the latter historically correct, in light of repeated accusations of Nubian secession, the risk of being interpreted as making such an accusation would be counter-productive to their cause.

Rather than framing their demands through the discourse of indigeneity, many activists have resorted to a minority rights discourse. Both discourses articulate the return to ancestral lands as an inherent right rather than as a favour. However, unlike indigeneity, the concept of religious minority is very much part of Egyptian legal traditions.[67] Seen from a global perspective, the shift in argument between a "rights as minorities" discourse and one claiming "rights as peoples" is nevertheless nothing new. Mobilisations mounted by indigenous peoples in Latin America have tended to shift in discourse over several decades before finally landing in one based on indigeneity.[68]

Furthermore, other activists tie the question of a Nubian return to the Palestinian right of return to historic Palestine.[69] Despite that the "right of return" throughout the Arab world is intricately linked to the Palestinian cause, many observers have nevertheless disputed the parallels between the Palestinians and Egyptian Nubians. As a result, they have criticised activists' appropriation of this

61 Interview C, February 2015.

62 Interview A, February 2015.

63 Interview A, February 2015.

64 Interview F, March 2015.

65 Interviews B and F, February and March 2015.

66 Interview A, February 2015.

67 Zuhur (n 21).

68 For more on the shift in discourse between these rights in the Latin American context, see J Jackson, 'Rights to Indigenous Culture in Colombia' in M Goodale and SE Merry, *The Practice of Human Rights* (Cambridge University Press 2007).

69 M Megahed, 'The Right to Return is Not Only Palestinian' Nubian Youth Democratic Union Website (23 April 2012) <http://www.y4nubia.blogspot.com/2012/04/blog-post_23.html> accessed 2 March 2017.

discourse.[70] These critics have primarily argued that, unlike Palestine, Nubia is not a freestanding, separate nation fighting against an occupying enemy. According to them, the "right of return" should only be associated with UN Resolution 194 on *Palestinian* return.[71] Given the symbolism of Palestine in Egypt and in the Middle East in general, the use of the Palestinian frame when advocating for a Nubian return can nevertheless be seen as a highly strategic decision.

5.2. Development and local understandings

One would imagine that the vast resettlement of Nubians in the 1960s would have triggered a large-scale political and social unrest among the Nubian population. However, in line with Egyptian nationalism, many Nubians seem to have supported the construction of the High Dam, feeling that they sacrificed their old homes for the "greater Egyptian good".[72] As Mossallam has argued, "the Nasserist hegemony was one the Nubians embraced, personalised and contributed to, rather than simply donned".[73] Feeling that demanding specific Nubian rights was, on the one hand, more associated with vulnerability and marginalisation than empowerment and, on the other, could be understood as disloyalty to the nationalist project, it appears as if some Nubians rather waited patiently for the government to address their situation.[74]

The development frame is historically and politically rooted in the displacement of Nubians during the 1960s. Former president Nasser employed the term "development" as a "tool to distract from social and political issues", and the ostensibly neutral language of development was explicitly used to justify the relocation of the Nubians.[75] In addition, many Nubians felt that they were making an enormous sacrifice for the benefit of the nation and therefore saw development as a right following relocation. Nubians thus began to use the development discourse to put forward claims from the state already in the early days of the relocation. As a 1971–1975 survey explained, because they were forced to leave their homelands,

> Nubians strongly believe that development is a right and not a favour. . . . hence, instead of showing the appreciation and gratitude expected by the administrators in return for their efforts to better the social-economic conditions of the settlers, the Nubians are employing tactics of protest and constant criticism against the administration while demanding far greater services and privileges than are given to any rural community in the country.[76]

70 R Khallaf, 'Right of Return' *Al-Ahram Weekly* (2006) <http://weekly.ahram.org.eg/2006/788/eg9.htm> accessed 2 March 2017.

71 M S el-Dawla, 'The Right to Return is Palestinian and not Nubian' *Journal of Arab Consciousness* (30 June 2011) <http://elw3yalarabi.org/modules.php?name=News&file=article&sid=9970> accessed 21 October 2015.

72 Allen (n 10); Mossallam (n 19).

73 Mossallam (n 19) 174. Cited in Allen (n 10) 51.

74 Interview B, February 2015.

75 Allen (n 10) 109.

76 H Tadros, 'The Study and Evaluation of the Rehabilitation Process in the Newly-Settled Communities in Land Reclamation Areas: Final Report Part One the Nile Delta' (American University in Cairo 1975) 19. Cited in Allen (n 10) 110.

Today, this discourse of development has been strategically reappropriated by Nubian activists demanding a return to ancestral lands. Even the 2010 ECHR petition to the UN explicitly mentions a right to development, which includes a demand of "establishing and assisting Nubians to establish development projects that can benefit them".[77] The discourse of development is thus the primary way that Nubians have been able to make their claims in what they perceive as more neutral language, which directly speaks to the government's unwillingness to recognise the role of indigeneity and ethnic minority. Some activists have nevertheless expressed harsh criticism of this strategy simply because, in their view, it risks reducing the issue to solely a land problem, rather than a social, political, and economic problem.[78]

In the process leading up to the adoption of the 2014 Egyptian Constitution, it was precisely through the employment of the development frame that Nubian activists managed to make their demands of return heard. In an unprecedented manner, they demanded the right to return to the land of Nubia (around the lake), and that the population be consulted in the decision-making process for development of their land.[79] The developmental aspect of a Nubian return is clear in article 236 of the 2014 Constitution, which states that

> The State shall guarantee setting and implementing a plan for the comprehensive economic and urban development of border and underprivileged areas, including Upper Egypt, Sinai, Matrouh, and Nubia. This shall be made with the participation of the residents of these areas in these development projects, and they shall be given a priority in benefiting therefrom, taking into account the cultural and environmental patterns of the local community, within ten years from the date that this constitution comes into effect, as regulated by Law. The State shall work on setting and implementing projects to bring back the residents of Nubia to their original territories and develop such territories within ten years, as regulated by Law.

For many Nubians, article 236 is an important milestone, not the least because it marks the first time constitution drafters included the term "Nubia". Others, wishing to emphasise the *right* of return, reject the article simply for its emphasis on development.

Following the constitutional breakthrough, the Ministry of Transitional Justice formed the Committee on the Rehabilitation and Reconstruction of Nubia in September 2014. The main task of this Committee is to implement the constitutional provisions on Nubia by drafting a specific law on return and setting out the details of such a return.[80] Until now, the Committee has developed three

77 ECHR (n 15).

78 Interviews B and D, February 2015.

79 F Emam, 'Being Nubian in Egypt, and in the Constitution' *MadaMasr* (23 December 2013).

80 Ahram Online, 'Egypt Forms Committee to Draft Law for Nubian Resettlement' *Ahram Online* (8 October 2014) <http://english.ahram.org.eg/NewsContent/1/64/112628/Egypt/Politics-/

draft laws on the "Rehabilitation and Development of Nubia", the most recent of which has been submitted to the Council of Ministers in February 2015.[81] The Committee's work was nevertheless significantly obstructed when current President Abdel Fattah el-Sisi, elected in May 2014, unexpectedly issued Decree 444 in November 2014. This decree establishes vast areas along the Egyptian border as military zones not to be inhabited, including 16 villages to which Nubians demand to return.

In August 2016, President Sisi additionally issued Decree 355 that allocated land, which is situated in the Nubian villages of Toshka and Forkund, to the new Toshka development project.[82] In October, the Egyptian government announced that it would sell parts of the Toshka development project in an auction as part of the government's "1.5 million project", which is Egypt's newest landmark agricultural mega-project. The project aims to convert 2,400 square miles of arid desert into farmland in an attempt to increase food security and boost Egypt's struggling economy.[83] As I will detail on page 44, Nubian activists have once again taken to the streets.

5.3. Tensions: global, local, generational

In relation to the 2014 Constitution, Nubian claims of return to ancestral lands were successfully mobilised, not through the use of an indigenous rights discourse, but instead by employing a discourse of *development*.[84] The allocation of Nubian lands for agricultural development nevertheless demonstrates that there is a tension between the Egyptian government's understanding of development and Nubian desires to return to their lands by way of development. The competing frames and modes of mobilisation suggest that tensions arise on primarily three interconnected levels when it comes to Nubians' demands of return to ancestral lands: global, local, and generational.

Research on human rights activism in authoritarian states has demonstrated that speaking openly about the lack of rights can be a hostile or threatening act

Egypt–forms–committee–to–draft–law–for–Nubian–rese.aspx> accessed 2 March 2017. See also M Shams El-Din 'Activists Call Sisi's Announcements on Nubia Insufficient' *Madamasr* (29 January 2017) <http://www.madamasr.com/en/2017/01/29/feature/u/activists-call-sisis-announcements-on-nubia-insufficient/> accessed 2 March 2017.

81 Interview D, February 2015. Draft laws on file with author.

82 Z el-Guindy, 'Nubian Protesters to Continue Sit-in Against Sale of Toshka land in Egypt's Aswan' *Al-Ahram Online* (20 November 2016) <http://english.ahram.org.eg/NewsContent/1/64/250385/Egypt/Politics-/Nubian-protesters-to-continue-sitin-against-sale-o.aspx> accessed 2 March 2017.

83 R Michaelson, 'Egypt's Nubians Fight for Ancestral Land Earmarked for Mega-project' *The Guardian* (13 February 2017) <https://www.theguardian.com/global-development/2017/feb/13/egypt-nubians-fight-for-ancestral-land-earmarked-for-mega-project> accessed 2 March 2017.

84 M Janmyr, 'Nubians in Contemporary Egypt: Mobilizing Return to Ancestral Lands' (2016) 25 *Middle East Critique* 127.

against a ruling authority seeking self-preservation.[85] As Lemaitre and Sandvik have argued, "political opportunities are dangerous when social movements both perceive the political system as open to challenge, and also understand this challenge to come with significant risk".[86] Indeed, ever since they started to articulate their demands publicly, many Nubian activists have been subjected to persistent intimidation and persecution, such as obstacles in carrying out legal procedures and even physical assaults.[87]

What the Nubian experience importantly shows is that, in Egypt, there is not the same type of appropriation of a global human rights discourse, in which local groups bring in local histories, understandings, and goals, as Speed has highlighted in her study of indigenous rights mobilisation in Mexico.[88] The web of connections between local activists and global actors as has been identified in the Latin American context with regard to claiming indigenous rights has been largely absent. Activists have thus often adopted a "low profile" when it comes to framing claims related to indigeneity.

The ECHR's experience petitioning the UN also sheds light upon the uneasy relationship many Nubian activists have with "global" human rights. It is clear that the progress in human rights achieved through this internationalisation was far less satisfying than expected – one activist even argues that it was not worth the risks.[89] Thus, prior to the 2015 UPR, no reports on the position of Nubians in Egypt were submitted, and the question remained unaddressed by the UPR Working Group. At the same time, the constitutional success prompted many Nubian activists to believe that the question of return could be handled domestically and outside the realm of global human rights.

President Sisi's two decrees nevertheless appear to have brought about a growing sense of hopelessness in which many youth activists feel unable to deal with the government. This has arguably re-ignited the question of internationalising the Nubian cause and prompted some Nubians to make the controversial decision to turn to regional mechanisms.[90] In response to the latest decrees, Nubian

85 MF Massoud, 'Do Victims of War Need International Law? Human Rights Education Programs in Authoritarian Sudan' (2011) 45 *Law & Society Review* 1.

86 J Lemaitre and KB Sandvik, 'Shifting Frames, Vanishing Resources, and Dangerous Political Opportunities: Legal Mobilization among Displaced Women in Colombia' (2015) 49 *Law & Society Review* 5, 33.

87 S Azer, 'Can the New Egyptian Government Deliver on the Promise of the Constitution to the Nubian People?' *Frontline Defenders* <http://www.frontlinedefenders.org/node/25624#sthash.blKNsWkM.jFNROgBf.dpuf> accessed 27 May 2015.

88 S Speed, *Rights in Rebellion* (Stanford University Press 2008).

89 Interview C, February 2015.

90 M Shams El-Din, 'Nubians May Turn to International Courts to Guarantee Return to Their Lands' *Madamasr* (19 October 2016) <http://www.madamasr.com/en/2016/10/19/feature/politics/nubians-turn-to-international-courts-to-guarantee-return-to-their-lands/> accessed 2 March 2017.

groups and civil society organisations are currently working on filing an official complaint against the Egyptian government before the ACHPR.[91]

Unsurprisingly, there is disagreement among Nubians on such international arbitration. Youth activists such as Mohammed Azmy, leader of the General Nubian Union, have argued that turning to "international courts" "is the only solution"; whereas, many others believe that it means direct confrontation with the state. Yet others are supportive of the action but are sceptical of its potential to achieve real change.[92] The failure of the UPR process is still fresh in the minds of many, as are Egypt's previous interactions with the ACHPR. In 2013, the Commission found the government guilty of physical and sexual assaults against a number of female journalists protesting in 2005, but merely demanded that Egypt re-open investigations into these cases and to compensate the victims.[93]

Moreover, engaging transnational movements and utilising an international human rights discourse can attract accusations of abandoning one's indigenous culture and preaching Western influences.[94] Nubian activists employing the human rights frame to further their demand of return faced repeated accusations of serving colonial goals and trying to divide the nation. Any appeal to international actors for assistance in claiming Nubian rights – what Nubian activists generally refer to as "internationalising the cause" – would not be seen as a legitimate form of domestic political contestation, but rather as a "geo-political threat to state security".[95] This is not the least evident in the smearing campaign that followed recent Nubian calls to hire a Danish lawyer to work on the Nubian case. Talk show host Ahmed Moussa said the calls "carry a threatening message for the Egyptian state" and questioned, "Who are these activists who represent our people? Who gave you the right to turn an Egyptian case into an international matter? Do these activists speak in the name of entities inside or outside Egypt?"[96]

The main struggle has not necessarily been one between the global and the local, but perhaps more so between generations. This fragmentation revolves around the key question of who has the right and authority to speak for and about Egypt's Nubians. Some have argued that there has been an intentional government strategy to use a divide and rule strategy within the community in order to weaken their ability to mobilise.[97] Additionally, there has long been an

91 MadaMasr, 'Nubians Escalate Demands to Return to their Lands, Plan for Protests' *Madamasr* (8 November 2016) <https://www.madamasr.com/en/2016/11/08/news/u/nubians-escalate-demands-to-return-to-their-lands-plan-for-protests/> accessed 2 March 2017.

92 Shams El-Din, 'Nubians May Turn To International Courts' (n 90).

93 Since the conclusion of the case, Egypt has not taken any action on the Commission's recommendations. African Commission on Human and Peoples' Rights, Communication 323/06 Egyptian Initiative for Personal Rights and INTERIGHTS v Egypt (12 October 2013).

94 L Chua, 'Pragmatic Resistance, Law and Social Movements in Authoritarian States: The Case of Gay Collective Action in Singapore' (2012) 46 *Law & Society Review* 713.

95 Kymlicka and Pföstl (n 24).

96 Shams El-Din, 'Nubians May Turn to International Courts' (n 90).

97 Interview F, March 2015.

open struggle between, on the one hand, the old generation and the young and, on the other, between the new elite of the Nubian community and the old one. According to one Nubian youth activist:

> The Mubarak-era Nubian elite consists of businessmen and the so-called traditional leaders of the Nubian community, who have through the years made many "deals" with the state, which have gone against the interests of the Nubian people. The new elite is trying to build its legitimacy within the Nubian community, while maintaining good relations with the state.[98]

The anger of the Nubian youth is thus not merely directed at the state, but also against the older generation and the elites. Older generation Nubians have frequently profiled their concerns as problems common to all Egyptians, for example, unemployment and lack of housing, and presenting any concerns as Nubian would therefore be seen as a clear "betrayal" of their Egyptian identity.[99] As explained above, many older generation Nubians also appear to have supported the construction of the High Dam and the subsequent Nubian resettlement.

Many of the older generation Nubians additionally appear cautious when it comes to international arbitration and seem more willing to give the government time to solve the issues domestically. As an expression of a will to seek middle ground, in September 2016, participants of a major conference dubbed "Return is a Right" gave the Egyptian government three months to comply with their demands "before the involvement of international courts".[100] During these months, older generation Nubians subsequently pressured politically for the removal of the decree that designated Nubian land as military zones.[101] Nubian youth, on the other hand, staged several protests, including the November 2016 convoy "The Nubian Return Caravan".[102] Here, more than 150 Nubians headed in 25 buses to Toshka and Forkund villages to stage a sit-in against President Sisi's decrees.

In early January 2017, the government arrested several protestors and threatened the head of the General Nubian Union with arrest unless he and his colleagues dissolved the Union. Referring to these same activists, President Sisi also called those "inciting strife" among Egyptians "people of evil".[103] A small victory was nevertheless reached when President Sisi that same month issued a decision to exclude the village of Forkund from the wider new Toshka development project.[104] While considered a breakthrough, many Nubian activists consider it not enough and continue calling for return to their lands and for the retraction of the decree concerning the military zones.

98 Emam (n 79).
99 Khallaf (n 70).
100 MadaMasr, 'Nubians Escalate Demands' (n 91).
101 Shams El-Din, 'Nubians May Turn to International Courts' (n 90).
102 Michaelson (n 83).
103 Shams El-Din, 'Activists Call' (n 80).
104 ibid.

6. Conclusions

This chapter has explored the competing frames of indigeneity and development when it comes to Nubian mobilisation regarding return to ancestral lands. In light of longstanding government attempts to quash any debates about Nubian return, the developments in recent years are remarkable. They were made possible largely due to a series of national crises, including the Egyptian Revolution in 2011, which opened up political space for an increasing number of youth activists.

Key mobilising strategies have involved framing their demands in the discourses of indigeneity and global human rights, and in more localised discourses such as development. Through the employment of the discourse of development, Nubian activists succeeded in their quest to have Nubian return explicitly mentioned in Egypt's 2014 Constitution. This constitutional success prompted many Nubian activists to believe that the question of return could be handled domestically and outside the realm of global human rights.

The militarisation of Egyptian society, as well as the shrinking space for civil society and political action under Sisi's presidency, have nevertheless brought about pressing concerns that the constitutional changes will not be implemented anytime soon.[105] These gains have recently been challenged by the Egyptian president's two decrees in 2014 and 2016 on militarising, and agriculturally developing, key land areas identified for Nubian return. This development has led to a re-invigoration of global human rights as a mobilising strategy. Nubian activists are currently attempting to bring the Nubian issue to the ACHPR.

The chapter further explored how political opportunities have been impeded by the fragmentation of Nubian activists. This fragmentation has caused tension on at least three interconnected levels: global, local, and generational. Any attempts at internationalising the cause by, for example, drawing on global human rights or engaging international actors has been persistently met with accusations of serving colonial goals and trying to divide the nation. A key question has been about who has the right and authority to speak for and about Egypt's Nubians, and there has long been an open struggle between the old generation and the young, and between the new elite and the old one.

Future research into the situation of Egypt's Nubians should essentially seek to deconstruct the tension between the global and the local, and particularly the generational and elite/non-elite dimensions of this tension. It should also closely follow Nubian mobilisation as this now once again takes an international form in the process leading to Nubian involvement in regional arbitration. In a broader perspective, scholars interested in indigenous rights should engage in the historical and political aspects of indigeneity in the Middle East and North Africa.

105 Interviews D and F, February and March 2015.

3 Politics of oneness and Twa's struggle for land

Questioning identity discourses in Rwanda

Katrijn Vanhees

Introduction

Throughout Rwandan history, discourses on identity have been imposed, appropriated, and radicalized by different actors in a quest for power. The use of identity discourses remains a contentious issue in current Rwandan society. Discourses about group identity in Rwanda mainly revolve around the Hutu and Tutsi binary. The third group, named Twa,[1] is often only attributed a bystander role in research on Rwanda. For instance, the genocide of 1994 has been meticulously researched from every possible angle, yet Twa's experiences are merely a footnote or are even extraneous to most of these studies or reports.[2] This might have a simple mathematical explanation, since Twa people only account for an estimated 0.41% of the current Rwandan population.[3] Originally identified as hunter–gatherers, the Twa community has been deprived of its forest area and finds itself in a permanent struggle for land.[4] Twa people claim to be descendants of the Pygmy community and see themselves as the first inhabitants of the Great Lakes region's forests. The Twa population is scattered over Rwanda, Uganda, the Democratic

1 For the purpose of this chapter, only the term 'Twa' (grammatical stem) will be used, although literature also refers to 'Batwa' (plural). This is in accordance with the popular use of 'Hutu' and 'Tutsi' in Western languages, instead of using 'abahutu' or 'abatutsi'. When literally citing respondents, the grammatically correct wording will be used. It is also important to note that some interviewees considered the term 'Twa' to be a pejorative appellation, which was used by other population groups to ridicule them.

2 For an exception, see for instance J Lewis, *The Batwa Pygmies of the Great Lakes Region* (Minority Rights Group International 2000) 23.

3 This figure of 2010 is an estimation by the NGO COPORWA. Recent accurate data on the exact number of Twa people in Rwanda are non-existent, which is a striking example of the fact that Twa are simply being brushed aside. S Vandeginste, 'Political Representation of Minorities as Collateral Damage or Gain: The Batwa in Burundi and Rwanda' (2014) 49 *Africa Spectrum* 3 5; COPORWA, *Potters Community of Rwanda. Five Years Strategic Plan (2010–2014)* (2010) 10; F K Ndahinda, *Indigenousness in Africa. A Contested Legal Framework for Empowerment of 'Marginalized' Communities* (TMC Asser Press 2011) 216; K Ramsay, *Uncounted: The Hidden Lives of Batwa Women* (2010).

4 Lewis (n 2) 13–18; COPORWA, 'The Socio-Economic Situation of the Historically Marginalized People in Rwanda' (2014) 16.

Republic of Congo, and Burundi. Nowadays, Twa face socio-economic challenges and the erosion of their rights.[5] The bigger picture shows that Twa people remain invisible because of ongoing structural discrimination and marginalization. These harsh living conditions have alarmed civil society, and in the effort to improve the lives of Twa, the question of indigeneity comes to the fore.

Rwanda has not ratified the Convention 169 of the International Labour Organization (ILO 169), nor does it undertake steps to implement the United Nations Declaration on the Rights of Indigenous Peoples (UNDRIP).[6] This chapter will not argue that Twa have to be recognized as indigenous, nor that they should not receive this recognition. Dealing with this question requires an extensive self-identification process within the Twa community and a comprehensive analysis to map their specific needs. The first part of this chapter will elaborate on the evolution of this self-identification process in the African context and the particular challenges Twa people may face when attempting to mobilize the indigenous peoples' framework in the Rwandan context. In general, the case of the Twa people helps to identify concrete difficulties during the pre-identification phase. Moreover, it introduces the question of how to accommodate identification claims that are made virtually impossible within a certain society.

Even though the Rwandan context is a very specific one and definitely an important case study for the analysis of identity politics, research rarely asks additional questions about how to deal with the socio-economic situation. This approach risks jumping to conclusions, since the categorization process paves the way to an essentialized analysis of a group's socio-economic position. This chapter explores the process of reifying a group's identity by highlighting two possible pitfalls when choosing 'indigenousness' as a category of analysis. Methods of identifying indigenous peoples have been criticized in the past for their lack of flexibility, on the one hand, and ignorance of intra-group dynamics, on the other.[7]

With regard to the first critique on inflexible identity processes, Twa as an identity is a social construction that is not immune to societal change. Therefore, Twa people are constantly manoeuvring to find their space in the socio-economic field that is Rwandan society. They do so by emphasizing, obscuring, and altering features of their lifestyle, which makes it possible for them to function in society. This transformation of Twa's socio-economic identity, their so-called way of living, will be studied in relation to evolving land tenure in Rwanda.

The second critique discloses intra-group dynamics in the Twa community along gender lines. Twa identity does not exist in an isolated world, nor does it

5 D Jackson, *Twa Women, Twa Rights in the Great Lakes Region of Africa* (Minority Rights Group International 2003) 4.

6 African Commission on Human and Peoples' Rights (ACHPR), *Report of the African Commission's Working Group on Indigenous Populations/Communities* (2010) 20.

7 J Corntassel, 'Who Is Indigenous? "Peoplehood" and Ethnonationalist Approaches to Rearticulating Indigenous Identity' (2003) 9 *Nationalism and Ethnic Politics* 75, 94.

hold a monopoly on what defines a group member's self-hood. Within the Twa group, other identities can be secondary to the group identity or in some situations even more dominant than the Twa identity. This may create tensions within a group that are caused by the opposing interests of different group members. To illustrate these intra-group dynamics in land issues, the relationship between gender and land within Twa communities will be analysed.

The first section of this chapter treats the relevant literature and legal documents that contextualize Twa's position in Rwandan society. In order to analyse intersectional dimensions of land ownership, 60 female members from four different Twa communities were interviewed during April 2015. These communities are located in the Southern and Eastern provinces of Rwanda. With the assistance of a community gatekeeper, Twa women were asked to participate in individual semi-structured interviews on land and gender relations within their community.

This chapter will begin by briefly explaining the controversy of translating the concept of indigenousness to the African context and more specifically to the Rwandan political climate. This will introduce Twa's position in Rwandan society from a historical and legal angle. The central part of the chapter will discuss the problematic complexities of defining Twa within the legal framework of indigenous peoples. This essentialism-based critique will point out the fluidity of Twa's identity, and it will shed a light on intra-group dynamics that may bring about contradicting interests within one group. Both analytical angles will explore land dimensions in the Twa communities. By shedding a light on these two possible pitfalls, the chapter aims to point out the consequences of essentializing a group's identity in the light of the identification process. It intends to avoid the re-occurrence of the stigmatization of Twa, a strategy previously issued by colonizers, Hutu and Tutsi in striving for domination. Therefore, this definitional process can lead to a reinforcing of discriminatory perceptions about Twa, both on an intra- and inter-group level. This in turn may eventually hinder accurate advocacy for the improvement of their socio-economic status.

1. One thousand hills, one single story: identity politics in Rwanda

Originally designed in a non-African setting, the notion of indigenousness has proven to be problematic when it is translated into other geographical and cultural contexts. One of the often-mentioned criteria to define the scope of indigenousness is that of 'first inhabitants'.[8] When applied to Africa, human occupation obviously goes way back in history, and therefore, most Africans can

8 J Gilbert, 'Indigenous Peoples' Human Rights in Africa: The Pragmatic Revolution of the African Commission on Human and Peoples' Rights' (2011) 60 *International & Comparative Law Quarterly* 245; K Lehmann, 'To Define or Not to Define: The Definitional Debate Revisited' (2007) 31 *American Indian Law Review* 509, 514.

be seen as autochthones.[9] This would inevitably lead to an erosion of the notion of indigenousness in the African context.[10] Hence, others have suggested that the idea of indigenousness in Africa only emerged after the Berlin Conference of 1884–1885, infamously known for the 'Scramble for Africa'. According to this idea, the concept of indigenousness was used as a counterpart for the colonizers' narrative, meaning that a dichotomy was created between colonizers and the original inhabitants of a certain territory.[11] Following this view, one could argue that since African states have been decolonized, the 'indigenous' peoples on the African continent are in the ruling position.[12] These discussions have led to the growing realization that the positivist, 'othering' approach, with characteristics such as the condition of priority in time and a well-delineated notion of indigenousness, had a neo-colonial flavour to it and is factually not meaningful in the African context.[13]

In reaction to this Western-centred view of indigenousness, the African Commission's Working Group of Experts on Indigenous Populations/Communities (ACWGIP) argued in 2005 that the focus should be on self-identification. This pragmatic approach would make it possible to divert attention from the problematic antecedence habituation discussion. According to the current definitional debate, claimants of indigenous rights are best positioned to define themselves as indigenous.[14] However, as American anthropologist Friedman put it aptly, 'self-definition does not occur in a vacuum, but in a world already defined'.[15] This idea of seeing indigenousness as a global and dynamic definitional process that is contextually constructed is itself contested. The notion of self-identification can be used and abused by both governments refuting official recognition of indigenous peoples and opportunistic groups seeking to rely on the broad spectrum of indigenous rights.[16] Furthermore, most post-independence African countries are not very keen on formalizing dissimilarities among their populations by recognizing indigenous peoples, because this brings

9 This observation was put forward by Alfonso Martinez, Chairperson–Rapporteur of the UN Working Group on Indigenous Populations (WGIP) in 1999, claiming that the framework of indigenous people cannot be applied to either an African or an Asian context. He preferred to categorize claims from these regions as minority claims instead of indigenous claims. Later, this position was also confirmed by R Hitchcock and D Vinding, *Indigenous Peoples' Rights in Southern Africa* (IWGIA 2004) 8; Lehmann (n 8) 513.

10 Lehmann (n 8) 522.

11 Ndahinda (n 3) 57.

12 R Niezen, *The Origins of Indigenism: Human Rights and the Politics of Identity* (2003) 72.

13 B Kingsbury, 'Indigenous Peoples in International Law: A Constructivist Approach to the Asian Controversy' (1998) 92 *The American Journal of International Law* 414; D Inman, 'Indigenous Peoples as Users of Human Rights. Pushing the Boundaries of Indigeneity and Influencing International Law' (2014) 8 *Human Rights & International Legal Discourse* 258, 266; Gilbert (n 8) 245–250.

14 Corntassel (n 7) 75.

15 J Friedman, 'The Past in the Future. History and the Politics of Identity' (1992) 94 *American Anthropologist* 837.

16 Lehman (n 8) 524, 528.

back painful memories of the 'divide and rule' tactic that was practised during colonization.[17] According to this line of thought, privileging certain groups above others might undermine national or even regional peace. In addition, the sense of nationality of post-independence or transitional states is a construct in itself, and governments are therefore wary of ideas that might interfere with and challenge the consolidation of the nation state.[18] Young nation states in Africa, therefore, often adhere to the idea of 'we-are-all-indigenous'[19] or apply a 'diversity in unity' approach.[20] Politicizing the concept of indigenousness makes legitimizing the different treatment of a specific group a highly debated issue, especially on the African continent. The questions of who defines such groups and how the definitional criteria are legitimized reveal important identity politics that occur on a global and national level.

These problems, translated to the Rwandan context, explain why Twa people in Rwanda cannot rely on the concept of indigenousness when advocating for their socio-economic rights. Even though they emphasize their unique identity within Rwandan society, they cannot get around the constitutionally based policy of oneness, so-called Rwandanicity *(ubumwe' bw' Abanyarwanda)*.[21] In order to unravel these clashing aspirations, the historical significance and meaning of identity politics in Rwandan society must be discussed first.

It is important to note that identities in Rwanda were first shaped by oral history during pre-colonial times and later entrenched by external and invasive historical narratives through anthropological studies during colonization. Consequently, written discourses on Rwandan identity have been appropriated or contested to legitimize different endeavours for political power. In other words, the colonial archive with its infamous divide and rule tactic has been internalized in the minds of Rwandan people and has often been instrumentalized for political aims. Furthermore, the notion of identity has been historically categorized as 'race, class, tribe, or ethnicity' in Rwanda.[22] Early historical writings on different identities in pre-colonial Rwanda range from a romanticized idea of harmony between various population groups to a society based on feudal order with dominant and subjugated groups. Despite this broad spectrum of interpretations, recent findings agree on the fact that group identities in Rwanda are not fixed, and a certain degree of social mobility between group identities has been acknowledged. Moreover, it has been broadly accepted that the colonizers of Rwanda re-shaped the Twa, Hutu, and Tutsi identities to racially and hierarchically structured ethnicities.[23]

17 Ndahinda (n 3) 26.
18 R Niezen, *The Origins of Indigenism: Human Rights and the Politics of Identity*; Kingsbury (n 13) 422.
19 Niezen (n 18) 7.
20 Ndahinda (n 3) 241.
21 Vandeginste (n 3) 15; *Constitution of the Republic of Rwanda* Preamble, Article 9, 13, 33.
22 Ndahinda (n 3) 215.
23 Ndahinda (n 3) 215.

In the history of Rwanda, it is impossible to deny the fact that power struggles linked to contextually moulded and clashing identities have been a leitmotif. The 1994 genocide can be considered a devastating highpoint of such extreme 'othering' politics. As a result, the current post-genocide Rwandan governing party, the Rwandan Patriotic Front (RPF), promotes the unification of the Rwandan people by silencing the existence of different identities in Rwandan society. The RPF justifies this policy as a necessary security measure for safeguarding internal peace. Criticizing the official version of Rwandan identity has been equated with propagating genocidal ideas, an act that is criminalized under the anti-genocide ideology law of 2008.[24]

It is within this context that Twa have had to tiptoe around the official discourse when advocating for the improvement of their livelihood. Identity is constructed by a deliberate selection and interpretation of historical events in order to justify current and dominant identities. This mechanism can be illustrated by looking at the way Twa people are commonly referred to, namely, as *'abasizwe inyuma n'amateka'*, which means 'people who have been left behind by history'. Even the Rwandan Constitution mentions the notion of 'historically marginalized communities' in article 82(2), which stipulates that eight members of the Senate should represent these communities in the National Parliament. Yet, in theory, the application of this term is not limited to Twa only, since they are not explicitly mentioned as such. As a result, only one Twa representative has been appointed by the president to the Senate.[25] The Twa identity of this senator is an open secret; nonetheless, it remains unclear who the other seven representatives from 'historically marginalized communities' are, since such an inquiry risks being associated with genocide ideology. In spite of pre-colonial sources indicating the significant role of certain Twa individuals in Rwandan history, the Twa identity has been consistently pushed aside by other dominant group identities, such as those of colonizers, Hutu and Tutsi.[26] As mentioned above, Friedman argues that identities are constantly evolving and reflecting power patterns in a society. According to him, 'Identity (. . .) is decisively a question of empowerment. People without history (. . .) are the people who have been prevented from identifying themselves from others'.[27] This theory of reincarnating the past in the present[28] partially explains the marginalized position of Twa people in society and the struggle for recognition of their rights in the context of the prevailing 'oneness' narrative of the current Rwandan ruling party. Through the appropriation of history by the current Rwandese rulers,

24 *Law No°18/2008 of 23/07/2008 Relating to the Punishment of the Crime of Genocide Ideology* Art.3.

25 Vandeginste (n 3) 8.

26 B Hartley, 'Rwanda's Post-Genocide Approach to Ethnicity and Its Impact on the Batwa as an Indigenous People: An International Human Rights Law Perspective' (2015) 15 *QUT Law Review* 51 60; Ndahinda (n 3) 230.

27 Friedman (n 15) 837.

28 Friedman (n 15) 853.

Twa in Rwanda are unable to expose their exclusion based on their differences and advocate for their socio-economic inclusion.

Another illustration of this strong attachment to the narrative of Rwandanicity is the government's effort to undermine any activist movement promoting the distinctness of the Twa identity. The post-genocide government condemns every non-governmental organization that amplifies Twa people's voices as a distinct identity. This policy is based on the Constitution of 2003, which promotes unity of the Rwandan people, and therefore propaganda of ethnic division is against the law. More specifically, article 54 stipulates, 'Political organizations are prohibited from basing themselves on race, ethnic group, tribe, clan, region, sex, religion or any other division which may give rise to discrimination. Political organizations must constantly reflect the unity of the people of Rwanda'. In addition, the Rwandan Parliament specified in 2008 the criteria and punishment of the crime of genocide ideology, as mentioned above.[29] Following this policy, the Rwandan Ministry of Justice denied the then-called NGO CAURWA ('Community of Autochthones Rwandans') official recognition and accused the organization of promoting genocide ideology because not only did they refer to the notion of 'indigenous' by using the word 'autochthones', but they also portrayed Twa as a separate ethnic group. In this tug-of-war with the power of identity at stake, the Rwandan government emerged as victor by forcing the organization to change their name to COPORWA ('Community of Rwandan Potters'). Paradoxically, by using the term 'Twa' themselves in their own communication, the Ministry of Justice implicitly acknowledged the existence of the Twa community in Rwandan society.[30]

2. Transformative features of Twa's socio-economic identity as a response to evolving land tenure

The ACWGIP pointed out in their report that the land of indigenous peoples is vital for the survival of these communities. The ACWGIP argued that 'the survival of their *particular* way of life depends on access to lands and natural resources' (emphasis added by author).[31] This section will argue that it is highly complex to identify a certain particular way of life in relation to land access for Twa. When describing the livelihood of the Twa community, three stereotypical keywords are often used: nomadic hunter–gatherers, landlessness, and marginalization. There is definitely an element of truth in this perception, yet caricaturing their identity makes it impossible to adequately address the complexity and versatility of their land situation. This will be demonstrated by discussing three land-related developments in the context of Twa's livelihood: the genocide of 1994, land

29 *Law No°18/2008 of 23/07/2008 Relating to the Punishment of the Crime of Genocide Ideology*.

30 L Matthews, 'The People Who Don't Exist' (2006) 30 *Cultural Survival Quarterly* 4.

31 The African Commission on Human and Peoples' *Rights, Report of the African Commission's Working Group of Experts on Indigenous Populations/Communities* (2005) 89.

commodification, and land scarcity. These events cut across Twa stereotypes and will unravel the depth and flexibility of their socio-economic identity. Before discussing the impact of these three land-related developments on the Twa community, the notion of 'land' should be clarified. Since 94% of Rwandan households are involved in subsistence agriculture,[32] land refers in this chapter to arable land (*isambu*). In the past few years, the government, religious institutions, and aid organizations have allocated plots to landless Twa communities; however, these plots are building lots that are not large enough to support a family.[33]

2.1. Land relations under stress: Twa's experiences during the genocide of 1994

Speaking about Rwanda's land tenure inevitably leads to a discussion of the role and impact of the Rwandan genocide of 1994.[34] During this violent turmoil, land relations came under stress and chaos ruled the country. Such catalysing moments that have the potential to completely transform land claims also opened up different manoeuvring spaces for Twa. Their outsiders' position transformed to a participative one on both sides of the war. Several Twa had to run for their lives during the turmoil, while others chose different, more active paths. Supposedly, 30% of the Twa population died or were murdered during and in the aftermath of the genocide. Yet, there is not much information available on how they participated and for what reasons, let alone that their losses have officially been acknowledged.[35] Their agency during the genocide ranged from passive victimhood to active perpetration.[36] Nevertheless, these events had an impact on the land situation of Twa people. Twa who fled during the genocide found their parcel seized by others when they returned:

> Before the genocide my family had sold a small piece of their parcel to another family. As a consequence of the chaos, our family had to flee during the war. However, when we returned to our village, we found out that they not only occupied the whole parcel but also alleged that they legitimately bought the whole plot before the genocide. We went to the local authorities to complain about the situation, but they did not listen to us. They minimized the case.[37]

32 J Crook, 'Promoting Peace and Economic Security in Rwanda through Fair and Equitable Land Rights' (2006) 94 *California Law Review* 1489.

33 J Woodburn, 'Indigenous Discrimination: The Ideological Basis for Local Discrimination against Hunter–Gatherer Minorities in Sub-Saharan Africa' (1997) 20 *Ethnic and Racial Studies* 345, 347.

34 Even before the genocide, there were large migration waves that created tension in the land tenure system. For instance, some women recounted that their family had lost land during the violent revolution of 1959 in which Hutu people took over power and drove many Tutsi into exile.

35 CC Taylor, 'Molders of Mud: Ethnogenesis and Rwanda's Twa' (2011) 76 *Ethnos* 183, 204; Lewis (n 2) 23–34.

36 Field research 2015, interview Twa 3, 4, 5, 18, 30, 35, 37.

37 Field research 2015, interview 38.

This sense of powerlessness was echoed in other stories, but it was not always caused by the inaction of administrative institutions. One interviewee narrated that the social context is too hostile to re-claim lost land:

> Before my father died, he had a piece of land in X. Nowadays, the land is occupied by force and used for free by repatriates [returning refugees after 1994]. We are too scared to go back there and claim our land. If one of us would go back there to claim the land, she or he will be poisoned![38]

Others took part one way or another in genocidal activities for various reasons and eventually had to pay a high price for their involvement. A Twa woman explained the following:

> My father stole a goat during the genocide from his Tutsi neighbour. After the genocide, he had to appear before the Gacaca.[39] They decided that, in order to compensate for the loss of the goat, he had to give his parcel to the remaining family members of his neighbour. This parcel was worth at least 4,000,000 Rwandese Franc.[40] The local authorities chased us away when we complained about this unfair punishment. Afterwards, we went to the district level, but they said that the family had sold the parcel for 3,500,000 Rwandese Franc[41] and that it would be impossible to claim it back.[42]

Not only men were involved in the genocide; female participation has long been silenced in Rwandan society and post-genocide reports. Contrary to popular belief, women were not on the sidelines.[43] Some testimonies made reference to female protagonists in the genocide. An interviewed woman testified that she was accused of looting. As a consequence, she had to sell her land in order to reimburse the victims.

This lack of information on Twa's experiences during the genocide is problematic because it ignores one of the root causes of Twa's current precarious land situation. As usual, Twa people are only attributed a bystander position, which makes their land issues invisible. Addressing their experiences during the 1994 events should help to understand their post-genocide land issues.

2.2. The impact of land commodification on Twa's socio-economic situation

Where before land tenure was based upon both legal regulations that date back to colonial times and informal norms, post-genocide Rwanda has embarked on

38 Field research 2015, interview 13.
39 Local community justice forum.
40 5,961.40 dollars.
41 5,216.20 dollars.
42 Field research, interview 31.
43 N Hogg, 'Women's Participation in the Rwandan Genocide: Mothers or Monsters?' (2010) 92 *International Review of the Red Cross* 69 70.

a wide-ranging land formalization process. In 2004, the Rwandan government designed a land policy that would make the land tenure system more transparent, efficient, and secure.[44] Key features of this policy were drafting a new land tenure law and systemizing the land administration by registering all plots. Parallel with the transformation of the land tenure system, Twa perceptions about land and its use changed, too. With the upcoming land market, land was progressively commodified and its monetary value increased. This process went hand in hand with a formalization of land ownership.[45] During colonial and pre-colonial times, Twa used to live in the forests as hunter–gatherers. Later, the woodland started to disappear slowly because of increased economic forestation activity by the colonizers and other Rwandan groups and the pressing need for arable land. Yet, the deprivation of their forest land was also aggravated by nature conservation projects, such as Nyungwe Forest National Park, that took place in the last decade of the 20th century.[46] Most Twa were not adequately compensated for the loss of their forest land, although some managed to obtain farmland. Over the years, Twa's identity shifted from being nomadic hunter–gatherers to a more sedentary existence. Evidently, this shift to a semi-nomadic lifestyle was not an entirely smooth process. Twa people were not used to managing land, and especially not familiar with the commercial side of the land market. During interviews, people often compared their views on land with those from previous generations. After decades of living a nomadic lifestyle, Twa only recently have started to truly value actual ownership of land, both legal and de facto possession.

In contrast with the land perceptions of their antecedents, the younger Twa generation is determined to valorise their knowledge about the value of land:

> How can we develop ourselves if we have to wake up every morning to work on the fields of other people? As long as we do not own any land, we, Twa women, cannot improve our situation. Every day we work on someone else's field for some money that we immediately consume the same day. The next day, the same story starts all over. So how can we develop ourselves?[47]

Before, Twa could be easily tricked into selling their parcels at a low price, not knowing the actual value and importance of land. This ignorance was combined with a desperate need for money. Moreover, some non-Twa people exploited the chaos after the genocide to make shady pre-genocide deals look legitimate. Several women stated during the interviews that they lost their land due to

44 *National Land Policy* 22.

45 JE Burnet and RISD, 'Culture, Practice, and Law: Women's Access to Land in Rwanda ' in L M Wanyeki (ed), *Women and Land in Africa: Culture, Religion and Realizing Women's Rights* (Zed Books 2003) 181.

46 Lewis (n 2) 6.

47 Field research 2015, interview 47.

stress sales. Their family 'sold' their land in exchange for food, such as a goat. The following account illustrates these kinds of unfortunate transaction:

> My husband's father used to frequent cabarets to drink beer. One day, he met a man at the cabaret, who gave him 2,500 RwFr[48] to rent the family's parcel [family of her husband], although they originally agreed on 3,000 RwFr.[49]Afterwards, the man asserted that he had bought the land. My father-in-law went to the abunzi[50] to complain about this situation, but they said that the man should only pay the outstanding amount of 500 RwFr.[51] I think they did not listen to him because we are abatwa and we do not have any say in such things.[52]

Consequently, Twa are often in a weak bargaining position on the land market because they are in dire straits when it comes to making ends meet. During one of the interviews, a Twa woman noted the following:

> I do not have access to land, because my family-in-law does not possess any plots. Even families who do own small parcels are selling them because they have a lot of problems and are very poor. They are forced to sell their land at a very low price, otherwise they would starve to death. My father-in-law used to own land, but some abahutu appropriated it. Abatwa were not developed enough at that time, [so] they could easily be cheated.[53]

Coming from a nomadic hunter–gatherer existence, the shift to a sedentary lifestyle did not happen naturally. This struggle became more aggravated with the gradual intensification of the land market. The revaluation of land is an important aspect of Twa's evolving perception and use of land. It shows that their particular way of living has transformed into another lifestyle than the stereotypical portrayal of Twa may suggest.

2.3. Ongoing land scarcity: a need for diversification of Twa's economic activities

Rwanda has a historical link with land scarcity, and the current population growth rate does not predict any improvement from a Malthusian perspective. Confronted with this land scarcity, owning land is an economic goal many Twa may never achieve. Therefore, Twa attempt to mitigate the challenges of sedentary life in a land-scarce context through the diversification of income-generating activities

48 3.67 dollars.
49 4.40 dollars.
50 Local mediation court.
51 0.74 dollars.
52 Field research 2015, interview 34.
53 Field research 2015, interview 37.

including off-land labour. One of their main economic activities is *guca inshuro*, which is a form of temporary employment. Most of the time, this involves working on the fields of others. The interviewed Twa stressed that, in spite of their stereotypical branding as hunter–gatherers, they do know how to cultivate. The availability of *guca inshuro* is highly unpredictable and poorly paid since supply is high. This labour is mostly manual, since the schooling level of Twa people is generally low.[54]

Another typical income-generating activity of Twa is the production of various artisanal products. The fabrication of clay pots is one of their most well-known artisanal activities. Unfortunately, pottery is today far from a lucrative business. The sale of traditional pots has been pushed out by the emergence of cheaper and hardwearing industrial pots. Twa complain that the sales figures of pots have plummeted, and that now, pots are barely worth between 50–100 RwFr.[55] One woman exemplified the matter by saying that 'for one big pot, they would only give you a cup of beans'. Therefore, Twa try to find other income-generating activities by, for instance, selling gathered wood, weaving little baskets (*agaseke*), and producing skewers (*burusheti*). There is currently a higher demand for skewers than pots, but unfortunately, both products only generate very low profit.

Summing up, this section has shown that Twa's identity does not exist in isolation. Contemporary societal changes continue to transform certain socio-economic aspects of Twa's identity, most notably their use of the land and their perceptions of it. Land ownership plays a pivotal role in defining Twa's socio-economic identity. When land relations come under stress, as they did during the genocide of 1994 or in times of land scarcity, Twa manoeuvre to secure their livelihood by developing survival strategies or diversifying their economic activities. These moments of visible agency that still impact their current land situation remain underexposed. This is problematic because it simplifies Twa's land situation as being caused by marginalization, a reasoning that preserves itself and does not allow for reflections about accurate solutions. In order to fully grasp the complex background of Twa's land use and perceptions about land, it will be necessary to look further than the stereotypical hunter–gatherer identity to accommodate the needs of Twa's transformed socio-economic status within the context of the indigeneity question.

3. Addressing intra-group realities: Twa's land access from a gender perspective

Whereas the section on pages 52–57 explored the common conditions that affect all Twa as a group, this part will point out the individualized socio-economic interests of group members. For this purpose, land relations will be analysed from

54 COPORWA, 'The Socio-Economic Situation of the Historically Marginalized People in Rwanda'.
55 0.10 dollars.

a gender perspective. Highlighting gendered land divisions will demonstrate the necessity of keeping an intersectional perspective in mind when talking about group identity in indigenous discourses.

Access to land is mainly achieved through two channels in Rwanda. First, land can be acquired via the commercialized land market, namely, by buying or renting land. Second, people acquire access to land through their social networks, which should be understood as the family unit and relations within their community. Examples of these kinds of acquisitions are the inheritance and donation of land. Entering the commercial land market is rare for Twa, since their economic position is not strong enough to be an active player on the land market.

Therefore, in most cases, Twa have access to land through a web of gendered relations. These relations should not solely be interpreted as the interaction between men and women in the context of the household. Women's claims to land are equally influenced by their interaction and association with other female members of the community.

Furthermore, women sometimes explained that they were allowed to use the parcel of a village neighbour (often a non-Twa) because people would pity their situation. This right of use was often compensated by manual labour or by sharing the harvest.

Nevertheless, in general, the family unit is the most common gateway to gain access to land. Within the family unit, land is passed on through the practice of inter vivos inheritance, the so-called *umunani*. According to the original interpretation of this practice, parents gave a parcel to their son on the occasion of his marriage, whereas daughters would only rarely receive a part of the family's land. If a daughter did receive land, it was usually a small plot that was left.[56]

> I have received umunani from my parents. I have three sisters and five brothers. We divided the land and my brothers took the biggest share. However, we, girls, we only got small plots of land. We did not say anything about it.[57]

This unequal division of the family land used to be broadly accepted in the community since women were supposed to live off the land of their husband's family.

The composition of the family unit drastically transformed after the genocide of 1994, since the majority of Rwandan families have thinned out through the loss of (mostly) male relatives. Family members were scattered throughout the country, and some are still today located outside the borders of Rwanda. Due to the transformation of family units, the Rwandan Parliament revised the Civil Code and enacted a new inheritance law in 1999 that recognized an equal inheritance right for all children, regardless of their sex.[58] This made it possible for female orphans and widows to inherit their share of the family land.

56 J Adriaenssens, *La Parenté, Le Mariage, La Famille Au Rwanda* (1964) 58.

57 Field research 2015, interview 58.

58 Law No°27/2016 of 08/07/2016 *Law Governing Matrimonial Regimes, Donations and Successions* Art.54.

Despite the fact that the preference for male heirs is still culturally prevalent nowadays, there are cases in which families would negotiate a more pragmatic division of the land. Sometimes the largest plot would be given to the child who needed it the most. Siblings who live further away from the family land could also agree that the brother or sister who resided nearby the plot would be allowed to use and exercise control over the land.

During the interviews, various Twa women mentioned conflicts in the family between siblings about the division of the family land. One of the reasons for these conflicts was the favouritism of male children when apportioning the land. Women complained that their family land was too small to divide to give each sibling a decent part. To complicate the matter even more, the Land Law of 2013 prohibits the division of land smaller than one hectare.[59] Therefore, many families decide to sell their parcel and divide the profit among the siblings, not necessarily in an equal way. Women explained that they used the proceeds of the sale to rent fields to cultivate or to buy food because in none of the cases was the profit sufficient to purchase a different parcel. In the majority of the cases, family land among the Twa community was non-existent or too small to divide. As explained on page 55, landlessness is a cross-generational issue for the Twa community. The interviewees often referred to the unfortunate situation of their parents and ancestors, who did not own any land either or possessed only a small parcel of bad quality.

In addition, women did not have a prosperous future in mind for their children because they would not be able to give *umunani* to them. These unfavourable family relations hinder Twa people in escaping poverty. Another concern that was often expressed during the interviews was the fact that Twa men could not provide their household with any land. As previously discussed, the pre-inheritance practice that favours male children used to be justified in Rwandan culture because women could live off their husband's parcel. However, Twa families rarely own sufficient land or, when they do, it is poor quality land. As a consequence, young men are left empty handed when they get married.[60] This is exactly the crux of the issue. As a consequence, Twa women do not have access to land through their affinal network, either. One of the interviewed Twa women said that her partner completely let her down during the construction of their house. She ended up selling her own *umunani* in order to finance the final construction works of the house. Others denounced the mismanagement of the land by their husband and the women's lack of power to raise their voices about it.

> My husband used to own land but he sold it, due to his foolishness! They gave him little money for it and he just spend it on meat and beer. In that time, women could not say anything about it because husbands had a strong position in the household.[61]

59 *Organic Law No°03/2013 of 16/06/2013 Repealing Organic Law N°08/2005 of 14/07/2005 Determining the Use and Management of Land in Rwanda* Art.30

60 M Sommers, *Stuck: Rwandan Youth and the Struggle for Adulthood* (Athens 2012) 122.

61 Field research 2015, interview 51.

Another weakness of the affinal network is men's unwillingness to officially register their marriage.[62] Since the revision of the Civil Code in 1999, spouses have had the right to inherit the matrimonial property. Unfortunately, the scope of the revised Civil Code is limited to officially married couples.[63] Half of the interviewed Twa women who were involved in a relationship stated that they were not officially married. Compared with national statistics, which state that 17.2% of the couples nationwide remain in unofficial marriages,[64] this number is considerably higher. Moreover, all interviewed unmarried couples had been cohabiting with their husband for at least four years and some of them even for over 20 years. Why, then, did Twa women not enter into an official marriage, which is potentially more beneficial for them? Interestingly, ignorance is not an explanation, since Twa women are well aware of the advantages of official marriage. They mentioned benefits such as a secured union, increased decision-making power in the household and, most importantly for their land access, the right to an equal share of the matrimonial property. The following quote from a 59-year-old Twa woman can illustrate this matter:

> Of course there are advantages! When you are officially married, your husband cannot treat you just the way he wants. And even if he does, you can go to the local authorities to complain about it. And there are even more advantages. When you have children together and your husband would say: 'You, my wife, I do not want you anymore', in that event your children can demand their umunani [pre-inheritance land] and they would let their mother stay on it.[65]

This automatic recognition of children was often mentioned as an important advantage of an official marriage. Interestingly, reasons for an informal marriage differed according to age. Older Twa women reported that when they met their husband, official marriage was not so relevant. In those days, great importance was attached to customary marriage, which involved the donation of a dowry (*inkwano*), which would solemnize the union and link both families of the pair. Younger interviewees told a different story. First, some couples do not formalize their marriage because they cannot comply with the legal requirements of a civil marriage, as stipulated by the Civil Code. For instance, the minimum age to enter into an official marriage (21 years old) is a formal obstacle for minors.[66]

62 This refers to a registered marriage as opposed to an informal, non-civil marriage. Rwandan people refer to the latter kind of marriage as an illegal marriage. This stigmatizing wording is only used in this chapter when literally citing interviewees. Preferable terms to describe this sort of marriage in a more neutral way are informal, de facto, or consensual unions or relationships.

63 *Law No 22 of 13/11/1999 to Supplement Book One of the Civil Code and to Institute Part Five Regarding Matrimonial Regimes, Liberalities and Successions Art 70.*

64 National Institute for Statistics Rwanda, *Demographic and Health Survey 2014–15* (2016) 8.

65 Field research 2015, interview 58.

66 *Law No 32/2016 of 28/08/2016 Governing Perons and Family* Art 168.

Second, many women explained that they could not afford the organization of a formal wedding ceremony due to their limited financial resources. Despite the organization of mass weddings by the government, figures on informal marriages have maintained a status quo over the years. Therefore, poverty alone cannot be a substantial explanation for the persistent existence of informal marriages. The interviewed women often complained that neither they nor the government could force their partner to officially register their union. This explanation reveals an ongoing gendered conflict in the household whereby both partners want to preserve their own interests. The outcome of the conflict depends on the bargaining power of both sexes.[67] In most cases, men refuse to enter into a formal marriage because they fear that granting their partner the status of official wife would create an instability in the household that would disfavour them. This fear is exacerbated by myths depicting official marriage as an institute that turns women into unbearable wives terrorizing their husbands. An informally married woman is more likely to obey her partner, since there is a constant threat of being abandoned without any right to claim a part of the property. This phenomenon places women in a stressful position that is difficult to escape. Opt-out options are often non-existent since the family network still tends to assign their resources to male members. Being involved in a formal marriage would require men to consult their partner and to even ask for permission concerning property transactions. For example, consent of both spouses is obligatory when selling immovable property that belongs to the marital patrimony.[68] Interestingly, this narrative was also appropriated by a Twa woman whose partner, unlike her, did not have access to land. She obtained a parcel of land through inheritance.

> No, I am not legally married. Why? Because I do not want to share my property with my partner. He did not contribute anything to the household and he does not own any land. Only our children are allowed to inherit my land.[69]

Moreover, the diversification of economic activities also has consequences for gender relations within the Twa community. The traditional role of the men as sole breadwinners has slowly disappeared due to the impossibility of maintaining their status as hunter–gatherers. As a consequence, women have attained a more central position in the household, an evolution which is not only a threat for internal group cohesion but also a source for gender-based violence.[70]

67 B Agarwal, 'Bargaining and Gender Relations: Within and Beyond the Household' (1997) 3 *Feminist Economics* 1, 4.

68 *Law No°22 of 13/11/1999 to Supplement Book One of the Civil Code and to Institute Part Five Regarding Matrimonial Regimes, Liberalities and Successions.*

69 Field research 2015, interview 47.

70 Jackson (n 5) 10; Ramsay (n 3) 10.

Furthermore, there is a lack of official land titles within the Twa community, yet those who were able to register their land were mostly men. Women complained during the interviews that they were not included in the land registration process.

There is no doubt that the glorification of civil marriage was originally intended to enhance gender equality. Nevertheless, the actual outcome of this policy reveals a different story. Since men are, in general, economically and socially in a stronger position, they have the option to use formal law and socially gendered practices to their own advantage. The outcome of this negotiation game has a highly unfavourable outcome for women, especially for Twa women, since informal marriages frequently occur within the Twa community. They are forced to remain in a very unstable and unpredictable living situation, without any vital escape options.

Conclusion

It would be an understatement to say that Twa's socio-economic situation is challenging. They suffer from poverty, a low education level, discrimination, and landlessness. During interviews, participants would frequently mumble that they would have to go to bed with an empty stomach again that day. These harsh living conditions are certainly not enviable. They have prompted non-governmental organizations and COPORWA to represent Twa's interests and to advocate for their needs. In doing so, the question of indigenousness has come to the fore. However, discussing whether Twa should be recognized as an indigenous people requires a long consultation process within the Twa community. In addition, their advocacy work is often stalled because of the current political climate in Rwanda. The Rwandan government has introduced the idea of oneness by prohibiting any identification as a distinct group within the Rwandan identity. This policy is motivated by the country's horrific past where explicitly profiling a group's identity has ended up in genocide. Nowadays, Twa's identity manifests itself in a disguised, so-called more neutral version of a 'community of potters'.

The second part of this chapter has elaborated on the ways that identifying as indigenous entails risks essentializing Twa's lifestyle. Their socio-economic situation is often too easily causally linked to the fact that they are part of a discriminated or historically marginalized group. Their current land situation is indeed significantly worse than that of other groups in Rwandan society; however, the reason behind this cannot be entirely based upon their identification as a marginalized group. Consequently, this chapter has explored how Twa socio-economic identity has changed through a survival strategy to adapt to an ever-changing society. This can be illustrated through analysis of the impact of evolving land tenure in Rwanda on Twa's land access. Three major societal processes have changed the livelihood of many Twa. To begin with, land relations became highly insecure during and after the genocide. The impact of this aspect of the genocide on Twa's livelihood has rarely been researched. During this period, some Twa manoeuvred actively by appropriating the assets of others.

Eventually, they had to pay a price in the aftermath of the genocide whereby they had to compensate victims by selling their land. Others adopted a more passive role or were themselves victims of land seizures. These untold stories help to explain Twa's current land situation, instead of solely focusing on their so-called marginalized bystander position. Second, the transformation of the land market has significantly influenced Twa's living situation. Twa people were originally hunter–gatherers with little knowledge of a sedentary lifestyle. This all started to change when conservation policies labelled forests as protected nature areas where Twa people were no longer welcome. Later, Twa people were confronted with the land commodification process that was intensified by the land registration. Only slowly did they start to realize the actual value of land. As a consequence, many Twa people were tricked by other non-Twa into selling their land at a low price. Most of these sales were driven by the urgency of providing basic needs for their family. Third, this process was exacerbated by the ongoing land scarcity due to population growth. Therefore, Twa people had to think of other ways to survive. Leaving behind their hunter–gatherer status, they moved to more sedentary income-generating activities such as pottery. However, with the introduction of cheaper industrial pots, this activity eventually became non-profitable. Land pressure forced Twa to divert their economic activities to manual labour on the fields of others in exchange for money or food. This diversification of economic activities has led to a changed socio-economic identity. The genocide, the formalization of the land market, and land scarcity all had an impact on the socio-economic identity of Twa. Their so-called marginalized position cannot simply be explained by a circular reasoning that is based on their stereotypical identity as hunter–gatherers or potters.

The third part has discussed the relevance of highlighting intra-group dynamics when talking about group identity in indigenous discourses. Again, this section focused on the land situation of Twa, but it more specifically drew attention to the impact of gender on land relations. Interviews with Twa women showed that women face more difficulties when securing their land access. Even though the Rwandan government has officially prohibited any discrimination based upon gender, land is still commonly passed on from father to son. Moreover, there seems to be a current tendency to remain in unofficial marriages. This phenomenon cannot simply be explained by pointing out Twa's ignorance about the benefits of civil marriage. The interviews showed that Twa are well aware that official marriage offers them a secure household, equal decision-making power in the household and, most importantly, the right to inherit the marital property. It is true that some Twa are simply unable to comply with the legal criteria that are put forward by the Civil Code, such as the minimum age. Moreover, others declared that they could not afford the ceremonial costs of a formal wedding. Yet, when analysing this matter more in depth, it seems that there is an unwillingness among men to register their marriage. Men intend to maintain their dominant position within the household, since an official marriage would mean sharing their decision-making power. Moreover, they do not see a formal marriage as fair since their partners did not bring any land to the partnership. This was not problematic in the past, since a woman still had a strong fall-back position in her own family and her claims to the conjugal land were weaker. However, with the establishment of the new Civil Code and the strengthening of spousal rights, this arrangement has become unbalanced at the expense of women's property rights. Therefore, these findings demonstrate that there are competing interests and gendered power relations within the Twa community with respect to land access.

The question of indigeneity becomes a possible strategy in the process of advocating for the improvement of Twa's socio-economic position. However, dominant identity discourses make it virtually impossible to express any desire to recognize their unique position within Rwandan society. The case study of Twa in Rwanda presents the question of how groups can mobilize the indigenous framework in societies that forbid such strategies. Moreover, through the analysis of their land situation, there is a need to accommodate their fluid socio-economic identity and to take intra-group and especially gender dynamics into account.

4 The impact of migration processes on indigenous peoples' rights

Challenges for identity and culture

Asier Martínez de Bringas

To date, very few rigorous attempts have been made within the social sciences to assess the strength and quality of indigenous peoples' rights in migratory processes.[1] This chapter considers the complex circumstances surrounding indigenous migration. Indigenous migration, either voluntary or forced, will be discussed in its broadest sense, including migration across the borders of states that divide indigenous territories and jurisdictions, as well as indigenous migration across continents.

There has been a dramatic change to the individual and collective rights of indigenous peoples in recent years, resulting from the ILO Convention Concerning Indigenous and Tribal Peoples 1989 (No. 169) and from the United Nations Declaration on the Rights of Indigenous Peoples (UNDRIP) adopted in 2007. These remarkable regulatory developments in the collective rights of indigenous peoples have meant that their claims, needs and demands have had a strong impact on the institutional apparatus of human rights at local, regional, national and international levels.

While the discourse on indigenous collective rights has seen a significant advancement, the discourse on migrants' rights and, by implication, the rights of indigenous peoples regarding migration-related issues, have not progressed to the same extent. On the contrary, the rights of indigenous peoples who migrate have been extremely weakened and restricted.[2] Yet, migratory processes also need to be considered from the point of view of human rights.[3] Civil, political, social,

1 We fundamentally refer to the strong and dense nature of indigenous collective rights, such as territory, autonomy and jurisdiction.

2 J Rodriguez and G Busso, *Migración Interna y Desarrollo en América Latina Entre 1980 y 2005: Un Estudio Comparativo con Perspectiva Regional Basado en Siete Países* (CEPAL, Santiago de Chile, 2009); L Velasco, 'Migraciones Indígenas Mexicanas a Estados Unidos: Un Acercamiento a las Etnicidades Transnacionales', in *Los Grandes Problemas de México. III. Migraciones Internacionales*, Francisco Alba and others (El Colegio de México, 2010) 317–354.

3 This study seeks to address this research gap. This was the main objective of the Research for Excellence project in which I participated entitled 'Migrations and indigenous peoples of Ecuador and Bolivia in Spain. Specific situations and perspectives in the Autonomous Communities of Andalusia, Murcia and Valencia' funded by the Regional Department of Economy, Science

economic and cultural human rights, individual and collective, are solid and consistent when they are approached from a theoretical point of view.[4] However, in the context of conflict-ridden, delocalised processes such as those of migration, these rights cease to have tangible effects.[5]

Migration policies are generally based on a political philosophy that adamantly portrays migrants as rootless, superfluous people who are out of place and display threatening behaviour and actions that should be prevented. Policies are predominantly aimed at containing and limiting migratory flows, and the legal status of migrant people is always marked by a *state of emergency*.[6]

Migratory flows are linked to the thorny concept of citizenship, a key legal category created by Modernity to regulate and qualify difference. It is expressed

and Innovation of Andalusia and the European Regional Development Fund (ERDF) (P07-HUM-03040). The main purpose of the working group that forms part of the Research for Excellence project was to analyse the socio-economic, cultural, political and legal vulnerability and lack of protection of the Ecuadorian and Bolivian immigrant population, with special emphasis on the indigenous populations of both countries. Four thematic areas were considered: (a) human rights and citizenship; (b) interculturality; (c) gender; and (d) community participation and management. The research was focused on three geographical areas in Spain, Andalusia, Murcia and Valencia, as these are regions characterised for receiving a large number of Ecuadorian and Bolivian indigenous immigrants. The project was divided into two phases, a research phase and an intervention phase. The research was aimed at diagnosing the general conditions of the indigenous population concerned, through the collection of information from indigenous people from Ecuador and Bolivia by conducting interviews and surveys. The questions dealt with the most urgent needs of this population group and with some forms of discrimination and violations of human rights that they experienced in the places where they lived with both migrant population and Spanish natives. The intervention sought to avoid research models that would separate the objects of study from the observing subjects, and an indigenous rights approach was adopted in the research process. To this end, seminars were organised to serve as meeting places between the indigenous migrants and the research team. In an attempt to have an impact on Spanish public policy in order to improve the living conditions of indigenous migrants in Spain, avenues were explored to strengthen dialogue and promote intercultural exchanges between the parties involved, as well as foster their empowerment. The research project lasted three years and involved 800 migrant participants, used an interdisciplinary methodology and placed special emphasis on indigenous migration in Spain. cf. D Sánchez and P Cruz, *Indigenous Peoples, Identities and Rights in Migratory Contexts* (Icaria 2011).

4 By theoretical point of view, we mean International Human Rights Law and its treatment of indigenous peoples.

5 Central to the debate was the 'implementation gap', as described by Stavenhagen as Special Rapporteur on the situation of human rights and fundamental freedoms of indigenous people. This problem relates to the difference between the formal recognition of an (indigenous) right and its practical application. In other words, even though certain rights have been formally recognised, indigenous communities see them violated in their life on a regular basis. Report of the Special Rapporteur on the situation of Human Rights and fundamental freedoms of indigenous people, UN doc. E/CN.4/2006/78/Add.2 (15 December 2005).

6 A De Giorgi, *Tolerancia Cero. Estrategias y Prácticas de la Sociedad del Control* (Virus 2005) 81–124; S Sassen, *Contrageografías de la Globalización. Género y Ciudadanía en los Circuitos Transfronterizos* (Editorial Traficantes de Sueños 2003) 65–82; S Sassen, *Inmigrantes y Ciudadanos. De las Migraciones Masivas a la Europa Fortaleza* (Siglo XXI 2013).

in the original dichotomy between the rights of citizens and the rights of migrants. Migrants are usually excluded from protections afforded to citizens and qualified as 'non-citizens', separate from the body of 'nationals'. Citizens' rights are therefore granted in a reductive manner.

There is a paradoxical and ambivalent relationship between human rights and citizens' rights. Whereas indigenous individuals and peoples are recognised by international law as holders of human rights, they are denied civil, political, economic, social and cultural rights by the laws of states. This is the paradox of citizenship.[7]

This chapter presents an in-depth study of how migratory processes impact the rights of indigenous peoples. It analyses the changes and transformations that occur in indigenous peoples' identity as a result of being compelled to migrate, and discloses the latent violence underlying forced migration. The chapter is divided into four sections. The first section discusses the difficulties encountered by social science and legal research in addressing the complexity of the migratory processes of indigenous peoples. The second section provides a mapping of these processes in order to understand and assess their complexity. The third section describes some of the particular problems involving the migratory processes of indigenous peoples. And the fourth section specifically addresses the impacts that these problems have on the rights of indigenous peoples.

The critical analysis in this chapter seeks to show the hard and conflicting aspects of indigenous migratory processes and to dismantle some myths about how many of these processes are narrated. The study is informed by previous research that adopted an interdisciplinary approach. Therefore, it is the outcome of an interaction between different epistemic branches, such as the sociology of law, international human rights law, anthropology and other branches of social science.

1. Problems involved in researching indigenous peoples' migratory processes

Two major problems arise when researching indigenous peoples' migration. They result from the general lack of concern about, and apathetic approach to, these issues.

7 The lack of citizenship implies, for instance, limits to migrants' political rights. See J Barbalet, *Citizenship: Rights, Struggle and Class Inequality* (Open University Press 1998); E Balibar, *¿Nosotros Ciudadanos de Europa?* (Tectnos 2003); Z Bauman, *Archipiélago de Excepciones* (Katz 2008); C Wihtol de Wenden, *Face aux Migrants: État de Droit ou état de Siege* (Textuel 2007); J de Lucas, 'Superar el Vínculo de la Nacionalidad: La Potencialidad del Artículo 15 de la DUDH' (2014) 35 *Revista de Derecho Migratorio y Extranjería* 29–42; 'Borders, Violence, Law' (2014) 2 *The Age of Human Rights Journal* 46–50.

The first problem is the lack of pertinent data about the subject, from the point of view of sociology, from which to infer principles and standards for political and regulatory action. While there is a large corpus of data to explain and interpret migratory flows in general, it is extremely difficult to obtain references to provide a portrayal of and interpret indigenous peoples' migratory processes. There is an epistemological gap in the sociology of migration[8] regarding indigenous migration flows, both within and across national borders. This is not a new issue. It can be traced back to the lack of reliable studies and censuses that could assist in understanding indigenous identities and worldviews and how these are rooted within national borders. In addition, the quantitative research conducted about indigenous peoples within states (such as indigenous censuses) rendered a distorted version of indigenous reality. Approaches to the 'indigenous issue' at state level have been typically characterised by a lack of data on the sociological understanding of indigenous identity in migratory processes and by the manipulation and politicisation of such data. A critical, rights-based, radical view on the relationship between indigenous peoples and migration has been precluded by all of the above elements. However, there have been some interesting developments following the regulatory changes arising from the recognition of indigenous rights. The population and housing censuses in Latin America are an indication of such recovery. In this region, there has been a gradual increase in the number of countries that have widely identified and recognised indigenous peoples within their borders by relying on self-identification.[9]

8 CEPAL, *Los Pueblos Indígenas en América Latina. Avances en el Último Decenio y Retos Pendientes Para la Garantía de Sus Derechos* (Naciones Unidas 2014); L Velasco Ortíz `Agentes Étnicos Transnacionales: Las Organizaciones de Indígenas Migrantes en la Frontera México–Estados Unidos´ (2002) 20 59 *Estudios Sociológicos* 335–370; M Sánchez Gómez and R Barceló, `Mujeres Indígenas Migrantes: Cambios y Redefiniciones Genéricas y Étnicas en Diferentes Contextos de Migración´ (2008) 14 *Amérique Latine Histoire & Memoire. Les Cahiers Alhim* <http://alhim.revues.org/2292>; J Rodriguez and G Busso, *Migración Interna y Desarrollo en América Latina Entre 1980 y 2005: Un Estudio Comparativo con Perspectiva Regional Basado en Siete Países* (CEPAL 2009); A Portes, 'Convergencias Teóricas y Evidencias Empíricas en el Estudio del Transnacionalismo de los Inmigrantes' (2005) 4 *Migración y Desarrollo* 2–19; P Cruz Zuñiga, `Pueblos Indígenas, Migración Transnacional e Identidades. Retos y Desafíos en la Migración de los Pueblos Indígenas de Ecuador Hacia España´ (2010) 18 34 *Revista Interdisciplinar de Movilidad Humana* 81, 98.

9 Whereas in the 1970s and 1980s only isolated, manipulated censuses were available; the 1990, 2000 and 2010 rounds increased the statistical visibility of indigenous groups, especially as a result of the demands and pressures of indigenous organisations, the positive responses of specialised government bodies and the support of international agencies, non-governmental organisations and academics, among others. cf. In this regard, CEPAL, *Panorama Social de América Latina 2006* (United Nations 2007); CEPAL/Celade, *Censos 2010 y la Inclusión del Enfoque Étnico: Hacia una Construcción Participativa con Pueblos Indígenas y Afrodescendientes de América Latina, Seminarios y Conferencias* (United Nations 2009); F Del Popolo and S Schkolnik, `Pueblos Indígenas y Afrodescendientes en los Censos 2010 de América Latina: Avances y Desafíos en el Derecho a la Información´ (2013) 40 97 *Notas de Población* 215; F Del Popolo and S Schkonik, `Indigenous

A second problem is the lack of a conceptual framework to locate the relationship between indigenous peoples and migration. The important contribution that an international sociology of migration processes could make to the debate on international migration, voluntary and involuntary migration, temporary migration, remittances and return flows remains outstanding with regard to indigenous peoples. Their specificities would change the understanding of their migration processes and raise significant questions in relation to indigenous peoples' rights in migratory contexts. For instance, would the important weight that territory typically has in indigenous peoples' worldviews and in the understanding of their overall rights allow the same significance to be given to territoriality and other rights after indigenous migratory processes have taken place? Or should the opposite be inferred, that indigenous rights would lose importance in migration contexts? Do remittances serve as bridges for communication and connection between indigenous migrants and their native communities? Or is it precisely in this process that indigenous migrants reach a point of no return, and their identity is disenfranchised? Do international indigenous rights become paper rights when they are located in migration contexts? All these issues highlight an important finding from the research used to support this chapter: migration processes result in fractured identities among indigenous peoples (at least, in the understanding of some rights), which leads them to reconsider their links to, and relationship with, their communities of origin.

2. Mapping the migratory processes of indigenous peoples

Given the difficulties outlined in the previous section, it would be very useful to map out how indigenous migrations occur and are expressed. To do so, it would be important to differentiate between ancestral territorial mobility and transnational indigenous migration[10] and to consider the indigenous rural/urban world dialectic resulting from these movements. *Indigenous ancestral mobility* refers to territorial mobility within ethnic borders. It describes how indigenous peoples have been fragmented by the territorial borders of different states. There are two major ways to interpret ancestral territorial mobility: (i) mobility associated with historical itineraries, which originates in traditional economic activities (textiles, crafts, etc.); and (ii) forced mobility within the indigenous territory: the case of extractive industries and other external actors present in indigenous territory.[11] Ancestral territorial mobility, which occurs among indigenous peoples who were fragmented by the borders established by the creation of national states in the

Peoples and Afro-descendants: The Difficult Art of Counting' in L Angosto Ferrández and S Kradolfer (ed), *Everlasting Countdowns: Race, Ethnicity and National Censuses in Latin American States* (Cambridge Scholars Publishing 2012).

10 CEPAL (n 8) 179–200; P Zuñiga, 'Comunidades Trasnacionales Indígenas' in A Torre and J Carrasco, *Al Filo de la Identidad. La Migración Indígena en América Latina* (Flacso 2008) 91–108; Pilar Cruz (n 7) 81–98.

11 CEPAL (n 8) 182–184.

nineteenth century, is directly connected to the cultural dimension of indigenous peoples. This leads to difficulties in visualising complex and collective identity processes within the territory of a single nation state.[12]

Transnational indigenous migration[13] entails reconstructing community ties beyond national, geographical, cultural and political boundaries, through constant exchanges between the communities of origin and destination. An example constitutes Ecuadorian and Bolivian indigenous people moving to Spain and maintaining links with the community of origin.[14] These ties are also institutionalised through indigenous migrants' organisations, which facilitate continuous interaction with the original communities.

The *rural world/urban world* dialectic is an expression of indigenous transnational migration. It involves leaving their community of origin in search of better opportunities in large Latin American urban centres. The tension between the indigenous rural and urban worlds causes indigenous peoples to

12 J Fox and G Rivera Salgado, 'Construyendo Sociedad Civil Entre Migrantes Indígenas' in J Fox and R Salgado (ed), *Migrantes Indígenas Mexicanos en los Estados Unidos* (Porrúa 2004) 9–74. This has been covered in national legal frameworks, but only superficially, without taking into account the provisions of Convention 169 of the ILO and the UNDRIP. Article 32 of ILO Convention 169 (Part VII 'Contacts and cooperation across borders') clearly states that it is a question of *national interest* to facilitate contact and cooperation between cross-border indigenous peoples, implicitly recognising that the *raison d'être* of these borders is to impinge on and attack a specific type of social organisation and cultural identity. It euphemistically speaks of economic and social fields, as well as specific indigenous fields such as the spiritual, environmental and cultural. If states do not enable this level of cooperation and contact between peoples separated by borders, the result would be forced migration, caused by broken agreements and violated rights. Again, the origin of indigenous migration in this case is the violation of (indigenous) rights. A possible solution for this situation would be to make the rights of migrants compatible with the specificities resulting from their status as *indigenous* migrants. Article 36 of the UNDRIP is more explicit in this respect, as it points to the planning and development of indigenous contacts as a right whose violation *produces the dynamics of indigenous forced migration*. Many aspects of indigenous migration have an ancestral founding memory, a fundamental cultural aspect that is carried and projected onto migratory processes. And it is also clear that this founding memory is based on the violation of indigenous rights, or on the systematic weakening of these rights. Our concern is therefore the violation of the original rights of migrant indigenous individuals.

13 The cross-border perspective is broader and more extensive than the transnational perspective, insofar as it covers movements beyond the nation state, including ethnic, cultural and regional border crossings that shape the difficulties experienced by the different indigenous peoples. In this regard, see Article 32 of ILO Convention 169, which is complemented by Article 36 of the UNDRIP from the point of view of assurance of rights.

14 This kind of migration entails mobility towards 'new' regions that have not been typically inhabited by indigenous peoples, such as Spain. cf. L Stephen, *Transborder Live* (Duke University Press 2007) 42–50; G Schiller, Basch and Szanton-Blanc, 'Towards a Transnational Perspective on Migration. Race, Class, Ethnicity and Nationalism Reconsidered' (1992) 645 *Annals of the New York Academy of Sciences* 25–52; F Krisman, 'Sin Coyote Ni Patrón: Why the Migrant Network Fails to Explain International Migration' (2005) 39 *International Migration Review* 4–44; G Maldonado, *Comerciantes y Viajeros* (Flacso 2004); G Eshelaman, *Haciendo la Lucha: Arte y Comercio Nahuas de Guerrero* (Fondo de Cultura Económica 1988) 234–238.

become fundamentally disengaged and disconnected from what constitutes the core of their collective rights, rooted in their ancestral territory, their forms of autonomous organisation, their justice systems and their own jurisdictional models. This complex matrix of rights is very difficult to reproduce and replicate in urban contexts. Territory-based indigenous rights thus turn into mobile rights through migration. This first transformation is projected onto all indigenous migratory processes as both a conflict and a problem. A sociology of indigenous migration should take into account these implications and connections. State public policies should address the vast impoverishment and difficulties experienced by indigenous peoples as a result of the growing urbanisation driven by migration processes.[15]

These ways of mapping indigenous migration can serve as a guide for understanding and contextualising the complex migratory processes of indigenous peoples, as well as the tensions between their rights.

Along with this mapping, four aspects should be studied in order to understand indigenous migratory processes. The first two aspects are related to the causes of indigenous migration. The other two are concerned with the consequences that migration has for the rights of indigenous peoples. The integration of these four complementary aspects can be considered as a single-purpose, systemic toolset that can be used to analyse the sociological complexity of indigenous migration. These aspects are (a) indigenous peoples as voluntary migrants, (b) indigenous peoples as forced migrants, (c) the impact of indigenous migration on the indigenous communities of origin, and (d) the impact of non-indigenous migration on indigenous communities.

First, it cannot be denied that some indigenous individuals and/or peoples voluntarily decide to migrate. However, the sources of information available in the field and the analysis of the actual practices of migration do not lead to the conclusion that *actual willingness* is an essential concept for understanding migration.[16] The notion that there is no such thing as freely chosen migration is more robust and consistent with the reality of global migration. There is a kind of coercion (for political, economic, ideological and environmental reasons, etc.), both in economic migrations and in forced indigenous displacement, which compels these individuals, communities and peoples to migrate.

15 CEPAL (n 8) 159–163; S Sousa, 'Entre la Aldea y los Rascacielos: Identidad, Inmigración y Territorialidad Indígena Urbana en Curitiba, Brasil' (2011) 41 2 *Revista Española de Antropología Americana* 391–416; M Sánchez and R Barceló, 'Mujeres Indígenas Migrantes: Cambios y Redefiniciones Genéricas y Étnicas en Diferentes Contextos de Migración' (2007) 14 *Les Cahiers Alhim. Amérique Latine Histoire & Memoire* <http: alim.revues.org/index410.html> accessed 27 July 2015; F del Popolo, A Oyarce and B Ribota, *Indígenas Urbanos en América Latina: Algunos Resultados Censales y Su Relación con los Objetivos de Desarrollo del Milenio* (CEPAL 2011); F Torres, 'Inserción Urbana y Migraciones Indígenas. El Caso del Área Metropolitana de Valencia' in D Sánchez Rubio and P Cruz (n 3) 19–241.

16 The main sources of information for the study of indigenous international migration originating in Latin America are the population records that are not used for statistical purposes,

Second, the concept of indigenous peoples as *forced migrants*, displaced from their original territories, is the most typical characteristic of indigenous migratory processes. There are many factors that cause indigenous migration. These include the dramatic level of poverty experienced in certain indigenous communities, which shows the close relationship and symbiosis between migration, indigenous identity and poverty. A number of contributory factors must also be added: the extreme violence suffered in indigenous territory; the severe environmental damage to the territory, which has the effect of serious violations of the right to health; the illegal possession, ownership and usufruct of the indigenous territory; and the lack of protection of collective rights. The emerging conflict with extractive industries also has a direct and immediate impact on the forced mobility of indigenous peoples.[17] These are some of the factors that account for indigenous migration.[18] This is the main starting point for this study: that indigenous migration processes are fundamentally triggered by right violations in the places where these peoples originally lived.[19]

This calls for raising awareness about the importance of indigenous collective rights for the reproduction and sustainability of their individual and collective lives, and shows the need to enforce states' obligations to respect and ensure these rights. This should be combined with the development of a broader regulatory framework for indigenous peoples' rights that takes into account the complexity of their migration processes: the rights of migrants, in other words, the rights everyone is entitled to merely because they migrate,[20] on the one hand, and the rights to be cross-referenced with the rights that indigenous peoples have as peoples, bearing in mind their identity and cultural dimension, on the

entry and exit records, and population censuses. The first two sources are administrative data that provide information on population flows. Censuses, however, measure the stock of migration at a given time in a particular geographic region. The 'willingness' variable cannot be obtained from these sources. cf. A Maguid, *La Emigración Internacional a Través de los Censos en Países de Origen: Evaluación de Resultados y Recomendaciones* (CEPAL 2008) 45–60.

17 A Martínez de Bringas, 'La Aplicación Extraterritorial del Convenio 169 de la OIT ante la Actuación de las Empresas Trasnacionales Españolas que Afecten a los Derechos Indígenas' (2009) *Revista Vasca de Administración Pública* 85 83–105.

18 I Palma, *Migración en la Época de Postconflicto: Vulneraciones de Derechos de las Poblaciones Excluidas e Impactos en la Participación* (Consejería de Proyectos 2006), 28–54; R Duarte and T Coello, *La Decisión de Marcharse: Los Pueblos Indígenas Migrantes de Guatemala y Chiapas* (Consejería de Proyectos 2008).

19 CIDH, *Informe de Seguimiento – Acceso a la Justicia e Inclusión Social: El Camino Hacia el Fortalecimiento de la Democracia en Bolivia* (2009) Doc OEA/Ser/L/V/II.135 40 7, 158; CIDH, *Tercer Informe sobre la Situación de los Derechos Humanos en Paraguay* (2001) Doc. OEA/Ser./L/VII.110 52, 4; CIDH, *Acceso a la Justicia e Inclusión Social: El Camino Hacia el Fortalecimiento de la Democracia en Bolivia* (2007) Doc OEA/Ser.L/V/II 34 253.

20 The principal international instruments that directly or indirectly refer to the protection of migrant rights are the International Convention on the Protection of the Rights of All Migrant Workers and Members of Their Families 1990 (from hereon: ICRMW); the International Covenant on

other hand.[21] In this regard, another distinction could be made between 'general human rights' (rights every individual is entitled to because they are human beings) and 'specific migrant rights' (rights every individual is entitled to as they migrate). The challenge being faced at present is to respect general human rights in migratory contexts. These rights are respected to a lesser extent when indigenous peoples migrate, as cases of multiple discrimination abound.

At present, however, there is a paucity of research to bridge the gap between the cultural aspects involving migrants, the causes of migration and the impact that migration has on a specific indigenous culture in transition. How the cultural dimensions of a given community and of a certain people are dislocated, relocated, reformulated and re-established as a consequence of migration remains to be analysed.

A third perspective from which to analyse indigenous migrations is to consider the impact that migratory processes have on the communities of origin, on the one hand, and on the indigenous peoples who migrate, on the other. The overall structure of indigenous migration processes is based on the constant aggression and systematic weakening of the rights that all individuals have as migrants and as members of an indigenous people. It needs to be considered how the decision of indigenous people to migrate has a structural impact on community ways of life, its modes of political articulation and organisation, and the means of collective production and reproduction. Every community exodus has serious repercussions for the structures of community life that remain in the original territory. Moreover, the indigenous peoples who migrate are also confronted with various difficulties – as further discussed in the next section of this chapter (pages 74–77).

A fourth perspective to be adopted could be to analyse the impact of non-indigenous migration on indigenous territory. Logically, this perspective focuses on the reverse side of the indigenous migrant subject; it is the counterpart of indigenous migration. The severe impact that the presence of third parties (colonists, transnational corporations, etc.) has on indigenous territorial areas compels some members of indigenous communities to search for better living conditions elsewhere. Therefore, although this encroachment is initially local in scope, it later causes indigenous migration. A comprehensive and specific analysis of this issue would require further elaboration of how to make indigenous rights

Civil and Political Rights 1966; The International Covenant on Economic, Social and Cultural Rights 1966; the Convention against Torture and Other Cruel, Inhuman or Degrading Treatment or Punishment 1984; the International Convention on the Elimination of All Forms of Racial Discrimination 1966; the Convention on the Elimination of All Forms of Discrimination against Women 1979; the Convention on the Rights of the Child 1990; the Protocol against the Smuggling of Migrants by Land, Sea and Air, supplementing the United Nations Convention against Transnational Organised Crime 2000; the Protocol to Prevent, Suppress and Punish Trafficking in Persons, Especially Women and Children, supplementing the United Nations Convention against Transnational Organised Crime 2000; and the International Labour Organisation's Convention No. 97 concerning Migrant Workers 1949.

21 I am strictly referring here to the rights set out in ILO Convention 169 and in the UNDRIP.

effective in the countries of origin, and how to find implementation mechanisms that are mandatory for states and for third parties that violate indigenous rights. These violations include the total lack of consultation with indigenous authorities about operations that take place in their territory.

In view of the four aspects discussed above, the key question that arises is how to defend certain rights designed to be exercised in the original indigenous territories when subjects have left their territories of origin.

3. Conflicts and difficulties in indigenous migratory processes

Indigenous migration is caused by multi-dimensional factors, but the absence of the protection of indigenous migrants' individual rights (granted, among others, by the ICRMW[22]) and collective rights (guaranteed under the ILO Convention 169 and the UNDRIP) is ultimately the main trigger for migratory processes. The lack of life opportunities in their territory drives indigenous peoples to migrate.

A critical and comprehensive study of indigenous migration processes requires considering the right violations in their countries of origin as a fundamental factor. Indigenous peoples' migration can be understood as a consequence of their loss of rights over their traditional territories.

In order to understand the difficulties associated with migratory processes in general, and with indigenous migration in particular, it is important to analyse the discourses used by states to justify not ratifying the ICRMW. Although these difficulties directly affect labour migrants, it should not be forgotten that the search for a better life (i.e. better social and employment conditions) is also one of the reasons behind indigenous migration. This is an additional factor to be taken into account in order to better understand the problems involved in indigenous migratory processes. Based on the content, critique and deconstruction of these discourses, some important observations emerge:

(a) The migrant issue is reduced by states to a purely quantitative problem, and therefore they fail to link it to existing legislation guaranteeing migrants' rights, such as the ICRMW. This connection is even more unlikely to be made with regard to 'indigenous issues', which are merely local in scope and not applicable to migration settings. This becomes apparent in connection with indigenous peoples, since their specific features from a migratory viewpoint have not been taken into account by human rights discourse.

(b) States' discourse emphasises the unbearable cost for them to guarantee the rights of migrants. This is why it is problematic for them to ratify the ICRMW, and they question its viability.[23] This discourse clearly ignores the

22 The International Convention on the Protection of the Rights of All Migrant Workers and Members of Their Families did not create any new rights; it only contextualised and applied classic civil, political and social rights to the statute and working conditions of migrant people.

23 A Morales, 'Migraciones, Tendencias Recientes y su Relación con la Crisis de Ciudadanía en América Latina y el Caribe', in *Migraciones Indígenas en las Américas* (Instituto Interamericano de Derechos Humanos 2007) 35.

contribution that migrants make to the host countries. Migrants are considered as transit populations without attributes. Their cultural specificity, their self-designation as being indigenous, forms part of their private idiosyncrasy, rather than of public discourse.

(c) States consider migratory processes to be a matter exclusively belonging to their internal sovereignty, not to be interfered with by international human rights law. This is clearly seen in relation to indigenous peoples, since indigenous issues are considered to concern only the countries of origin of these peoples and to be totally unrelated to the host countries.

(d) Migration is reduced to a mere jurisdiction issue, of timid utilitarian calculations. As a result, national workers always have priority over migrant workers when faced with a situation of scarcity.[24] When migratory processes are approached from a utilitarian-production perspective, cultural specificities cannot be considered, as these are viewed as private matters of migrants outside the remit of the law.

(e) Migration is regarded solely as a production-related phenomenon. This rules out family reunions within the countries receiving migrants, as contemplated in the ICRMW.[25] Migration processes are reduced to being mere private choices, with no responsibilities or consequences for family members or other people who depend on migrants. The whole organic-community dimension, which is inherent to indigenous migrants, is rendered invisible by state policies that regulate migratory flows.

(f) The practice of deporting undocumented immigrants has become normalised as a requirement of the rule of law, contrary to fundamental rights guaranteed by the ICRMW. As can be seen from the reports of the International Organization for Migration (IOM),[26] the Special Rapporteur on migrants, and the Special Rapporteur on the situation of human rights and fundamental freedoms of indigenous people,[27] this is most palpable in the case of indigenous migration, since indigenous peoples are extremely vulnerable in migratory processes in relation to highly important issues such as healthcare, social services, housing[28] and identity,[29] and regarding the rights of indigenous

24 Oyarce, F del Popolo and J Martínez Pizarro, 'International Migration and Indigenous Peoples in Latin America: Old Issues, Emerging Problems and the Need for a Multinational Approach in Migration Policies', document presented at the XXVI International Population Conference of the International Union for the Scientific Study of Population (IUPAC), (Morocco, 27 September to 2 October 2009).

25 Article 8 ICRMW.

26 C Yescas, *Indigenous Route: A Framework for Understanding Indigenous Migration* (IOM 2008), Seminar report entitled 'Pueblos Indígenas y Migraciones: Retos y Oportunidades', held in Geneva by the OIM and the secretary of the FPCI on 6–7 April 2006.

27 R Stavenhagen, *Report of the Special Rapporteur on the Situation of Human Rights and Fundamental Freedoms of Indigenous People* (2005) E/CN.4/2006/78/Add.2, among others.

28 UNHRP, *Indigenous Peoples' Right to Adequate Housing: A Global Overview* (United Nations 2005).

29 C Yescas, *Indigenous Route: A Framework for Understanding Indigenous Migration* (IOM 2008) 45–53.

women, who experience the worst conditions. Physical and sexual abuse urgently needs to be prevented in these migratory processes.[30] From the point of view of economic precariousness and vulnerable living conditions, indigenous peoples suffer from multiple discriminations in migratory processes because of their indigenous status. Multiple discrimination is much more pronounced in the case of indigenous women.

(g) The ILO Convention 169 has strong appeal for undocumented migrants, and this is extremely burdensome for states. In addition, ratifying the ICRMW would require controlling the activity of states in order to assess the degree and quality of implementation, which would be impossible to achieve today.[31] In the case of indigenous peoples, few states would allow an extraterritorial application of the ILO Convention 169 for countries receiving indigenous migrants.[32]

Another important element necessary to understand the complexity of indigenous migration is the *variable nature of identity* in the migration process. The elasticity and multiple aspects of indigenous migrant identity are not reflected in the law. Regulations tend to have a static and rigid understanding of (indigenous) identity, which fails to reflect its actual character when contextualised in migration.[33] Analysing the migratory process requires defining whom indigenous migrants are; how territory and autonomy are conceived in this process, as they are related to key rights for these groups; and how political organisation, leadership and institutions are articulated. As a consequence of migration, all these elements are understood differently from how they are considered in the places of origin as well as in legal human rights texts.

A serious discrepancy therefore exists between the way indigenous peoples are defined and understood within the ILO Convention 169 and the UNDRIP, on the one hand, and how they are conceived and relocated by the experience of migration, on the other. From the very beginning, indigenous migration is

30 S Mejía Flores, 'Mujer Indígena y Violencia' (2003) *México Indígena* 2 5 41–47; Ana Silvia Monzón, *Las Viajeras Invisibles: Mujeres Migrantes en la Región Centroamericana y el sur de México* (PCS-Camex 2006); *Mujeres Mayas, Xinkas, Garífunas y Afrodescendientes en Guatemala. Exclusión y Desafíos* (ONUMujeres 2012); *Derechos Humanos de las Personas Migrantes* (COPREDEH 2012); S Mezzadra, *Derecho de Fuga* (Traficantes de Sueños 2005), 25–30; CEPAL, *Mujeres Indígenas en América Latina: Dinámicas Demográficas y Sociales en el Marco de los Derechos Humanos* (United Nations 2013); United Nations, *México ante la CEDAW. Observaciones Finales del Comité para la Eliminación de la Discriminación contra la Mujer* (Naciones Unidas 2012); CEPAL (n 8) 233–258.

31 A Morales (n 23) 74–77.

32 Meeting of experts and migration officers, held at the University of Seville in July 2011, within the Research for Excellence project of which this study forms a part.

33 A Ruiz Balzola, 'Los Rumores Trasnacionales: Infidelidades, Afectos y Orden Social en la Migración de las Mujeres Kichwa Otavalo' in David Sánchez Rubio and Pilar Cruz (n 3) 145–166; *Tejedores de Mapas. Una Familia Kichwa Otavaleña en la Migración Transoceánica* (Flacso 2015), 35–36.

defined by the socio-cultural systems of the place of origin. The economic, social and demographic aspects of indigenous migration are in permanent tension with the socio-cultural roots of indigenous peoples.

4. The impact of migratory processes on indigenous rights

This chapter argues that the violation of indigenous peoples' rights is the main factor that drives their desire to migrate. Evidence of how migratory processes impact on indigenous rights, both individually and collectively, can be inferred from the interviews and discussion groups that were held. They show how such rights are either diluted, reduced, transformed or reconfigured.[34]

The vague and diffuse answers given by indigenous migrant subjects to the question of indigenous identity were striking. Many specific elements of indigenous identity had been lost during the migration process. Others had flexibly adapted to the difficulties and complexities of de-territorialisation. The respondents were largely unaware of the dissolution of some of their rights.

Moreover, the research showed a strong polarisation between the discourse of indigenous rights, the dense re-politicisation with which it is presented in the native countries of indigenous migrants, and the concrete reality of 'indigenousness' as experienced by the de-territorialised migrant subjects. In the present study,[35] this became apparent when considering the two constituent processes that took place in Ecuador and Bolivia, as well as the heated debate on indigenous rights that was triggered by these processes. No reciprocal response has been offered in Spain to the intense debate on identity, collective rights, interculturality and plurinationality that has taken place in the countries of origin. The concerns of indigenous migrant subjects in receiving countries were rather different from these. Indigenous identity in these host countries was gradually expressed in various ways, such as by creating indigenous associations in Spain where these population groups can learn their indigenous languages, hold festivals and rituals, display their own customs and articulate their relations with the public authorities of the cities and towns in which they have settled. Identity takes shape through festivals and language, together with other political expressions such as the use of public space, thus separating themselves from the processes of autonomy and territorial ownership that occur in both Ecuador and Bolivia.

Indigenous migration has been, and continues to be, an object of concern and analysis in theoretical and academic settings, in which discourses are often generated that rarely come close to reflecting reality. The abstract way in which researchers address indigenous migratory processes means that the issues of

34 cf the research project `Migrations and indigenous peoples of Ecuador and Bolivia in Spain. Specific situations and perspectives in the Autonomous Communities of Andalusia, Murcia and Valencia´ (n 3).

35 cf D Sánchez and P Cruz (n 3), where the results of the research that support this chapter are presented.

concern for them do not coincide with those that matter to the actual subjects involved. Ultimately, the questions about indigenous identity are re-elaborated from the outside as defined concerns by researchers, from an *a priori* theoretical–intuitive basis. This is done without conducting a real investigation of the specific aspects that are relevant to indigenous migrant subjects, or the ways in which they understand and conceive themselves in the process of migration. Another point can be deduced from this observation: the result of the approach taken in these research projects, which investigate rootless, exiled identities from a rights perspective, is the opposite to what was intended. The reason is that the subject of rights is turned into an object of study, whose discourse and expression is based on theoretical conceptions. In other instances, assumptions are made about the discourse of indigenous identity, without taking into account the true object of research: how migratory processes modify identity discourse, and to what extent these subjects are affected by factors and problems that hinder and radically alter their way of life. Finally, in some cases, migration appears as a real option when the identity issue no longer serves to maintain the life assumptions and opportunities of indigenous people as it had done before.

Some key elements can be deduced from these research findings in order to provide a systematic account of the tensions that result from being both a migrant and a member of an indigenous community.

The first element concerns the perception that indigenous subjects have of their migratory process. There is a general perception (either tacitly or openly expressed) that mobility entails the loss of the essential points of reference for identity, such as territory (an essential notion for understanding the rest of indigenous rights), language, individual forms of organisation, symbolic dimensions of life, legal systems, spirituality, and so on. The main aspects of indigenous identity change to become micro-identity issues: being a migrant becomes more important than being indigenous. However, this transformation does not involve a loss of identity, but an adaptation to new contexts and a reformulation of forms of expression. Within this framework, the imaginary play of identities tends to develop pan-identity supporting elements that become stronger as a consequence of migration. For example, indigenous migrants from Ecuador in Spain establish forms of solidarity and ties with other non-indigenous Ecuadorian migrants, thus dissolving the dense identity dimensions usually found among indigenous peoples in Ecuador. In this way, they invent new ways of expressing identity together with other migrants, based on the attributes and constraints that characterise migratory processes. This does not entail that their identity bonds are dissolved, but they are reconstructed during the migratory process.[36]

The migration process structurally affects indigenous migrants, both in their ways of appropriating identity and in the decisions they make that affect their status as migrants. Concerns about cultural identity take a secondary place when

36 P Cruz, 'Pueblos Indígenas, Migración Trasnacional e Identidades. La migración de Pueblos Indígenas de Ecuador Hacia España' in D Sánchez and P Cruz (n 3) 53.

the need for economic survival is the first priority; in this way, identity depends on the constraints of their setting. There is a close dialectic here between each individual's cultural and economic circumstances, as each of these dimensions are structurally conditioned and moderated by the other.

The second element that could be part of the research agenda for upcoming projects relates to how the community-family dimension is experienced and perceived in the context of indigenous migration. Pertinent future research questions would then be how is the community organised and transformed into a family unit in a migratory context such as that the European Union? To what extent does the context of migration drive the notion of community towards a formal structure such as that of family? What are specific indigenous features, if any, of the ways in which life and communal living are structured? How is identity adapted and modulated in Western settings, which are systematically organised in family units? To what extent is the communal expressed, and how? What solidarity networks are generated in this context, and with whom? The answers to these questions are important from the point of view of indigenous rights, since they point to one of its most important qualities: the collective. The question would then be how is the collective maintained and reproduced in migration contexts, where the Western family structure is imposed, which does not necessarily involve that which is organic and community based?

The answers to these questions would help to understand the complexities of cultural references in a migration context. It is also true that these are difficult to assess and verify. In the course of this research, some issues have emerged as important for understanding the way in which identity adapts, becomes diffused and is transformed.[37] Indigenous identity clearly requires constant re-adaptation as a consequence of migration. This readjustment does not destroy the identifying components of a community but transforms them. These contexts demand a more intercultural perspective in future research.[38]

The third element refers to the idea of how a certain generational split in a community of indigenous migrants affects or can affect the production, reproduction and development of identity ties. The general impression is a progressive loss in the reproduction and transmission of cultural values and identity from one generation to another, which is more manifest among the younger generations. Core indicators are the loss of the language among the younger generations, lack of leadership and political training, the absence of real initiatives regarding establishing their indigenous culture beyond folklore offshoots and the lack of a true commitment to the indigenous political movement in Latin America.

37 I refer to issues such as indigenous peoples' identity; territory and autonomy; and political organisation, leadership and indigenous institutions.

38 This is precisely one of the aims of this edited volume: to explore new directions in research on indigenous peoples and their rights from a realistic and interdisciplinary perspective. Interculturality is one of the fundamental elements in the study and analysis of indigenous rights; it must be studied from different disciplines as sociology of law, (legal) anthropology, political sciences and linguistics.

It can be sociologically verified[39] that physical distance always translates into inequality in migratory processes. That is, the greater the distance, the weaker the connection between indigenous migrants and their communities in the countries of origin, the greater the inequality, and thus, the more rapid and intense the loss of cultural ties. Consequently, the forms of indigenous identification have more diffuse expressions, and the imaginary of the re-politicisation and struggle for indigenous rights becomes more blurred.

A fourth and final element concerns migrant associations in `contexts of transnational migration´, and how these associations allow, facilitate and promote the production and reproduction of their own forms of identity – thus, to what extent these associations function as political platforms for cultural reproduction. Among the associations selected for the interviews, two profiles could be distinguished: one profile is less political, oriented towards the reproduction of some elements of the indigenous identity, and the other profile is more political and strongly indigenous, where identity can serve as a means of understanding the migrant dimension of its members.

A number of findings can be clearly inferred with regard to migrant associations. There is a gap between discourse and reality in the more political associations. Again, the discourse of the associations extols and promotes elements of indigenous identity that are not experienced as such in the daily lives of migrants. The fabric of the indigenous migrant associations interviewed tends to re-elaborate a process of re-identification from the core of the indigenous discourse, making that gap between reality and discourse more obvious. If the preservation and reproduction of the indigenous language have been considered essential to give substance to and sustain indigenous identity, this becomes more evident in migration processes, because the densest components of identity that are linked to their ancestral habitats and territories disappear or are less present.

There is also a strong influence of political leadership in indigenous migrants' associations. The leaders are systematically the elites of the indigenous migrant group, who intellectualise indigenous discourse in migration settings. This again denotes a split between the intellectualised indigenous discourse and everyday reality. This trend is understandable when one considers the importance gained by indigenous rights gained in the international arena in recent years.

Migrant associations have also been seen to function as a resource to search for work, rather than as a factor for the promotion of indigenous identity. The competition for resources in migration settings is key to understanding the needs and claims of migrants, their existential attitudes and their ways of appropriating meaning in migratory processes. Cultural reproduction is closely linked to the economic capabilities and living conditions of migrant subjects. This is an important finding to avoid naïve attitudes when developing social policies, rights policies and international aid policies. These policies should focus on identity

39 S Sassen, *Una Sociología de la Globalización* (Katz 2007).

issues, based on an understanding of the importance of cultural processes and rights in the lives of indigenous migrants, in order to reproduce appropriate living conditions in migration contexts.

5. Conclusions

This chapter identifies many conflicts and challenges in terms of understanding indigenous migratory processes. I will now recapitulate some of them to help comprehend and transform the dialectic and conflictive relationship that migratory processes have with the indigenous world, in order to shed light on a possible rights policy in this area.

Firstly, there is a scarcity of research on indigenous migratory processes *from the point of view of the culture and identity of these peoples.* Migration processes, as research material, are usually approached in the abstract from an eminently socio-economic perspective. Analyses tend to focus on the indigenous migrant subject as a problem rather than as a subject of rights. The *original violence in indigenous territories* is often the reason for indigenous peoples to leave their territories and trigger the migratory process. The conflict with industries has a direct and immediate expression in the mobility of indigenous peoples. Until recently, *identity and migration* were two unrelated issues within the structural knowledge of migration processes. From a rights perspective, cultural identities have not been taken into account in the overall analysis of migratory phenomena.

The above is intended to be an urgent plea for the social sciences to carry out research on the importance of cultural identities in migration processes. This includes how identity influences the decision to migrate; how this option is handled by state apparatuses, other agents and operators who act as mediators in the process; how identity is adapted to the difficulties and complexities of migration itself; how identity is located and redefined after having been established in host countries for a number of years; and what are the specific features of certain identities in migratory processes that have not been taken into account until now.

Secondly, in recent years there has been a strong upturn in the construction and institutionalisation of the rights of indigenous peoples, both nationally and internationally. However, this development is not consistent with the way in which these rights are expressed in the real world of these communities' lives. The consequence is a strong gap between the existing discourse concerning the rights of indigenous peoples, on the one hand, and the discourse regarding migration in general, which fails to consider indigenous migrants as subjects of rights, on the other.

The human rights of indigenous migrants need twofold protection, due to their dual status as migrants and indigenous. This will pose a major challenge in years to come. Indigenous migrant subjects face two kinds of problems: those related to their identity as migrants and those related to their indigenous identity. At different levels, cooperation policies, social policies, human rights policies and legislation on foreigners are jointly responsible for addressing these problems. Public policies should take into account the enormous heterogeneity of indigenous peoples and their situations (the causes of migration, itineraries and consequences), which implies that there is not a single solution for all of them. It is necessary to deepen the knowledge on the migratory processes of indigenous peoples in order to attempt different approaches to these dramatic situations from a rights perspective.

Thirdly, the discourse of the rights of indigenous peoples, as it has been constructed in the international sphere, poses serious difficulties to be understood and implemented at local level. As a result, the issue becomes much more problematic if indigenous rights are transferred onto migrant subjects who are delocalised from their original habitats and territories. Indigenous rights that give collective substance to indigenous identity (territoriality, autonomy, jurisdiction, systems of indigenous law) have been conceived statically and are rooted in the original niches of community life. Indigenous migration therefore requires that these rights be thought about flexibly, uprooted from their original foundations, in order to adapt to the needs of migratory processes. It is necessary to establish cross-referential paths, compatible with the rights of migrants. This change raises serious problems for states, as they are used to developing human rights legislation on the basis of an analytical distinction between indigenous peoples and migratory processes of indigenous peoples. However, migratory processes are at the core of numerous human rights violations and structurally overlap with other important issues, such as identity and recognition. Some indigenous peoples are compelled to migrate to be able to live and survive, and this jeopardises the viability of numerous rights.

In this sense, there is still a strict incompatibility between the logic of rights and the political foundations of legislation on non-citizens.

Another conflict, derived from the previous one, is the extraterritorial application of human rights. This involves thinking of indigenous rights in terms of how they could be exercised in territories different from those for which they were originally conceived, as a consequence of the mobility of right-holders: indigenous peoples.[40] This transforms the responsibilities of states[41] in the field of human rights. In states that lack an original indigenous population (such as Spain), but which are now required to develop policies to welcome and guarantee the rights of indigenous migrants in their territory, there is a shift towards the two aspects involved in these rights: the migrant and the indigenous. This refers to the old problem of giving local solutions (at the level of the nation state) to conflicts that are irreversibly global (transnational migrations).

Fourthly, it is necessary to think of how migratory processes might have an impact on indigenous communities' identity. That is, to what extent migration

40 A Martínez de Bringas, 'La Aplicación Extraterritorial del Convenio 169 de la OIT ante la Actuación de las Empresas Trasnacionales Españolas que Afectan a Derechos Indígenas' (2009) 85 *Revista Vasca de Administración Pública* 83–104.

41 It should not be forgotten that on 15 February 2007, the Spanish State formally deposited the instrument ratifying ILO Convention no. 169 on Indigenous and Tribal Peoples, the main international binding instrument for ratifying states.

processes strengthen and reinforce migrant identities, or to what extent they have the opposite effect. Migration processes can strengthen both one's own and others' development models. But they can also highlight the purely assimilationist concerns of the host state, which allows no other formula for migrant identities than integration into the local cultural frameworks and codes.

Fifthly, indigenous women are the major victims of indigenous migratory processes because they face the worst conditions, not only with regard to non-indigenous receiving communities, but also with respect to the indigenous men who accompany them in migration processes. Physical and sexual abuse of indigenous women is to be most urgently prevented. Indigenous women are also the great custodians of indigenous knowledge and ancestral heritage, which is extremely important for the reproduction of the collective and cultural identity of indigenous peoples. For all these reasons, it is necessary to strengthen the presence of states in relation to healthcare services (sexual and reproductive), especially for women.

Part II

Innovating the law

Part II.A Dealing with legal tensions in light of indigenous peoples' rights

5 A dual perspective on the right to enjoy the benefits of scientific progress

Fons Coomans

1. Introduction

The right to enjoy the benefits of scientific progress (hereafter: REBSP) is an important human right. However, it is a neglected and unexplored right from a conceptual perspective. Also in the practice of states and international organizations, the monitoring activities of human rights treaty bodies, the activities of NGOs and in scholarly human rights work, it is underdeveloped.[1] Yet, the right is of increasing importance in a global economy, characterized by fast technological and scientific developments. In the present world, research and development institutes and industries are mostly based in the North and the new economies in the South. Moreover, the processes and products of research activities are also mainly applied and processed in developed economies. Such a situation is not conducive to realizing the REBSP and the right to development as universal rights for all people everywhere on this planet. In addition, for a long period of time the idea of sharing the benefits of scientific progress has been looked upon as a one-way stream: scientific knowledge as a product of research and development of institutes and companies based in the developed world (the 'North'). Such processes and products have been patented in most cases. The underlying tacit presumption is that all progress in sciences and knowledge needs to be protected and validated through legal, monetary and trade measures. This one-sided approach is no longer tenable in a global and plural society based on respect for other cultures and their identity. Increasingly, there is recognition of the role, importance and value of traditional non-Western knowledge, science and wisdom of local and national origin, for example, of indigenous and minority groups. The underlying idea therefore of this chapter is to pose the question of how to give substance and meaning to the REBSP by using a dual approach: through industrialized and technological knowledge *and* through non-Western, local knowledge linked to the identity, traditions and cultural heritage of local people.

1 See generally the Report of the UN Special Rapporteur in the field of cultural rights, F Shaheed, *The Right to Enjoy the Benefits of Scientific Progress and Its Applications*, UN Doc A/HRC/C/20/26 (14 May 2012), and the Special Issue of the *European Journal of Human Rights*, 2015-4.

From this dual approach, the REBSP can be seen from an individual perspective: knowledge as property owned by individuals and companies and protected by patent law. The other perspective is a collective one: science and knowledge as manifestations of the culture of a group, related to their self-determination, identity and well-being often reflected in customary norms.

The present contribution aims at unpacking the REBSP, which means identifying, analysing and explaining a number of key issues that need to be tackled in order to make this right more concrete. Its objective is to contribute to a better understanding of the issues that are directly and indirectly related to the nature and content of this right as a human right from a dual perspective. It will discuss the question of how the benefits arising from different types of science and knowledge may be shared and how the right holders may be protected. As an approach, this chapter will apply a human rights analysis to provide an answer to this question. In order to achieve this, it will first focus on the legal basis of the REBSP. Next, the normative content and scope of the REBSP will be dealt with in relation to a number of economic, social and cultural human rights. Finally, it will discuss a number of challenges that the international human rights community has to face in order to make the REBSP 'real' and relevant. The research method applied in this contribution will be analytical and normative, exploring the substance, meaning and scope of this right in relation to other human rights.

2. The legal basis of the REBSP

As a human right, the REBSP is usually seen as belonging to the group of cultural rights which are at the tail end of both the Universal Declaration of Human Rights and the International Covenant on Economic, Social and Cultural Rights (ICESCR).[2] They belong to the groups of economic, social and cultural rights, which are often categorized as second-generation rights. We find explicit references to the REBSP in the Universal Declaration (Art. 27(1)) and the ICESCR (Art. 15(1b)). The latter, as a legally binding provision, must be read in conjunction with the notion of progressive realization of economic, social and cultural rights, which is part of Article 2(1) ICESCR.[3] On the regional level, the Protocol to the American Convention on Human Rights in the Area of Economic, Social and Cultural Rights (Protocol of San Salvador, 1988)

2 See, for example, J Symonides (ed), *Human Rights: Concept and Standards.* (UNESCO Publishing and Ashgate 2000), chapter 5 on cultural rights; A Eide, 'Cultural Rights as Individual Human Rights' in A Eide, C Krause and A Rosas (eds), *Economic, Social and Cultural Rights: A Textbook* (2nd ed, Martinus Nijhoff Publishers 2001) 289–301.

3 For an overview of the drafting history of both Article 27 Universal Declaration and Article 15 ICESCR, see WA Schabas, 'Study of the Right to Enjoy the Benefits of Scientific and Technological Progress and Its Applications' in Y Donders and V Volodin (eds), *Human Rights in Education, Science and Culture: Legal Developments and Challenges* (UNESCO Publishing and Ashgate 2007) 275–286.

also briefly provides for the right 'to enjoy the benefits of scientific and technological progress'.[4] The Arab Charter on Human Rights (2004) contains a similar provision.[5] Finally, the ASEAN Human Rights Declaration recognizes this right in Article 32.

The body of substantive human rights treaty law dealing with the REBSP is thus quite limited. In UNESCO's standard-setting instruments, we find more detailed and explicit provisions on topics that do touch upon the REBSP. In 1997, UNESCO's General Conference adopted the Universal Declaration on the Human Genome and Human Rights. This Declaration, an authoritative, although non-legally binding text, contains a number of clauses that are particularly relevant from the perspective of promoting the REBSP. This instrument recognizes that individuals should benefit from applications of research on the humane genome, in particular aimed at offering relief from suffering and improving the health of individuals.[6] Furthermore, the Declaration provides for solidarity and cooperation between states aimed at enabling developing countries to benefit from the achievements of scientific and technological research to be applied to the benefit of all. In this regard, the capacity of developing countries to carry out research on human biology and genetics should be developed and strengthened.[7]

In 2003, UNESCO's General Conference adopted yet another standard-setting instrument on the relationship between genetics and the use of personal data for scientific research, in particular medical research. This is the International Declaration on Human Genetic Data. This instrument stipulates that benefits resulting from the use of human genetic data collected for medical and scientific research should be shared with society as a whole and the international community. It further lists a number of benefits, most of them related to health issues.[8] A similar provision was included in the Universal Declaration on Bioethics and Human Rights, adopted by UNESCO in 2005.[9]

The instruments adopted by states within the framework of the UN and UNESCO are important, because they elaborate on the generally worded REBSP in the ICESCR and Universal Declaration, although their subject matter mainly relates to medical research and its effects on health. It is important to note that these instruments contain and depart from a human rights inspired approach. This means that activities undertaken in the field of scientific and medical research should always respect, protect and contribute to the fulfilment of human rights.

4 Article 14.
5 Article 42.
6 Universal Declaration on the Human Genome and Human Rights, Article 12, available at <www.unesco.org>.
7 Article 19.
8 International Declaration on Human Genetic Data, Article 19, available at <www.unesco.org>.
9 Universal Declaration on Bioethics and Human Rights, Article 15, available at <www.unesco.org>.

From the perspective of traditional knowledge and science the most important international human rights provision is Article 31 United Nations Declaration on the Rights of Indigenous Peoples (UNDRIP).[10] It is useful quoting it here:

1 Indigenous peoples have the right to maintain, control, protect and develop their cultural heritage, traditional knowledge and traditional cultural expressions, as well as the manifestations of their sciences, technologies and cultures, including human and genetic resources, seeds, medicines, knowledge of the properties of fauna and flora, oral traditions, literatures, designs, sports and traditional games and visual and performing arts. They also have the right to maintain, control, protect and develop their intellectual property over such cultural heritage, traditional knowledge, and traditional cultural expressions.
2 In conjunction with indigenous peoples, States shall take effective measures to recognize and protect the exercise of these rights.

Article 31 is the first full recognition of the traditional knowledge, science and cultural expressions of indigenous peoples as human rights in an international legal document. States are the main duty bearers to implement this right. Its importance as a standard-setting provision is beyond doubt and fits in with the general trend within public international law of supporting the demands of indigenous peoples, away from the remains of colonialism, such as the right to self-determination.[11] The recent American Declaration on the Rights of Indigenous Peoples (2016) provides for a similar provision.[12] It is noteworthy that both UNDRIP and the American Declaration do not refer to the right of indigenous peoples to share in the benefits of scientific progress or traditional knowledge.

Article 2 of UNESCO's Convention for the Safeguarding of the Intangible Cultural Heritage (2003) also covers traditional knowledge. It provides:

1 The 'intangible cultural heritage' means the practices, representations, expressions, knowledge, skills – as well as the instruments, objects, artefacts and cultural spaces associated therewith – that communities, groups and, in some cases, individuals recognize as part of their cultural heritage. This intangible cultural heritage, transmitted from generation to generation, is constantly recreated by communities and groups in response to their environment, their interaction with nature and their history, and provides them with a sense of identity and continuity, thus promoting respect for cultural diversity and human creativity. (. . .)
2 The 'intangible cultural heritage', as defined in paragraph 1 above, is manifested inter alia in the following domains: (a) oral traditions and expressions,

10 United Nations Declaration on the Rights of Indigenous Peoples (2007), UN Doc A/RES/61/295.
11 J Anaya, *Indigenous Peoples in International Law* (Oxford University Press 2004) 4.
12 Article XXVIII. See <www.narf.org/wordpress/wp-content/uploads/2015/09/2016oas-declaration-indigenous-people.pdf> for the text of the Declaration.

> including language as a vehicle of the intangible cultural heritage; (b) performing arts; (c) social practices, rituals and festive events; (d) knowledge and practices concerning nature and the universe; (. . .)

This provision relates knowledge to the protection of the cultural identity and heritage of the group to which people belong.

Equally important are legally binding documents which are not human rights texts, but which certainly have human rights implications. These include in particular the legal framework created through the adoption of the Convention on Biological Diversity and its protocols.[13] The objectives of this Convention, as stated in Article 1, are

> the conservation of biological diversity, the sustainable use of its components and the fair and equitable sharing of the benefits arising out of the utilization of genetic resources, including by appropriate access to genetic resources and by appropriate transfer of relevant technologies, taking into account all rights over those resources and to technologies, and by appropriate funding.

In addition, Article 8(*j*) provides for the obligation of State Parties to

> respect, preserve and maintain knowledge, innovations and practices of indigenous and local communities embodying traditional lifestyles relevant for the conservation and sustainable use of biological diversity and promote their wider application with the approval and involvement of the holders of such knowledge, innovations and practices and encourage the equitable sharing of the benefits arising from the utilization of such knowledge, innovations and practices.

Furthermore, the Nagoya Protocol (2010) to the Convention on Biological Diversity aims at promoting fair and equitable benefit sharing arising from the utilization of genetic resources.[14] Its Article 5(5) states that

> Each Party shall take legislative, administrative or policy measures, as appropriate, in order that the benefits arising from the utilization of traditional knowledge associated with genetic resources are shared in a fair and equitable way with indigenous and local communities holding such knowledge. Such sharing shall be upon mutually agreed terms.

From a utilitarian perspective, the latter two instruments aim at protecting biological diversity by using traditional knowledge and local cultures, sharing the benefits arising from the utilization of genetic resources. These aims are close

13 For an overview and background information, see <www.cbd.int>.

14 Text available at <www.cbd.int>.

to the human rights notions of respect for cultural identity and diversity, self-determination, participation and inclusion of stakeholders that are relevant to indigenous and local communities.

3. An analysis of the normative content and scope of the REBSP

3.1. Use of terms

Before discussing the normative content of the REBSP, it is useful to elaborate on the meaning of some of the terms used in Article 27(1) Universal Declaration, Article 15 (1b) ICESCR and terms that are relevant with a view to understanding the indigenous perspective on this right (Art. 31 UNDRIP). Terms in these provisions that are in need of clarification include 'science', 'progress' and 'benefits'.

It is quite difficult to present an appropriate definition of 'science', taking into consideration the different fields of science (natural sciences, social sciences, humanities) and within these fields the various disciplines. For present purposes, I propose to use a definition adopted by UNESCO in 1974. According to the Recommendation on the Status of Scientific Researchers,[15]

> The word 'science' signifies the enterprise whereby mankind, acting individually or in small or large groups, makes an organized attempt, by means of the objective study of observed phenomena, to discover and master the chain of causalities; brings together in a co-ordinated form the resultant sub-systems of knowledge by means of systematic reflection and conceptualization, often largely expressed in the symbols of mathematics; and thereby furnishes itself with the opportunity of using, to its own advantage, understanding of the processes and phenomena occurring in nature and society.
>
> (ii) The expression 'the sciences' signifies a complex of fact and hypothesis, in which the theoretical element is normally capable of being validated, and to that extent includes the sciences concerned with social facts and phenomena.

This definition of science departs from the idea that science is a rational matter which can be developed by using systematic methods. The UN Committee on Economic, Social and Cultural Rights (UNCESCR), in its General Comment on the right of everyone to benefit from the protection of the moral and material interests resulting from any scientific, literary or artistic production of which he is the author, defines 'scientific production' as creations of the human mind, such as scientific publications and innovations, including knowledge, innovations

15 Recommendation on the Status of Scientific Researchers, adopted on 20 November 1974, para 1a. available at <www.unesco.org>. See also Schabas (n 3) 286.

and practices of indigenous and local communities.[16] This seems to be a more nuanced and balanced definition that takes into account that science and knowledge may have different origins, ratios and backgrounds.

In an article published in 1995, Arun Agrawal discussed different notions of knowledge, in particular indigenous and scientific knowledge.[17] He quoted from an article by Warren who dealt with the divide between scientific and indigenous knowledge:

> Indigenous knowledge is local knowledge – knowledge that is unique to a given culture or society. Indigenous knowledge contrasts with the international knowledge system generated by universities, research institutions and private firms. It is the basis for local-level decision-making in agriculture, health care, food preparation, education, natural resource management, and a host of other activities in rural communities. Such knowledge is passed down from generation to generation, in many societies by word of mouth. Indigenous knowledge has value not only for the culture in which it evolves, but also for scientists and planners striving to improve conditions in rural localities.[18]

Worldviews underlying traditional and local knowledge emphasize:

- the interdependence of socio-economic and ecological spheres
- cyclical processes in natural and social domains
- collective identification with place/land/ancestral territory
- recognition that knowledge is also embodied in practice, action, morality, spirituality (as opposed to abstracted and objectified).[19]

A typical feature of indigenous knowledge is the concept of guardianship of knowledge, instead of ownership, for the benefit of future generations and the preservation of the cultural heritage.[20]

Agrawal concludes that it makes no sense to create dichotomies between Western and indigenous knowledge systems. Instead, one should talk about multiple domains and types of knowledge with different logics and epistemologies.[21] In this respect, it is interesting that the Universal Declaration on Cultural Diversity

16 General Comment No 17, UN Doc E/C.12/GC/17, para 9.

17 A Agrawal, 'Dismantling the Divide between Indigenous and Scientific Knowledge', 1995 *Development and Change* 413–439.

18 DM Warren, *Using Indigenous Knowledge in Agricultural Development,* 1990, World Bank Discussion Paper 127, quoted by Agrawal, 420.

19 Report of the international expert workshop on the contribution of indigenous and local knowledge systems to the Platform on Biodiversity and Ecosystems Services, UN Doc IPBES/2/INF/1, 25 September 2013, 14.

20 S Frankel, 'Attempts to Protect Indigenous Culture through Free Trade Agreements', in CB Graber, K Kuprecht and JC Lai (eds), *International Trade in Indigenous Cultural Heritage: Legal and Policy Issues,* (Edward Elgar 2012) 118–143, 120.

21 Agrawal (n 17) 439.

refers to the need to foster synergies between modern science and local knowledge, for example, in the field of environmental protection and the management of natural resources.[22] Sillitoe has argued that the relationship between science and indigenous knowledge is not characterized by separation or hierarchy, but rather by a spectrum or continuum of dynamic relationships reinforced by trends towards globalization.[23] One may argue that in an era characterized by globalization, different types of knowledge, indigenous and scientific, may interact to tackle global issues, such as climate change. This mixture of knowledge makes it difficult to claim exclusive ownership of knowledge, for example, through intellectual property law. For example, indigenous ecological methods to cultivate forests may be combined with responsible ways to cultivate new types of tree or restore native tree species that are appropriate for reducing erosion and deforestation, rehabilitate regional ecosystems and counter global warming.[24]

The word 'progress' indicates that science develops in a certain way directed towards creating positive effects for humans, society as a whole and life on earth in general. The word progress may also be linked to the progressive realization of social, economic and cultural rights as laid down in Article 2(1) ICESCR. This entails higher standards of living aimed at the full realization of these rights. Progress thus assumes a well-defined route towards positive results.

The word 'benefits' certainly has a qualitative connotation. It includes effects that positively affect man and society. In the framework of international human rights law, these effects should be understood as contributing to the protection and fulfilment of human rights in a broad sense.

3.2. Right holders and duty bearers

In order to define the content and scope of a human right, it is essential that the actors who can claim a right be identified. In other words, who are the holders of the REBSP? First, it is evident that individuals are entitled to this right as it is an individual human right recognized by the international community of states. Does the REBSP also have a collective dimension; that is, can the right be claimed by groups? One could think of ethnic minorities that could invoke the REBSP in order

22 UNESCO Universal Declaration on Cultural Diversity (2001), Annex II, para 14.

23 P Sillitoe, 'Globalising Indigenous Knowledge' in P Sillitoe, A Bicker and J Pottier (eds), *Participating in Development: Approaches to Indigenous Knowledge* (Routledge 2002) 108–138, 108–113.

24 Indigenous Knowledge, The Key to Biodiversity Conservation, *Cultural Survival Quarterly Magazine,* March 2015, <https://www.culturalsurvival.org/publications/cultural-survival-quarterly/indigenous-knowledge-key-biodiversity-conservation>. See also the 2015 Paris Agreement on Climate Change, which 'Recognizes the need to strengthen knowledge, technologies, practices and efforts of local communities and indigenous peoples related to addressing and responding to climate change, and establishes a platform for exchange of experiences and sharing of best practices on mitigation and adaptation in a holistic and integrated manner' (page 19 V, Non-Party Stakeholders, para 136).

to protect and preserve their culture and language by using information technology. Is it a problem that the Covenant only recognizes individual rights in Article 15(1c) ICESCR and not collective forms of ownership? This is indeed an omission due to the fact that when the Covenant was drafted, little or no attention was given to the rights of groups and their collective interests. This has been rectified to some extent by the UNCESCR in its General Comment 17, in which it recognized that communities can also be considered as right holders under this provision.[25]

Collective rights of indigenous peoples have been recognized in the UNDRIP.[26] As already referred to, Article 31(1) of this Declaration stipulates the right of indigenous peoples to their traditional knowledge, as well as the manifestations of their sciences, technologies and cultures. Although not explicitly included, this provision contains interesting clues for arguing that indigenous groups are holders of the REBSP. However, there is currently in international human rights law a lack of legally binding recognition of traditional knowledge as legitimate scientific progress and consequently, a weak protection of the rights of indigenous groups to enjoy the benefits of their traditional knowledge and control the genetic resources that belong to them.[27] However, one could argue that one of the features of the Nagoya Protocol is to create recognition and establish a link between the traditional knowledge of indigenous groups about genetic resources and its application by potential users through modern forms of science and technology.[28] The focus of all the instruments mentioned is not on the individual, but rather on the community. It is not clear however, how a community should be defined. It may have different meanings in the context of traditional knowledge, such as the broader indigenous group, a tribe belonging to such a group, a village or farmers' community, a religious community or collective of spiritual leaders who have knowledge about traditional healing practices. From an individual human rights perspective, the REBSP is a timeless expression of a fundamental entitlement of the human person. From a collective perspective, it aims at safeguarding the link between the group and its cultural heritage, including its traditional knowledge.[29]

Another question that may come up is whether there is a right of others to enjoy the benefits of indigenous knowledge and, if there is, how should this be balanced against a tentative right of an indigenous community to receive moral and material benefits from others for the knowledge it possesses. This question will be discussed below in section 4 where community protocols under the Nagoya Protocol will be highlighted.

25 GC no 17 (n 16) para 8.
26 GA Resolution 61/295, 13 September 2007, contained in UN Doc A/RES/61/295.
27 This element is also missing from ILO Convention 169 Concerning Indigenous and Tribal Peoples in Independent Countries (1989).
28 See GS Nijar, Traditional Knowledge Systems, International Law and National Challenges: Marginalization or Emancipation, 2013 *European Journal of International Law*, 1205–1221, 1207.
29 UNCESCR, General Comment No 17, UN Doc E/C.12/GC/17, para 2.

Who are the duty bearers of the REBSP? It is beyond doubt that states are the primary duty bearers. This is clear, for example, from Article 15(2) ICESCR that refers to the steps to be taken by states to achieve the full realization of the REBSP. These steps shall include those necessary for the conservation, development and diffusion of science and culture.[30] Pursuant to the Convention on Biological Diversity and its Nagoya Protocol, states that have ratified or acceded to these instruments are the duty holders. They are under an obligation to take legislative, administrative and policy measures with a view to ensuring that benefits arising from the utilization of genetic resources that are held by indigenous or local communities are shared in a fair and equitable manner with those communities.[31] One example is South Africa's Biodiversity Act, which was adopted to give effect to the Convention on Biological Diversity.[32]

More controversial is the question whether corporations have obligations to make the benefits of scientific progress available to society. One key obstacle to such an obligation is, of course, the system of intellectual property law whose aim is the protection of the intellectual property rights of inventors, scientists and corporations that have allocated resources for research and development aimed at making profit. One could argue, for example, that there is an inherent tension between the REBSP and strict rules on the protection of patents on essential medicines.[33] The Agreement on Trade-Related Aspects of Intellectual Property Rights (TRIPS) of the World Trade Organization (WTO) recognizes as its objective the transfer and dissemination of technology to the mutual advantage of producers and users of technological knowledge in a manner conducive to social and economic welfare.[34] This phrase thus implies the idea of making scientific knowledge available for the benefit of society.

According to the UN Special Rapporteur in the field of cultural rights, intellectual property law may be used to protect the traditional knowledge against abuse by others. The other approach would be to prevent patenting of indigenous knowledge by third parties (such as companies).[35] There seems to be general agreement that intellectual property law has failed in addressing the needs and

30 Compare Article 31(2) of the UN Declaration on the Rights of Indigenous Peoples which runs as follows: 'In conjunction with indigenous peoples, States shall take effective measures to recognize and protect the exercise of these rights'.

31 Article 5(2) Nagoya Protocol.

32 See R Chennells, 'Traditional Knowledge and Benefit Sharing After the Nagoya Protocol: Three Cases from South Africa' 2013 *Law, Environment and Development Journal*, 163–184, 168.

33 See, for example, the resolution adopted by the UN Sub-Commission on Human Rights on Intellectual Property Rights and Human Rights, Resolution 2000/7.

34 See Article 7 TRIPS Agreement, available at <www.wto.org>. The WTO is not a specialized agency of the UN.

35 Report by the UN Special Rapporteur in the field of cultural rights, UN Doc A/70/279, para 35 (2015).

interests of indigenous groups in protecting traditional knowledge.[36] Indigenous groups and local communities consider intellectual property over cultural heritage, traditional knowledge and cultural expressions as collective ownership, rather than individual ownership.[37] Article 15(1)(c) ICESCR provides for the right of everyone to benefit from the protection of the moral and material interests resulting from any scientific, literary or artistic production of which he or she is the author. From the perspective of protecting the rights under Article 31 UNDRIP, states have an obligation to guarantee that indigenous and local communities have a fair share in the revenues of marketing traditional knowledge by companies, for example, the industrial production of medicinal plants or the use of indigenous seeds for improving foodstuffs produced on an industrial scale. States have an obligation to provide for the collective administration by indigenous peoples of the benefits derived from the marketing of their traditional knowledge.[38] This is very much in line with the obligations of states under the Convention on Biological Diversity and its Nagoya Protocol discussed on page 93. For indigenous groups, the protection of traditional knowledge through using intellectual property law (especially patents) is problematic for several reasons. Intellectual property law aims at protecting individual rights and corporate interests and is unable to cover community values and knowledge, which are composed of a combination of spiritual and cultural tangible and intangible expressions. Furthermore, intellectual property law is ill equipped to deal with customary forms of ownership, tenure and access. Finally, patents are tools to reflect the market value of knowledge and fail to include the spiritual and cultural value of knowledge.[39]

3.3. The substance of the REBSP

To what does the REBSP entitle? In other words, what is its object or substance? Clues for defining the object can be derived from the definition of terms discussed on pages 94–96. From a Northern view, the benefits of scientific progress would mainly refer to the results of processes of research and development activities that originate from advanced industry and research institutes. However, there is no doubt that the object of the REBSP is still rather undefined, but also quite broad. The REBSP gets substance and meaning in relation to a number of, especially, economic, social and cultural rights. An analysis in terms of availability, accessibility, acceptability and adaptability

36 Frankel (n 20) 122; Report by the UN Special Rapporteur in the field of cultural rights (n 1) para 38.

37 J Rowland, 'The New Legal Context of Indigenous Peoples' Rights: The United Nations Declaration on the Rights of Indigenous Peoples' 2013 *American Indian Culture and Research Journal* 148.

38 UNCESCR, General Comment No 17, UN Doc E/C.12/GC/17, para 32.

39 D Posey, 'Upsetting the Sacred Balance' in P Sillitoe, A Bicker and J Pottier (eds), *Participating in Development* (n 23) 24–42, 32–33.

is an appropriate framework to define its substance. For example, it is important that new ICT knowledge used in education and teaching is adaptable to different historical, social and cultural contexts of societies in which it is used, and that it is inclusive and non-discriminatory. It is also clear that the object of the right will be quite hybrid and varied in order to include the substance of several other rights, such as the right to health, food, information, education and intellectual property rights. For example, it will include access to chemical knowledge through medicines, information technology through computers and agricultural knowledge through modified food. Results of modern information technology may also foster the enjoyment of cultural rights, such as the right to take part in cultural life through the digital display of art. This hybrid nature makes it difficult to define the substance of the right as one that is permanent and clear-cut. It will change and expand over time through new scientific developments that impact on the enjoyment of substantive rights with the REBSP as a facilitating tool.

As for all human rights, the REBSP entails both freedoms, that is, a domain where the state and others should not interfere, and entitlements to services to be made available by the state. An example of the former is the use of the results of scientific research in modern surveillance systems, such as cameras, by state organs to survey the daily lives of people in the public domain. This may conflict with the right to privacy. Another example is the use of scientific medical research to trace hereditary diseases. Do parents have a right to use medical research to select healthy embryos to prevent the transmission of hereditary diseases from parents to children? This question may be approached from different angles, such as a legal and human rights perspective, but it also has serious ethical and religious dimensions. Should the state abstain from interference in the free exercise of medical experimental research; should it prohibit such research or perhaps regulate it?[40] How does stem cell research relate to the protection of the right to life?[41] The ethical dimension of such a discussion is important because ethics gives us the language with which to frame the questions that need to be asked. Ethical issues belong to the essential framework that shapes human rights.

An example of a service to be made available by the state and educational institutions is the use of modern information technology in teaching methods in schools and universities as a component of the right to quality education. Examples include Open Access sources and reading materials and teaching through Massive Open Online Courses (MOOCs).

In relation to the right to have access to health services and treatment, one may think of the right to have access to essential medicines produced by

40 For a discussion see A Plomer, *The Law and Ethics of Medical Research: International Bioethics and Human Rights* (Cavendish Publishing Limited 2007).

41 In May 2008, the Brazilian Supreme Court dismissed a case calling into question the constitutionality of Article 5 of Brazil's Biosecurity Law (that permits scientific research with embryonic stem cells for medical purposes) claiming a violation of the right to life. See <www.conectas.org/en/noticia.php?not_id=245>.

applying the results of scientific research. From a Southern, traditional knowledge perspective, this right may also entail the right to recognition of traditional, complementary and alternative medicine and healing practices. Article 24 UNDRIP provides protection to such traditional health practices and services.[42] There is currently a trend of recognizing the value of systems of traditional medicine and wisdom, which often constitute the basis for the treatment of modern diseases.[43] Traditional knowledge is embodied in practice, rituals, customs, morality and spirituality, as opposed to abstracted and objectified scientific data.[44] For example, the rituals of a traditional rainmaker in Nigeria would belong to such knowledge and wisdom.

In relation to the right to food and the right to be free from hunger, the questions can be asked of which form of scientific progress should be promoted and distributed, to the benefit of whom and how should such a goal be achieved?[45] A human rights approach would require that small and poor farmers must be seen as the main beneficiaries of a REBSP perspective on realizing the right to food and food security. An approach that would advocate strengthening intellectual property rights on plants, seeds and genetic resources in general would be contrary to such a goal because poor farmers would be excluded from accessing them. In other words, the direction of scientific progress in the area of food should be carefully chosen by governments angled by their obligations to realize the right to food.

A related issue is the question of the patentability of plants, seeds and biological processes for the production of genetic resources. On the basis of Article 27(3) TRIPS Agreement (to be discussed on page 105), member states of the WTO may exclude these from patentability with a view to preventing that these genetic resources are appropriated for commercial activities without the consent of farmers and communities who have developed them, and without a fair share in the benefits. This is in line with the idea of benefit sharing for indigenous and local communities as developed in the Convention on Biological Diversity and its Nagoya Protocol discussed on page 93.[46] Meanwhile, the idea has developed that (access to) plant genetic resources for food and agriculture are a global public good. The benefits thereof must be shared among those farmers and communities that produce them. This is the object and purpose of the FAO Treaty on Plant Genetic Resources for Food and Agriculture that entered into force in June 2004.[47] From a human right perspective on the REBSP, it is important that the focus of benefit sharing is on improving food security and the standard of living

42 See M Stuttaford and others, 'The Right to Traditional, Complementary, and Alternative Health Care' 2014 *Global Health Action* 24121.

43 C Stephens and others, 'Disappearing, Displaced, and Undervalued: A Call to Action for Indigenous Health Worldwide' 2006 vol 367, *The Lancet* 2025.

44 D Posey (n 39) 28–31.

45 See the extensive analysis by O De Schutter, 'The Right of Everyone to Enjoy the Benefits of Scientific Progress and the Right to Food: From Conflict to Complementarity' 2011 *Human Rights Quarterly* 304–350.

46 ibid. 321–325.

47 Discussed by De Schutter, 325–327.

of small local farmers, but also that conservation and a sustainable use of agrobiodiversity should belong to the common heritage of humankind for the benefit of present and future generations.[48]

3.4. The nature and scope of obligations

As a corollary of the notion of freedoms and entitlements, it is commonly accepted that every human right entails negative obligations not to interfere in the enjoyment of a right and positive obligations to actively contribute to the realization of a right. The definition of the nature of obligations can be further developed by applying the so-called typology of obligations, developed in the academic literature, to clarify and fine-tune the obligations emanating from a specific human right. These are the obligations to respect (a negative one), to protect (a positive one) and finally to fulfil (also a positive obligation).[49] The obligation to respect requires states parties to refrain from interfering directly or indirectly with the REBSP. The obligation to protect requires states parties to take measures that prevent third parties (such as corporations) from interfering with the REBSP, for example, by establishing and regulating a regime for the approval of genetically modified organisms or protecting expressions of knowledge (about health practices) and culture (arts, literature) of indigenous groups and local communities. The obligation to fulfil requires states parties to adopt legislative, administrative and promotional measures aimed at the full realization of the REBSP, such as promoting the positive results of medical research to a wider audience by encouraging people to change their behaviour in a way that is more beneficial to their personal health (campaign to deter smoking). Another example of a fulfilment-bound obligation would be to develop a policy that sets the aims and priorities of state-financed scientific research. The main obligation resulting from the REBSP would be to develop and implement a science policy at both the national and international level aimed at laying down the principles that underlie scientific research and traditional knowledge. Such a policy would include the duty to respect the freedom of individuals to seek information about scientific progress, protect individuals from the harmful consequences of sciences and ensure equality among the beneficiaries of scientific progress and its applications.

It is increasingly being recognized that when states act beyond national borders, or when their acts or omissions affect the enjoyment of human rights of people in other countries, human rights obligations resulting from treaties may apply. This type of obligation has been labelled international obligations by the UNCESCR in its General Comments[50] and extraterritorial obligations in the

48 ibid. 342–344.

49 See, A Eide, 'Economic, Social and Cultural Rights as Human Rights' in A Eide, C Krause and A Rosas (eds), *Economic, Social and Cultural Rights: A Textbook*, (n 2) 9–28, 23–25. This typology is also used by the UNCESCR in its General Comments.

50 See, for example, UNCESCR, General Comment No 14 on the right to the highest attainable standard of health, UN Doc E.C.12/2000/4, para 38–42.

academic discourse.[51] The legal basis for such obligations may be derived from Article 2(1) ICESCR, which refers to international assistance and cooperation, and Articles 55 and 56 of the UN Charter. International obligations may be particularly relevant from the perspective of the REBSP. For example, the question might be raised whether Western states, that host pharmaceutical corporations, have positive (international) obligations under human rights law to promote access to essential medicines in poor developing countries to cope with a health crisis. The 2011 Maastricht Principles on Extraterritorial Obligations of States in the Area of Economic, Social and Cultural Rights, an authoritative expert opinion, provide in Principle 29 that:

> States must take deliberate, concrete and targeted steps, separately and jointly through international cooperation, to create an international enabling environment conducive to the universal fulfilment of economic, social and cultural rights, including in matters relating to bilateral and multilateral trade, investment, taxation, finance, environmental protection, and development cooperation.[52]

The legal issue at stake here is, for instance, whether the patent regime on drugs can be accommodated to meet the needs of developing countries. This question has been taken up by the WTO in its 2001 Doha Declaration on the TRIPS Agreement and Public Health with regard to the use of compulsory licences for the production of pharmaceuticals for use in foreign markets.[53] From a human rights perspective, the key question is whether a balance can be struck between intellectual property law and human rights law.[54] Does the REBSP have an international dimension in the sense of an obligation to make the results of scientific research and its application in pharmaceutical production available beyond the traditional patent holder to the benefit of sick people in poor countries? The term 'benefit' should be understood here as meaning the availability and accessibility (non-discriminatory access; physical access and affordability) of essential medicines. General Comment no. 12 on the right to health identifies developed states, but also multinational corporations and international organizations, as key actors in this process. Another example of this question is how drug-resistant patients suffering from neglected diseases, such as tuberculosis, get access to new effective drugs. The problem here is that such new drugs are hardly available because

51 See M Langford and others, *Global Justice, State Duties: The Extraterritorial Scope of Economic, Social and Cultural Rights in International Law* (Cambridge University Press 2013).

52 The text of the Maastricht Principles is available at <www.etoconsortium.org>.

53 WTO General Council Decision of 30 August 2003, Doc WT/L/540. This decision laid the foundation for the amendment of the TRIPS Agreement by including a new Article 31*bis*.

54 See *The Impact of the Agreement on Trade-Related Aspects of Intellectual Property Rights on Human Rights*, Report of the High Commissioner, UN Doc. E/CN.4/Sub.2/2001/13, § 10–15. See J Sellin, *Access to Medicines: The interface between patents and human rights: Does one size fit all?* (Intersentia 2014).

pharmaceutical companies do not prioritize research for developing such drugs, because these are not profitable.[55]

Another element of the 'international' dimension of the REBSP is the call for the transfer of technology from developed countries to developing ones, which is part of the so-called Agenda for Development currently under discussion in the World Intellectual Property Organization (WIPO). One of its preliminary recommendations aims at encouraging member states, especially developed countries, to urge their research and scientific institutions to enhance cooperation and exchange with research and development institutions in developing countries, especially Least Developed Countries.[56] With the intention to strengthen the intellectual property institutional capacity of developing countries, member states agreed to accelerate the process on the protection of genetic resources, traditional knowledge and folklore, without prejudice to any outcome, including the possible development of an international instrument or instruments.[57] Attention given to traditional knowledge in the Agenda, however, is very limited. The emphasis is on intellectual knowledge and property developed in industrialized countries.

From a dual perspective on the REBSP, the key issue is that often indigenous groups do not benefit from the traditional knowledge that Western scientists and corporations use for new Western inventions for the treatment of diseases or the growing of seeds for new food crops. The idea of the Nagoya Protocol is to actually lay down obligations to make sure that the rights of owners of genetic resources are secured against illegal use by third parties (bio-piracy) and they can share in the benefits of processing this knowledge. How this can potentially be organized will be discussed in the next section.

4. Challenges

In order to make the REBSP more visible, tangible and meaningful from a dual perspective, the following challenges have to be addressed.

One of the major challenges is to identify what the REBSP means in a globalized economy characterized by rapid developments in science and technology and a weakened role for governments. In other words, how should this right be made operational? This relates to the issue of inequality between rich and poor nations, also in terms of political and economic power. There is a growing gap between 'have' and 'have-not' countries in science and capacity to apply scientific advances. One key question will be how the limited capacities

55 See L London, H Cox and F Coomans, 'Multidrug Resistant TB: Implementing the Right to Health through the Right to Enjoy the Benefits of Scientific Progress' 2016 *Health and Human Rights Journal*, 25–41.

56 The 45 Agreed Recommendations under WIPO Development Agenda, para 26, available at: <www.wipo.int/ip-development/en/agenda/cdip_recommendations.html>. See also the proposal for a WIPO Development Agenda submitted by Argentina and Brazil, WIPO Doc WO/GA/31/11.

57 WIPO Development Agenda, para 18.

of developing countries can be strengthened in order to benefit from scientific progress that is adaptable to their national and local needs. What exactly are the scientific needs of developing countries? Does the international community (rich states, international organizations, such as the World Bank, WIPO, UNDP) have responsibilities and/or obligations under human rights law to assist in the realization of the REBSP? For example, there may be a need for compensation or differential treatment of developing countries to bridge the digital gap. How can such an idea be made more concrete, for instance, through the promotion of the use of communication technology in education by giving developing countries preferential treatment in access to electronic learning environments?

Challenges are certainly big in the domain of the relationship between the REBSP and intellectual property rights. How to reconcile this human right with the regime of protection of monopoly property rights that is aimed primarily at the protection of commercial interests? Is it possible to integrate the REBSP in intellectual property regimes, such as TRIPS? Or, alternatively, does the REBSP prevail over intellectual property rights, because it relates to the protection of human dignity? In this context, it is interesting that there are conceptual linkages and similarities in foundational principles between the ICESCR and the TRIPS Agreement. Article 27(3) TRIPS Agreement provides:

> Members may also exclude from patentability:
>
> (. . .)
>
> Plants and animals other than microorganisms, and essentially biological processes for the production of plants or animals other than non-biological and microbiological processes. However, members shall provide for the protection of plant varieties either by patents or by an effective *sui generis* system or by any combination thereof.

This means that states are under no TRIPS obligation to protect traditional knowledge through a system of patents. It has been suggested by some developing countries that instead, a system of national rules and arrangements may be appropriate to make sure that traditional knowledge is used in such a way that it may contribute to achieving fairness and equity for all owners, users and consumers.[58] In this respect, it has been suggested to apply UNDRIP as an interpretive tool for the concept of benefit sharing included in Article 8(*j*) CBD discussed on page 93.[59] More generally, the Preamble to UNDRIP recognizes 'that respect for indigenous knowledge, cultures and traditional practices contributes to sustainable and equitable development and proper management of the environment'.

58 See WTO doc IP/C/W/370/Rev.1 (9 March 2006) 16–17 (Protecting Traditional Knowledge Under a *Sui Generis* System).

59 F Cittadino, 'Applying a UNDRIP Lens to the CBD: a More Comprehensive Understanding of Benefit-Sharing' 2014 *Indigenous Policy Journal*.

A further challenge is to develop a human rights based approach to the implementation of the REBSP. In addition to the identification of right holders and duty bearers, this would also require giving meaning to the notions of non-discrimination, participation of all stakeholders (especially indigenous and local communities), transparency, accountability issues and establishing (legal) remedies. One of the key issues in this respect is to involve the private sector in this process, meaning corporations and private research institutes. A typical feature of the Nagoya Protocol is that traditional knowledge associated with genetic resources that is held by indigenous and local communities is accessed with the prior and informed consent (PIC) or approval and involvement of these groups and that mutually agreed terms have been established.[60] The requirement of obtaining PIC is crucial for the acceptance of any agreement on the use of indigenous knowledge. It is clearly a human rights obligation, which can also be found in Article XXIII American Declaration on the Rights of Indigenous Peoples and Article 19 UNDRIP. More elaborate and specific guidelines on the collaboration between scientific researchers (especially ethnobiologists) and indigenous communities that are based on equality of partners, trust and transparency have been adopted by the International Society of Ethnobiology.[61] These may serve as a framework for collaboration and benefit sharing between all stakeholders.

Instead of relying on property laws, including intellectual property, it is suggested to use a different approach to regulate and protect knowledge about genetic resources held by indigenous and local communities. This approach is built on the notion of traditional knowledge as *sui generis* rights often incorporated in customary laws of the communities themselves. The notion of customary laws as an instrument to implement state obligations arising from the Nagoya Protocol has been included in its Article 12(1). The advantages of using customary norms as guidelines for implementing Nagoya Protocol obligations entail that such norms and practices are often closely related to the spiritual, sacred or ceremonial characteristics of traditional knowledge and to the broader notion of preserving the cultural identity of the group.[62] It is submitted that specific rules of the customary laws of indigenous groups reflect norms of international human rights law, such as the right to self-determination, cultural rights and other rights contained in the UNDRIP and the ICESCR.[63] According to Tobin, there is ample evidence of international (human rights) law, regional laws regulating access to genetic resources and national *sui generis* regimes which constitutes state practice entailing the recognition of customary laws as the main body of rules providing for the protection of traditional knowledge rights of indigenous groups.[64] The recent

60 Article 7 Nagoya Protocol.

61 International Society of Ethnobiology (2006), ISE Code of Ethics (with 2008 additions), <http://ethnobiology.net/code-of-ethics/>. See also Posey (n 39) 36–38.

62 BM Tobin, 'Bridging the Nagoya Compliance Gap: The Fundamental Role of Customary Law in Protection of Indigenous Peoples' Resource and Knowledge Rights' 2013 *Law, Environment and Development Journal* 142–182, 151.

63 Article 3, 11, 12, 24, 26, 31 UNDRIP; Article 15 (1) and (2) ICESCR; Tobin (n 62) 155.

64 Tobin (n 62) 156.

WIPO Draft Articles on the Protection of Traditional Knowledge also recognize that customary laws may play a role in achieving a fair and equitable sharing of benefits from the use of traditional knowledge.[65] Such laws as *sui generis* category should recognize the special nature and status of indigenous knowledge and science and protect against infringements by third parties. Customary law rules may be included in domestic legislation, with the potential of creating a wider scope of application on the one hand, but also the possibility of freezing the existing static application on the other. However, Frankel has rightly pointed out that a coordination mechanism between customary rules for the protection of indigenous knowledge and national intellectual property laws is necessary with a view to solving potential conflicts.[66]

Another human rights requirement is the need to have safeguards for the full involvement and participation of stakeholders in access to and use of traditional knowledge relating to genetic resources and to have an equitable sharing of the benefits resulting thereof. This is closely related to the standard of PIC of indigenous and local communities in agreements about access to and use of traditional knowledge. Article 12(3)(a) Nagoya Protocol provides for so-called community protocols as instruments to lay down conditions and terms by the indigenous groups themselves about access to and use of traditional knowledge on genetic resources by third parties. Community protocols have been defined as

> Instruments that facilitate culturally rooted, participatory decision-making processes within communities with the aim of asserting rights over their communally managed lands, resources and traditional knowledge. Community protocols are based on communities' customary norms, values and laws, and set out clear terms and conditions to governments and the private, research, and non-profit sectors for engaging with communities and accessing their local resources.[67]

It is submitted that such protocols may play an important role as foundations for agreements between indigenous groups and commercial parties, which should be characterized by fairness, equity, justice and respect for human rights.[68] One example is a biocultural community protocol providing for the collective management of the traditional knowledge of the Kukula traditional health practitioners of Bushbuckridge, South Africa. The healers possess different forms of traditional knowledge about the use of local medicinal plants. They decided to join forces through a community protocol to, *inter alia*, lay down an agreement for access to and use of their medicinal plants and knowledge by third (commercial) parties

65 Doc WIPO/GRTKF/IC/32/Facilitators Text Rev2 (2 December 2016).

66 Frankel (n 20) 123–124.

67 B Lassen and J von Braun, 'Community protocols: Bridging the stakeholder divide' *Business 2020* (November 2015) 26–27, 27 <https://www.cbd.int/doc/newsletters/news-biz-2015-11-en.pdf>.

68 See also Chennells (n 32) 181–182; Tobin (n 62) 158.

and the monetary benefits resulting thereof. On the basis of this protocol, the community concluded an agreement with a local cosmetic company for access to and use of some of their genetic resources and associated traditional knowledge for the development of cosmetic products.[69] It can be said that such protocols may be qualified as human rights proof, provided that they are not contrary to international human rights law. For example, community protocols reflecting customary laws must not discriminate against the rights of women to share in the benefits resulting from traditional knowledge.

Moreover, it has been suggested that traditional knowledge and its application can play an important role in furthering sustainable development.[70] The latter can be considered to be in the common interest of humankind.[71] Indigenous knowledge about biodiversity and the prevention of global warming can be beneficial for the protection of the common interest. For example, traditional knowledge addressing desertification or water management and water quality should be accessible to all because it is in the common interest. It would then make sense if the international community covers the cost of rewarding the holders of such knowledge. It is submitted that indigenous communities must be financially supported by a common trust fund for sharing this type of knowledge with the international community. Consequently, from a dual perspective on the REBSP, the challenge is to adjust the current (trade) rules in the areas of food, agriculture, health, education, environment and information with a view to incorporating concepts of traditional knowledge of indigenous and local communities. Leading in this regard should be the need to provide for a fair and even-handed share for those communities in the benefits generated by distributing the material and immaterial products of such knowledge.

As the process of clarification of the normative content of the REBSP is still at an early stage, it might be helpful to pave the way by compiling state practice, domestic legislation, cases and examples, remedies, case law, practice of intergovernmental organizations, actions by NGOs, customary rules and practices of indigenous and local communities and so on. Based on these materials, a manual should be drafted under the auspices of the Parties to the Convention on Biological Diversity which indicates what different approaches to the REBSP are possible and what the similarities and differences are. Such a manual may also contain some guidelines for implementing the REBSP at the domestic level.

69 R Sibuye and others, 'The BushBuckridge BCP: Traditional Health Practitioners Organize for ABS in South Africa', in *Biodiversity and Culture: Exploring Community Protocols, Rights and Consent* (International Institute for Environment and Development 2012) 101–108, 106, available at <www.abs-initiative.info/fileadmin/media/Knowledge_Center/Pulications/BCPs/Biodiversity_and_Culture_Exploring_Community_Protocols_Rights_and_Consent_-_IIED_-_2012.pdf>.

70 'Traditional Knowledge, Innovation and Practices', available at <www.cbd.int/traditional>.

71 C Voigt, 'Delineating *the* Common Interest in International Law' in W Benedek and others (eds), *The Common Interest in International Law* (Intersentia 2014) 9–27, 22–23.

5. Concluding remarks

The dual perspective on the REBSP recognizes and entails that a full and comprehensive implementation of this human right requires the acceptance and incorporation of the idea that progress in science and the development of knowledge may originate from modern (industrialized) societies, on the one hand, and traditional knowledge systems based on the cultural identity and legacy of non-dominant groups, on the other hand. Human rights law must facilitate this dual approach and develop it further through cross-fertilization and complementarity of the two knowledge and science concepts. This may imply less emphasis on individual property rights dimensions of knowledge and more on common approaches to protecting and maintaining public goods and the collective cultural heritage and identity. This dual perspective on sharing the benefits of scientific progress relates to the interdependence and interconnectedness of state- and non-state actors in a global society. The right to share in such benefits fits well into the process of (economic) globalization. Effective enjoyment of this right requires integration of 'modern' and 'traditional' knowledge and science, for example, in matters of health, food, the environment and culture. In such a way, the REBSP may become a valuable tool for making economic, social and cultural rights of all, in particular those people living in developing countries, a reality and contribute to achieving global justice.

6 Protecting traditional cultural expressions

Copyright tensions and human rights opportunities?

Kelly Breemen

Introduction

This chapter analyses the issue of protection of traditional cultural expressions (TCEs) as one that evokes questions across legal boundaries, notably in the context of copyright law and human rights law.[1] Particular attention will be paid to the tensions and opportunities that follow from the relationship between indigenous and non-indigenous views on the topic. As such, it will become clear that crossing boundaries between different branches of the law is imperative, and that the study of indigenous peoples' rights is particularly useful for a researcher of information law such as the present author.

The first section introduces the issues and describes relevant concepts. The second section examines the challenges of an intellectual property approach – with a focus on copyright law – to the protection of TCE subject matter. The third section analyses the relevance of principles of the human rights framework for TCE protection arguments, focusing on cultural and indigenous rights. Due to the limited scope of the chapter and its explorative aim, the second and third sections only briefly discuss main points of both aspects of the discussion. In a concluding section, the chapter ties the links between the two contexts together. Copyright's engagement with the protection of TCEs is connected to what indigenous rights, cultural rights and their underlying principles contribute to the protection discussion. How can tensions between indigenous and non-indigenous views on TCE protection in a copyright context be informed by a human rights perspective, taking advantage of the opportunities that follow from cultural and indigenous rights interpretations and principles, to further the discussion?

1. The issues, history and concepts at stake in the story of TCE protection

For many decades now, the question has surfaced of how to protect age-old, culturally significant and often sacred expressions of traditional culture from

1 This chapter draws on early research for the author's PhD thesis conducted in 2015. The thesis was finalised in January 2018 (Institute for Information Law [IViR], University of Amsterdam).

unauthorised (mis)use and reproduction. Examples of such use range from the copying of sacred Australian Aboriginal designs on carpets[2] to using a song from the Suy Indians in Brazil for an advertisement.[3] The discussion on protecting indigenous peoples' traditional knowledge and TCEs is not new. Calls for protection from third party copying and use have already received attention in scholarly literature and at the international policy level of the World Intellectual Property Organization (WIPO) for many years now.[4]

At first sight, TCE protection tends to be approached as an intellectual property issue. Intellectual property is an important global topic and area of international economics and trade. Generally, the first attention for protection of TCEs in an international copyright context emerged during the preparations for the revision of the Berne Convention for the protection of Literary and Artistic Works – one of the main international copyright treaties – in Stockholm in 1967.[5] This revision process had roots in both a historical and contemporary context, being visibly influenced by the developments of the post-World War II and decolonisation period. Newly independent countries felt pressure to join the Berne Convention, but the young Asian and African states were also critical of the perceived universality of the existing system, with its origins in 18th century[6] Europe.[7] As a consequence, they took up representing their (copyright) interests as developing countries,[8] while indigenous peoples began making claims regarding their traditional knowledge and TCEs.[9]

2 See the often-cited carpet case, C Haight Farley, 'Protecting Folklore: Is Intellectual Property the Answer?' (1997) 30 *Connecticut Law Review* 1.

3 See A Seeger, 'Singing Other Peoples' Songs: Indigenous songs are often considered "public domain" – yet a mainstream musician can turn them into "individual property"' (1991) 15 *Cultural Survival Quarterly* <www.culturalsurvival.org/ourpublications/csq/article/singing-other-peoples-songs-indigenous-songs-are-often-considered-public> accessed 26 July 2017, on the specific example of singing other peoples' songs.

4 There is also criticism to the protection of TCEs, including public domain and freedom of (artistic) expression concerns. It is often argued that cultures have traditionally interacted and exchanged elements, and that this does not necessarily mean that cultures disappear. However, for indigenous peoples, the historical context of one-sided taking and their cultures being used as objects often does mean that third party taking is felt as harming the meaning and distinctive character of their cultures.

5 A Lucas-Schloetter, 'Folklore' in S von Lewinski, *Indigenous Heritage and Intellectual Property. Genetic Resources, Traditional Knowledge and Folklore* (Kluwer Law International BV 2008) 350; M Perlman, 'From "Folklore" to "Knowledge" in Global Governance: On the Metamorphoses of the Unauthored' in M Biagioli, P Jaszi and M Woodmansee (eds), *Making and Unmaking Intellectual Property: Creative Production in Legal and Cultural Perspective* (The University Press of Chicago 2011) 116.

6 The British Statute of Anne of 1710 is generally called the first 'copyright law.'

7 M Domman, 'Lost in Tradition?' in CB Graber and M Burri-Nenova (eds), *Intellectual Property and Traditional Cultural Expressions in a Digital Environment* (Edward Elgar Publishing Limited 2008) 9.

8 S Von Lewinski, 'Traditional Knowledge and Folklore: A New Topic in the International Arena' in FW Grosheide and JJ Brinkhof (eds), *Intellectual Property Law 2002. Articles on The Legal Protection of Cultural Expressions* (Intersentia 2002), 189, 190.

9 S Von Lewinski, 'The Protection of Folklore' (2003–2004) 11 *Cardozo J Int'l & Comp L* 747, 747.

During the early stages of discussions on TCE protection, an international approach was preferred over national laws due to cross-border practices of copying and dissemination of such knowledge and creativity, largely to industrialised countries.[10] Indeed, there has been a considerable change in perception regarding indigenous peoples' knowledge and cultures. Where they were previously perceived as 'backward societies,' indigenous communities have increasingly been viewed as 'keepers' of the world's treasures. These treasures include "knowledge of medicinal plants, unique arts and expressive traditions, natural resources (. . .) and traditional concepts of worldview that often have no counterpart in the language of the dominant societies to which indigenous groups belong."[11] The result has been increased (commercial) interest in manifestations of such traditional knowledge and TCEs, resulting in 'taking,' using and copying this material.

What is striking is the terminology that indigenous peoples and advocates use. The sensitivity and feelings of loss and disregard that third party practices trigger among indigenous peoples are illustrated by terms of survival, stealing and "same old tactics of assimilation" with outsiders "trying to assimilate our culture into their world because it is fashionable in their eyes and will make money."[12] For a large part, these feelings seem to be caused by failures to ask permission, consult the communities concerned and, in a way, treating them as dehumanised and objectified passive sources instead of equal partners in cultural exchange.

All in all, the protection of TCEs seems part of broader indigenous struggles regarding their contemporary place in dominant societies, which also prominently feature land and resources issues. Interests and claims comprise, but go beyond, protection of TCEs for economic reasons, also including matters of dignity, identity, spirituality and continued practice, if so desired. Furthermore, attention for indigenous issues triggered the examination of the interplay between intellectual property and human rights at the international level. This shows the fundamental character of the underlying issues at stake in the protection debate regarding traditional knowledge and TCEs. This chapter aims to show that TCE protection is not merely an isolated intellectual property topic, that differing worldviews lead to tensions[13] and that a cultural and indigenous rights perspective can help to understand the fundamental aspects of TCE protection and to inform protection approaches by providing a set of 'benchmark' principles.

10 Perlman (n 5) 116; Domman (n 7) 10.

11 M Riley (ed), *Indigenous Intellectual Property Rights. Legal Obstacles and Innovative Solutions* (AltaMira Press 2004) ix.

12 E Coleman, *Aboriginal Art, Identity and Appropriation* (Ashgate Publishing Limited 2005), 2, citing G Yunupingu, 'The Black/White Conflict' in V Johnson, *Copyrites: Aboriginal Art in the Age of Reproductive Technologies*, Touring Exhibition 1996 Catalogue (National Indigenous Arts Advocacy Association and Macquarie University 1996) 55.

13 KAF Johnston and M Heathcote, 'The Quest for 'Real' Protection for Indigenous Intangible Property Rights' (2014) 9 *Journal of Intellectual Property Law and Practice* 345, 345.

1.1. Indigenous heritage and the conundrum of categorisation

A central difficulty when discussing the protection of TCEs is *what* exactly has to be protected. This question has given rise to definitional challenges that indicate a first tension between non-indigenous and indigenous views on the scope of protected immaterial goods. In 'intellectual property terminology,' this scope is determined by a delineation of the *subject matter* to be covered by the protection rules. For indigenous heritage, such delineations of protectable content tend to bring with them a number of sensitivities, such as dividing inherently connected elements of indigenous knowledge and culture into separate categories.

Objections to dividing cultural elements which are intrinsically linked were already noted early on in discussions on the topic by Erica Daes in her much-cited report on the protection of indigenous heritage.[14] One of the main characteristics of TCEs is that they form part of indigenous peoples' perception of the world as an "integrated whole,"[15] in which each aspect is considered interrelated.[16] In this holistic worldview, the land itself is central, from which all art and science originate, forming an expression of the people concerned.[17] The interrelated perspective of this worldview is reflected by the importance attached to relationships between all elements of the world, such as "the land, animals, plants, humans, their ancestors and spirits." These relationships are embodied in indigenous heritage, and culture and knowledge are seen as closely linked to territory.[18] This makes dividing the protection of cultural expressions and knowledge, and separating it from the traditional lands of the communities concerned, contestable.[19]

A division of traditional knowledge, genetic resources and TCEs for regulatory purposes, and differentiation on the basis of intellectual property, art and science for protection approaches, have been called artificial precisely because of the interrelated nature of these elements.[20] As work on the issue takes place within WIPO's international intellectual property context, intellectual property law's distinction between various areas and their specific subject matter has likely influenced the categorisation of indigenous heritage. In other words, indigenous worldviews and relationships seem forced to be

14 E Daes, *Discrimination Against Indigenous Peoples. Study on the Protection of the Cultural and Intellectual Property of Indigenous Peoples* (Commission on Human Rights, Sub-Commission on Prevention of Discrimination and Protection of Minorities 1993), 7; E Daes, *Protection of the Heritage of Indigenous People* (United Nations Publication 1997) 3.

15 T Janke, *Our Culture: Our Future. Report on Australian Indigenous Cultural and Intellectual Property Rights* (Australian Institute of Aboriginal and Torres Strait Islander Studies and the Aboriginal and Torres Strait Islander Commission 1998), 2.

16 S Von Lewinski, 'Adequate Protection of Folklore: A Work in Progress' in P Torremans (ed), *Copyright Law: A Handbook of Contemporary Research* (Edward Elgar 2007), 215.

17 Daes, *Protection of the Heritage of Indigenous People* (n 14) 3.

18 Janke, *Our Culture: Our Future* (n 15) 8.

19 Daes, *Discrimination Against Indigenous Peoples* (n 14) 39.

20 Daes, *Protection of the Heritage of Indigenous People* (n 14) 3.

translated into dominant ones in order to fit within 'Western'-style categories and frameworks.[21] Intellectual property law distinguishes, for example, between copyright's literary and artistic works, patent law's novel inventions and trademark's distinguishing signs. In this sense, traditional knowledge concerning plants and medicinal application would seem related to patent law's (pharmaceutical) inventions or applications, whereas TCEs are likened to copyright law's literary and artistic works.[22]

Following this distinction, WIPO's Intergovernmental Committee (IGC) on Intellectual Property and Genetic Resources, Traditional Knowledge and Folklore has attempted to define the scope of TCEs in its Draft Articles for a treaty on the protection of TCEs, the latest version of which are of 2017, distinguishing between a number of categories.[23] Per category, an unlimited list of examples is included. It is rather copyright-like to give a list of items that would fall under the subject matter of the protection regime.[24] However, the scope of WIPO's draft treaty does not seem too restrictively formulated, reducing the risk of a static approach. Still, an approach more in line with indigenous peoples' own view would underline the importance of self-identification, or indeed self-determination, of what constitutes indigenous peoples' heritage.[25] It has been argued that indigenous heritage is a living inheritance, and that "[u]ltimately, any definition of Indigenous Cultural and Intellectual Property should reflect the perspective of a particular Indigenous group."[26] The Mataatua Declaration of 1993, one of the early intellectual property initiatives of indigenous groups and representatives themselves, also stresses the necessity of self-definition.[27]

1.2. Diverging views on objectives and outcomes of regulation

Intellectual property law's focus is mainly on *protection*, in the sense that it provides for possibilities of *excluding* others from using and copying the artistic

21 Rosemary Coombe has mentioned the example of copyright licences, which require a translation of indigenous systems of permission into a copyright licence system. This, then, would diminish the characteristic social relationships of cultural expressions. See RJ Coombe, 'The properties of culture and the possession of identity: postcolonial struggle and the legal imagination' in B Ziff and V Rao (eds), *Borrowed Power: Essays on Cultural Appropriation* (Rutgers University Press 1997), 92. See also RJ Coombe, *The Cultural Life of Intellectual Properties. Authorship, Appropriation, and the Law* (Duke University Press 1998) 229.

22 Both for reasons of time and space, and in order to compare tensions between indigenous and non-indigenous views under copyright law vis-à-vis human rights opportunities, this chapter also focuses on TCEs only. The broader context is however still kept in mind.

23 See in Article 2, Use of Terms.

24 Compare, for example, Article 2(1) of the Berne Convention.

25 Compare Daes, *Discrimination Against Indigenous Peoples* (n 14), 39. See also B Sherman and L Wiseman, 'Towards an Indigenous Public Domain' in L Guibault and PB Hugenholtz (eds), *The Future of the Public Domain* (Kluwer Law International 2006) 273–275.

26 Janke, *Our Culture: Our Future* (n 15) 3.

27 See provision 1.1: "In the development of policies and practices, indigenous peoples should: [d]efine for themselves their own intellectual and cultural property."

work, trademark or invention in question due to (temporary) monopoly rights. This enables right holders to prevent use of others and constitutes therefore a defensive type of right.

Customary rules regarding indigenous peoples' heritage seem more oriented towards *usage* requirements rather than monopolising the underlying works or knowledge. This is in line with the indigenous reality and worldview of centralising relationships as mentioned above. In other words, traditional knowledge and TCEs are impersonal: they are communally shared and governed, and there is not one owner who benefits from exclusive protection rules. Rather than protection, ownership and exclusivity, customary rules on traditional knowledge and TCEs are characterised by "bundles of relationships,"[28] custodianship, responsibilities and communal interests.[29] There seems therefore more involved than straightforward protection of exclusivity in this multi-layered system of sharing, usage conditions and custodianship.

Still, the appeal of (intellectual property-like) *protection* of TCEs to indigenous peoples is clear when protection is considered as the ability of indigenous peoples to *control* traditional knowledge and TCEs according to their own worldviews as governed by their customary rules and to exclude third parties from use without due regard of customary laws or use without consultation and benefit sharing. Such control interests indicate some similarity with an author's control over third party use, for example, through copyright licences. Apart from such control concerns, *preservation* and *promotion* are two other interests that seem vital to indigenous peoples' struggles in a broad way and the creation of TCEs in specific. Indeed, in Peter Jaszi's study on traditional art in Indonesia, key concerns of traditional artists included the transmission of their art to future generations.[30] An underlying need is respect and recognition for indigenous peoples' TCEs in societies, which is not a need that is easily addressed through legal means.[31]

2. An intellectual property and copyright perspective: copyright tensions

Due to TCEs' initial likeness to immaterial works as covered by intellectual property laws such as copyright law and WIPO's competence regarding international intellectual property issues, it seems 'natural' that WIPO has decided to work

28 Daes, Protection of the Heritage of Indigenous People (n 14) 4.

29 See on this impersonal, collective nature of TCEs among others: Daes, *Protection of the Heritage of Indigenous People* (n 14); Coombe, 'The Properties of Culture' (n 21); Coombe, *The Cultural Life of Intellectual Properties* (n 21); Haight Farley (n 2); Janke, *Our Culture: Our Future* (n 15); and Von Lewinski, 'Adequate Protection of Folklore' (n 16).

30 P Jaszi, *Traditional Culture: A Step Forward For Protection in Indonesia: A Research Report* (Institute for Press and Development Studies 2009) 14, 22.

31 ibid., 22: "It is impossible, however, to legislate respect. A failure to afford recognition where it is due is primarily a matter of ethical, rather than legal, dimensions."

on the protection of traditional knowledge and TCEs in its IGC.[32] This does however mean that WIPO's approach tends to draw on the concepts of classical intellectual property rights.[33] While the attention for protecting traditional knowledge and TCEs on the international level in the intellectual property environment of WIPO is not surprising, in academic literature many scholars have concluded that intellectual property laws such as copyright are not suitable to that end for a number of organisational and fundamental, technical reasons. Von Lewinski explains this as follows:

> This pragmatic approach, i.e. of using an existing international organization that traditionally has been dealing with matter similar to, but certainly not fully matching, traditional knowledge and its background has, from the outset of discussions within WIPO, reflected the *clash of concepts* of traditional intellectual property on the one hand and the claimed protection for traditional knowledge on the other hand.[34]

The fundamental, technical unsuitability of copyright law includes tensions regarding property and ownership concepts; the possibility of alienating rights; copyright requirements such as originality, fixation, authorship; and duration. Apart from such technical difficulties, the applicability of the main copyright theories and justifications to the protection of TCEs is also questionable on a foundational level. Reasons to protect traditional knowledge and TCEs comprise specific concerns that are part of a broader, more fundamental struggle, including land and self-determination issues. Applying a protection model that draws on diverging reasons and protection theories inevitably leads to tensions. These tensions are elaborated on later in this section.

The central concept of the public domain exemplifies another difficulty, one that was already briefly touched upon on page 111, footnotes 3 and 4: from a copyright perspective, unprotected and age-old works are in the public domain. This is one of the main examples where reconciling – central features of – a dominant legal system with indigenous views is prone to challenges. When conceiving of copyright law as a system where (individual) authors' interests and the public interest in a common public domain have to be balanced, indigenous peoples' interests are caught in the middle, making it difficult to have their communal claims heard.[35] WIPO's Draft Articles on the protection of TCEs address this 'gap' by legislating

32 S Von Lewinski, 'Comments on Susy Frankel: "'Ka Mate Ka Mate' and the protection of traditional knowledge" – an international perspective' in R Cooper Dreyfuss and JC Ginsburg, *Intellectual Property at the Edge. The Contested Contours of IP* (Cambridge University Press 2014), 216, referring to Article 2(viii) of the Treaty on the WIPO: "'intellectual property' shall include the rights relating to: (. . .) and all other rights resulting from intellectual activity in the industrial, scientific, literary or artistic fields."

33 Von Lewinski, 'Comments on Susy Frankel' (n 32) 216.

34 ibid. [italics added].

35 A Pask, 'Cultural Appropriation and the Law: An Analysis of Legal Regimes Concerning Culture' (1993) 8 *Intellectual Property Journal* 57, 63; M Battiste and J Youngblood Henderson, *Protecting Indigenous Knowledge and Heritage. A Global Challenge* (Purich Publishing Ltd 2000) 150.

specific rules that do take TCEs' specific characteristics as a starting point. The potential result of protection for previously unprotected works has led to criticism of limitation of the public domain and thus of cultural life around the world.[36] Here, one can clearly see the tension between indigenous and non-indigenous views on the public domain, and between the interests of indigenous peoples versus interests of creative industries and freedom of expression interests.

2.1. Property and ownership: tensions between indigenous and non-indigenous views

Copyright law, as one aspect of the intellectual *property* regime, presents an obvious issue for TCEs: it deals with property and ownership. However, as touched upon on pages 113 and 115, for TCEs, the relationships between peoples and their land, knowledge and cultural expressions differ from the concept of property, with its economic and commodity-based focus and implications. This difference seems to be a central underlying difficulty causing a disconnect between the dominant intellectual property system and immaterial traditional knowledge and TCEs.[37]

Traditional knowledge and TCEs are generally not considered commodities to be owned by a particular person. Considering the (social) relationships that are central to TCEs as property does not adequately address the role of this material in indigenous communities. TCEs tend to be impersonal and collective in nature and not first and foremost valued for economic reasons.[38] Rather, works are produced to serve the whole community. Therefore, since benefit for the society as a whole is involved, it is the collective that 'holds' the knowledge and cultural expressions and has an interest in its use and decisions thereon.

Usually, though, an individual, family or group within the community is designated via customary rules as custodian of specific pieces of knowledge or traditional culture.[39] The privileges that come with holding the knowledge 'on trust' for the community, for example, use and reproduction, generally last while the custodians "act in the best interests of the community."[40] And,

36 J Band, 'Will The Vulcan Salute Live Long And Prosper? The Rush To Lock Up "Cultural Expression"' (6 March 2015) <www.techdirt.com/articles/20150305/11261930217/will-vulcan-salute-live-long-prosper-rush-to-lock-up-cultural-expression.shtml> accessed 25 July 2017: "(. . .) the treaty could interfere with cultural life around the world, pulling out of the public domain material that is incorporated in countless novels, paintings, films, sculptures, operas, and other musical compositions. This is because these works are based on stories, legends, dances, rituals and other forms of expression that the treaty could protect without a limitation on term."

37 Battiste and Henderson (n 35) 145.

38 Daes, *Protection of the Heritage of Indigenous People* (n 14) 3–4.

39 Daes, *Protection of the Heritage of Indigenous People* (n 17) 4; Janke, *Our Culture: Our Future* (n 15) 8–9; T Janke, *Minding Culture. Case Studies on Intellectual Property and Traditional Cultural Expressions* (WIPO 2003), 14; Von Lewinski, 'Adequate Protection of Folklore' (n 16) 216. These rules determine who may use or reproduce certain specific elements, in what way and under what circumstances, as certain material is for example sacred and only to be shared in a limited way.

40 Daes, *Protection of the Heritage of Indigenous People* (n 14) 4; Janke, *Our Culture: Our Future* (n 15) 8.

importantly, custodianship comes with responsibilities.[41] As the traditional material is embedded in and governed according to specific customary rules, this shows that ownership is not an adequate concept. A system of custodians and communal responsibilities rather than autonomous, individual owners of the intangible material in question is unfamiliar to dominant property-based legal regimes. Some kind of trusteeship in the interest of the community as a whole seems to better describe the relationship between TCEs and source communities.[42]

2.2. Transfer and alienation of rights

Connected to this different view of property and ownership is the consequence of designating cultural expressions as property: the ability to transfer and alienate rights to the intangible material in question. An individual author is free to decide upon this. However, when the material benefits the community as a whole, "layers of rights"[43] and multiple members of the community become involved in the governance of the material.

Rights to heritage are generally perceived as communal rights,[44] and only the collective can give consent for sharing of the heritage through community-specific procedures, consent which is always limited in time and revocable. *Sharing* implies that the "heritage can never be alienated, surrendered or sold, except for conditional use."[45] As relationships are central, traditional knowledge or TCEs lose their meaning outside these specific relational contexts, with sale even understood as terminating the relationships.[46] It is communal material, held in trusteeship by custodians for the benefit of the community as a whole, and described as existing mainly outside "the modern marketplace."[47] As Battiste and Youngblood Henderson state,

> The idea of individualistic, market-driven legal components creating property rights in the creative interaction of human beings with their world leaves little room for respect for or protection of creation that does not divide creativity into transferable segments capable of having value in economic terms.[48]

41 Von Lewinski, 'Adequate Protection of Folklore' (n 16) 216. Having received this knowledge means that the custodian has to use or keep it in compliance with customary rules, thus repaying the gift through acting according to his or her responsibilities. Not doing so, and breaching customary rules, would set into motion a sanction regime to repair any damage to social relationships that might have occurred. This is also noted by Janke with regard to the Aboriginal law and culture; see Janke, *Minding Culture* (n 39) 15.

42 Daes, *Protection of the Heritage of Indigenous People* (n 14) 4; Janke, *Our Culture: Our Future* (n 15) 8.

43 Haight Farley (n 2) 32.

44 Daes, *Protection of the Heritage of Indigenous People* (n 14) 4.

45 ibid.

46 Battiste and Youngblood Henderson (n 35) 71.

47 Battiste and Youngblood Henderson (n 35) 147.

48 ibid.

On the other hand, framing the protection of TCEs in an intellectual property narrative implies that the material is reduced to property. In other words, it is turned into alienable "commodities," "shift[ing] authority over knowledge objects away from those who produced and towards those who have capital to acquire them."[49] Again, different perceptions of alienation of seemingly alike material lead to tensions between intellectual property systems' focus on commodification of immaterial innovations and creations versus the general absence of such a motivation for indigenous knowledge, innovation and creativity.[50] Such knowledge is, for example, created for spiritual, cultural and social purposes, for which customary laws govern use, access and reproduction. These purposes are captured in interests in protection of integrity and recognition and consultation as source communities.

2.3. Originality, fixation, an identifiable author and duration

Although copyright law is not internationally harmonised, there are a number of generally agreed-on characteristics and requirements. In scholarly literature, a number of these tend to be highlighted due to the difficulties they present for TCEs. These are originality, fixation,[51] an identifiable author and 'limited' duration of protection. They illustrate the different perceptions of 'literary and artistic' works in a copyright sense on the one hand, and indigenous peoples' TCEs on the other hand.

Firstly, copyright's threshold criterion of originality[52] might not be very high in practice,[53] but theoretically, it presents an obvious challenge for age-old works that have been transmitted through generations. This is especially the case because originality is required for each one specific expression. Generally, certain distinctive input of the author is required.[54] This is a clear (theoretical)

49 Jaszi (n 30) 92–93 in his section on intellectual property and alienation: further implications of a property regime.

50 P Drahos, 'When Cosmology Meets Property: Indigenous People's Innovation and Intellectual Property' (2011) 29 *Prometheus* 233, 233.

51 NB: This is only a prerequisite for copyright protection in certain countries. Article 2(2) of the Berne Convention allows member state legislation, but does not require contracting states to make protection dependent on fixation or expression in some material form.

52 See extensively on the originality requirement and Aboriginal art: B Sherman, 'From the Non-original to the Ab-original: A history' in B Sherman and A Strowel (eds), *Of Authors and Origins. Essays on Copyright Law* (Clarendon Press 1994), 118–125.

53 See SJ Van Gompel, 'Creativity, Autonomy and Personal Touch: A Critical Appraisal of the CJEU's Originality Test for Copyright' in MMM van Eechoud (ed), *The Work of Authorship* (Amsterdam: Amsterdam University Press 2014), 95–143, on this low threshold in copyright law as confirmed by the Court of Justice of the European Union (CJEU), where he analyses the following line of case law: *Infopaq International v. Danske Dagblades Forening* (case C-5/08, 2009), para 37; *Bezpečnostní softwarová asociace – Svaz softwarové ochrany v Ministerstvo kultury* (case C-393/09, 2010); *Football Association Premier League & Others v QC Leisure & Others* (case C-403/08, 2011), para 97; *Painer v Standard VerlagsGmbH & Others* (case C-145/10, 2011), para 87; *Football Dataco Ltd & Others v Yahoo!* (case C-604/10, 2012), para 37); and *SAS Institute Inc. v World Programming Ltd* (case C-406/10, 2012), para 45.

54 Sherman (n 52) 119: "There must be something of the creator in the final product which can be said to be distinctively his or hers."

example of the difference between copyright elements and the reality of indigenous artistic practices. *De facto*, the latter tend to be copies of existing works, passed on through generations.[55] Such material is often appreciated precisely for the accurate depiction and continuation of the TCEs in question, for example, for reasons of spirituality or education.[56] Here, a disconnect is visible between copyright aims of stimulating new creations, and indigenous creativity, forming part of a collective heritage, where artists form "collective voices." They strive to preserve the heritage they are entrusted with, rather than to innovate or deviate.[57]

Of course, indigenous culture is not static, but it develops dynamically at its own pace.[58] Similarly, not all TCEs can automatically be considered 'unoriginal' in a copyright sense. Where allowed and appreciated, works from indigenous artists that add original elements or draw on inspiration derived from centuries-old TCEs *could* be protected by copyright.[59] However, this does not include the large mass of TCEs that are transmitted across communities' generations and are 'copied' repeatedly. Still, considering indigenous cultural works per definition as merely static copies failing to meet the originality requirement of the copyright regime also falls short of taking the nuances of indigenous cultural life into account. In any case, this requirement of originality shows a first potential tension.

Secondly, in certain countries,[60] only works that are fixed in some way are copyrightable. This presents an obvious challenge for indigenous traditions or cultural expressions that often exist only intangibly and are transmitted orally to future generations, such as stories, dance or music. A fixation requirement limits protection options for TCEs that are not fixed in a material 'carrier'.[61] As it is the very nature of almost all TCEs to exist unfixed within their source communities,[62] this shows another tension between dominant understandings of copyrightable works in certain countries and the reality of indigenous creativity. Furthermore, one of the main questions here would be what effect the act of fixation could have on the content of the work of traditional culture in question,[63] as this is a perhaps rather unnatural practice for indigenous communities.

55 See for an example from indigenous songs: S Mills, 'Indigenous Music and the Law: An Analysis of National and International Legislation' (1996) 28 *Yearbook for Traditional Music* 57, 65.
56 Haight Farley (n 2) 21.
57 Lucas-Schloetter (n 5) 385.
58 Haight Farley (n 2) 21.
59 Lucas-Schloetter (n 5) 385.
60 According to Article 2(2) of the Berne Convention, member state legislation may determine whether protection depends on fixation in some material form. This is, for example, the case in the United States (Section 102 of the US Copyright Act of 1976, 17 U.S.C.) and the United Kingdom (Article 3(2) of the Copyright, Designs and Patents Act 1988, (Chapter 48)).
61 Lucas-Schloetter (n 5) 383.
62 S Scafidi, *Who Owns Culture? Appropriation and Authenticity in American Law* (Rutgers University Press 2005) 31.
63 As Scafidi wonders, "What does fixation save, and what might it destroy?" Scafidi (n 62) 34.

Another copyright challenge facing TCEs is the concept of authorship and, consequently, who can claim and hold the rights following from the act of having made a work. For recent works, this may not be problematic, but it is a difficult task to search for an identifiable author of age-old works that have been transmitted through community generations for centuries.[64] However, in practice, there is generally not one person that claims authorship. This complicates the notion of authorship status. Even if a TCE is produced by an individual artist who is the custodian of that specific expression, it is still for the benefit of the community as a whole and usually involves continuing existing traditional practices, thus keeping the heritage 'alive.'

It has been argued that demanding identifiable persons with authorship status to determine the right holder of the copyright, or to grant rights at all, is problematic. Reshaping traditional creativity in such a way that it is compatible with the legal context of copyright law would disregard indigenous views on authorship and ownership.[65] Riley has called the struggle for recognition of rights to cultural property as an indigenous group a "search to recover collectivity."[66] Again, this shows tensions between dominant legal systems and indigenous peoples' worldview, position and needs. Copyright law does have the possibility of joint authorship, yet the contribution of the joint authors is determinant: merely ideas are not enough to pass the joint authorship test; there has to be a certain creative, contributing expression. This is a difficult requirement for large group authorship. Copyright law has also increasingly faced challenges to its conceptions of authorship outside traditional knowledge debates, for example, in the case of film productions[67] and increasingly large-scale scientific research projects,[68] where there are many collaborators.

Finally, the time-limited duration of the protection is a copyright characteristic that poses a challenge for TCEs: it lasts until 70 years after the death of the author maximally.[69] This could be viewed as a certain trade-off between author interests and the public interest in a public domain of cultural works. It is inherent to copyright protection that it is not indefinite but that works

64 T Kono (ed), *Intangible Cultural Heritage and Intellectual Property. Communities, Cultural Diversity and Sustainable Development* (Intersentia 2009) 17.

65 J Anderson, 'The Politics of Indigenous Knowledge: Australia's Proposed Communal Moral Rights Bill' (2004) 27 *UNSW Law Journal* 1, 6.

66 AR Riley, 'Recovering Collectivity: Group Rights to Intellectual Property in Indigenous Communities' (2000) 18 *Cardozo Arts and Entertainment Law Journal* 175, 177–178.

67 P Goldstein and PB Hugenholtz, *International Copyright. Principles, Law, and Practice* (Oxford University Press 2010) 244.

68 L Bently and L Biron, 'Discontinuities Between Legal Conceptions of Authorship and Social Practices' in MMM van Eechoud (ed), *The Work of Authorship* (Amsterdam University Press 2014) 239–243.

69 The Berne Convention requires a minimum term of protection of 50 years after the death of the author, i.e. in Article 7(1). In Europe, recital 12 and Article 1 of Directive 2006/116/EC on the term of protection of copyright and certain related rights determine this is 70 years.

enter the public domain and are then freely usable, which is guaranteed by this delineated protection period.[70] However, for TCEs that go back centuries in time, a protection system that expires 70 years after the death of the author is not very useful.

As TCEs tend to play a role in indigenous societies over many years and throughout generations, it seems incompatible with their simultaneously ancient and contemporary significance that these expressions would enter the public domain after a certain period of time. According to indigenous advocates, it is not the individual author's benefit which is at stake in eternal protection of TCEs, but that of communities that exist throughout the passage of time.[71] However, extension of the term of protection for 'general' copyright is already hotly contested. Suggestions for a protection regime that is potentially unlimited in time[72] will likely provoke similar – or even more – fierce reactions, especially when it leads to taking previously public domain material *out* of the public domain.[73]

2.4. Copyright theories and TCE protection arguments: a relationship shaped by complexity

When looking at the theories or justifications that are generally accepted to underlie copyright protection, a further tension is visible with interests and arguments for TCE protection.[74] This tension seems to encompass central differences between indigenous and non-indigenous views on creative production, 'creative life' and reasons to protect creativity. The two main copyright rationales are the utilitarian tradition, on the one hand, and the natural law or authors' rights tradition, on the other. They cover utilitarian and incentive theories, and natural law, labour, personality and *droit d'auteur* theories, respectively.

In short, the distinction between the two traditions is that they are either economics or morals oriented. The utilitarian and incentive theories for copyright protection are concerned with notions of efficiency, practicality and an emphasis on diffusion of works for utilitarian welfare reasons. They are focused on regulating information markets in a practical and effective way. To this end,

70 Intergovernmental Committee On Intellectual Property And Genetic Resources, Traditional Knowledge And Folklore 2008, p 20.

71 Haight Farley (n 2) 17.

72 WIPO's Draft Articles of 2017 suggest in draft Article 8 on the term of protection that protection may/should/shall "last as long as the traditional cultural expressions fulfill/satisfy the [criteria of eligibility for protection] according to this [instrument], and in consultation with beneficiaries.]" Protection against distortion or mutilation, harming the reputation of the source community or region, could last indefinitely. In an alternative option 3 for this draft Article, it is suggested that protection of TCEs, "at least regards their economic aspects," should/shall be limited.

73 Band (n 36).

74 See on this also J Hughes, 'Traditional Knowledge, Cultural Expression, and the Siren's Call of Property' (2012) 49 *San Diego Law Review* 1; SR Munzer and K Raustiala, 'The Uneasy Case for Intellectual Property Rights in Traditional Knowledge' (2009) 27 *Cardozo Arts and Entertainment Law Journal* 37.

copyright protection via a temporary exclusive monopoly is generally thought to lead to incentives to innovate, create, disseminate or preserve literary and artistic works. This would benefit society as a whole. On the other hand, the natural law, labour, personality and *droit d'auteur* theories to justify copyright protection rely primarily on the bond between author and work, and rewarding the labour of the author by allowing him or her to reap the benefits of that labour via temporary exclusive rights. A typical aspect of this tradition is its set of moral rights, including for example an attribution right and a right to object to distortion of the work.

Market considerations and benefit for the public are not initially thought of to adequately underlie a protection system that responds to actual indigenous interests, which stretch beyond economic ones. Furthermore, a justification that relies on incentives would run counter to the argument that indigenous peoples have not traditionally needed these to further their traditional creativity. As a result, the utilitarian tradition cannot grasp other values that may be at stake in the context of TCEs and their functions in indigenous communities, such as a spiritual role or a role as an inheritance rather than as commodities.

As for the natural law or authors' rights protection arguments, the general notion of centralising the bond between the author and the work seems to resonate with the importance attached to TCEs in indigenous communities, forming part of the land and communal relationships in a holistic way. However, a difficulty here is the individual and author-centric nature of the natural law, labour, personality and *droit d'auteur* theories. Applying these theories and justifications to communal works and interests would require significantly stretching them.

To recap, there seem to be two main issues: a difference between indigenous and non-indigenous creative production and 'creative life,' on the one hand, and a difference between indigenous and non-indigenous systems and reasons to protect, on the other.[75] 'Mainstream' legal concepts, language and theories are not equipped to adequately respond to indigenous peoples' needs and distinctive cultural characteristics. To fit indigenous peoples' creativity into existing categories and rationales seems artificial and presumes a degree of mainstream narrative authority over indigenous peoples' cultures. However, not engaging with the language and requirements of existing laws leads to a lack of protection for indigenous creative productions.

3. What can a human rights perspective tell us: human rights opportunities?

Against the historical background of centuries of indigenous struggles, it becomes apparent that TCE protection cannot be considered in isolation as 'just another intellectual property issue.' Yes, indigenous peoples might have economic interests with regard to their TCEs, economic development might have

75 See also Jaszi (n 30) 73 on this tension between copyright theories and TCE protection.

been mentioned in a copyright sphere as a reason for TCE protection from early on, and the debate and issues concerned may have certain copyright-like features. But beyond that, there is 'something more' at stake that cannot be fully grasped within a copyright context.

A human rights perspective will show that this elusive part of TCE protection could be viewed as part of a broader context, one that touches upon such fundamental notions as dignity and self-determination. It is therefore useful to look at considerations of human rights law. Telling the story of TCE protection from a human rights perspective provides us with the opportunity to help grasp the fundamental nature of TCE protection and understand its wider implications. It can also help to frame arguments for TCE protection beyond a primary focus on copyright(-like) rationales.

Human rights and intellectual property law share a certain space concerning the topic of TCE protection. The interplay between the two areas originates in debates at the international level about indigenous peoples' rights. In fact, discussions regarding indigenous peoples' knowledge have been a prime incentive for scrutinising the relationship between human rights law and intellectual property law in general.[76] It was the "emphasis on the neglected rights of indigenous peoples" that first displayed "the serious normative deficiencies of intellectual property law from a human rights perspective."[77] In subsequent years, the UN and WIPO have tried to close this gap in their respective areas. The UN has focused on developing indigenous rights, WIPO on protecting traditional knowledge and TCEs. More recently, there has been an exchange of concepts and expertise. For example, former UN Special Rapporteur on the rights of indigenous peoples James Anaya has connected indigenous fundamental rights and concepts with intellectual property issues at several WIPO sessions.[78]

3.1. TCE protection through a cultural and indigenous rights looking glass

This section will explain the relevance of a cultural and indigenous rights perspective for the protection of TCEs by discussing four central human rights principles: dignity, non-discrimination, self-determination and participation. This is necessarily a selection, and of course, many more principles, perspectives and rights could

76 LR Helfer and GW Austin, *Human Rights and Intellectual Property: Mapping the Global Interface* (Cambridge University Press 2011) 34, 48.

77 LR Helfer, 'Human Rights and Intellectual Property: Conflict or Coexistence?' (2003) 5 *Minnesota Intellectual Property Review* 47, 52.

78 SJ Anaya, 'Intellectual Property and Genetic Resources: What is at Stake for Indigenous Peoples?', Keynote Address at the Indigenous Panel of WIPO's IGC (February 2014) <www.wipo.int/edocs/mdocs/tk/en/wipo_grtkf_ic_26/wipo_grtkf_ic_26_indigenous_panel_james_anaya.pdf> accessed 25 July 2017; SJ Anaya, 'Indigenous Peoples' Rights to Genetic Resources and Traditional Knowledge', Presentation at the Indigenous Panel of WIPO's IGC (4 February 2013) <www.ip-watch.org/weblog/wp-content/uploads/2013/02/IGC-Statement-UN-Sp-Rapporteur-Ing-Peoples-Feb-2013.pdf?0c235b> accessed 28 July 2017.

be included. These four principles are chosen because they touch upon core indigenous issues and in this way show that a cultural and indigenous rights perspective is a valuable, if not essential, addition to the TCE-protection discourse.

3.1.1. Dignity

Various roles can be ascribed to the notion of dignity. McGonagle has distinguished the following roles: a foundational role, as a basis for other rights (used for claiming violations of rights); a role as a value, in particular as an operative public value (for aspirational or incentive purposes, such as promotion of values that the whole society should share); or a role as a principle (securing a place next to other fundamental principles).[79] Here, we will focus on the latter: dignity as a central underlying principle of human rights law. The inherent dignity of human beings features in the preambles of the Universal Declaration of Human Rights (UDHR),[80] the International Covenant on Civil and Political Rights (ICCPR) and the International Covenant on Economic, Social and Cultural Rights (ICESCR). The importance of the dignity principle is also emphasised in Article 1 UDHR, which contains dignity as one of the main underlying principles or 'foundational blocks' of human rights law.[81]

The principle of dignity is central to claims of cultural integrity and the right to maintain and develop own cultural identities. These are notions of central relevance for TCE protection. They are closely connected to such rights as non-discrimination,[82] self-determination, the right to take part in cultural life of Article 15(1)(a) ICESCR and the rights of minorities of Article 27 ICCPR.[83] The latter two rights, informed by non-discrimination and self-determination, essentially safeguard the existence and survival of distinctive cultures and ways of life by guaranteeing rights to practise and protect these cultures and lifestyles.

The International Labour Organization's (ILO) Convention No. 169 on Indigenous and Tribal Peoples also merits particular mention, as its main theme is to remove previous assimilationist orientations and to recognise "the aspiration of these peoples to exercise control over their own institutions, ways of life and economic development to maintain and develop their identities, languages and religions."[84] In the United Nations Declaration on the Rights

79 T McGonagle, 'Safeguarding Human Dignity in the European Audiovisual Sector' (2007) 6 *IRIS Plus* 1, 3.

80 Via its preamble and emphasis on dignity, the UDHR has been called a 'member' of the "large family of dignity-based rights instruments" adopted during and since World War II. MA Glendon, *A World Made New. Eleanor Roosevelt and the Universal Declaration of Human Rights* (Random House 2001), 175.

81 ibid., 174, 178.

82 See CERD, 'General Recommendation No. 23 on Indigenous Peoples' (1997) UN Doc A/52/18, especially para 4.

83 See generally SJ Anaya, *Indigenous Peoples in International Law* (Oxford University Press 2004), 134-37 on Article 27 as a cultural integrity norm.

84 ILO Indigenous and Tribal Peoples Convention, 1989 (No. 169), preamble paragraph 4 and 5; Anaya, *Indigenous Peoples in International Law* (n 83) 59.

of Indigenous Peoples (UNDRIP), dignity is not an aspirational, preambular principle, but safeguarded in a substantive provision. Article 15 underlines indigenous peoples' collective right to the inherent dignity and the diversity of their cultures, traditions, histories and aspirations. Both indigenous rights instruments further contain extensive provisions that contribute to the protection of the cultural integrity, dignity, diversity and identity of indigenous peoples.[85] This rights framework is indispensable for any approach to TCE protection in a broad sense: it forms a basis not just for arguments for the protection of TCEs, but also for their maintenance, development and for their expression at all. Although they thus seem to form a clear normative framework for such diverse aspects of TCEs, there are also limitations to these instruments. The first is that ILO Convention No. 169 has only been ratified by a fairly small number of countries. The second is that UNDRIP is a Declaration that is legally non-binding, which means that without implementation by nation states, its provisions run the risk of being paper tigers.

One of the main arguments to protect TCEs is to prevent them being diffused, used out of context and copied by 'outsider' third parties without consent and due account of their cultural significance in order to safeguard the inherent dignity of indigenous communities and their cultures. This seems to resonate with the human rights principle of dignity. The connection between indigenous peoples' dignity, cultural integrity and identity on the one hand, and their heritage, traditional knowledge and TCEs on the other, is continually stressed throughout the literature on the topic, as well as in panels and sessions at the United Nations and WIPO.[86] The discussion on TCE protection is clearly a part – and an example – of the broader indigenous struggle for recognition and respect for their inherent dignity. Arguments for protection, including control, maintenance and development, of TCEs can therefore draw on the fundamental human rights principle of dignity.

3.1.2. Equality and non-discrimination

The equality principle is visible throughout the corpus of human rights law. The leading thought behind it is the conviction that differential treatment based on the distinctive characteristics of a person, or of the groups to which that person belongs, is unjust.[87] Equality is one of the 'foundational blocks' of

85 See, for example, Articles 2, 4, 5, 8, 9 and 28 ILO Convention No. 169 and Articles 5, 8, 9, 11, 12, 13, 14, 15, 16, 31 and 33 UNDRIP.

86 The Report of the 23rd session of the Working Group on Indigenous Populations recommends for example that the protection of indigenous peoples' cultural heritage "[P]romote[s] respect for the dignity and cultural integrity of indigenous peoples who conserve and maintain their cultural heritage, and respect[s] and recognize[s] their rights, particularly human rights, under international and national law." Working Group on Indigenous Populations, 'Report of the 23rd Session', which had as main theme "Indigenous peoples and the international and domestic protection of traditional knowledge" (2005), 12.

87 S Skogly, 'Article 2' in A Eide, G Alfredsson, G Melander, LA Rehof, A Rosas (eds), *The Universal Declaration of Human Rights. A Commentary* (Universitetsforlaget AS 1992), 57.

the UDHR.[88] The right to non-discrimination is laid down bindingly in Article 2(1) of the ICCPR and Article 2(2) of the ICESCR. Article 2(1) ICCPR has been called an "umbrella clause," with a function in "the systematic interpretation of the Covenant."[89] For the ICESCR, the concepts of non-discrimination and equality as following from Article 2(2) are said to be the central themes to the Covenant as a whole and particularly useful for economic, social and cultural rights claims.[90] In both Covenants, the right to non-discrimination has an accessory character. This means that the right, and potential violations, only comes into play in conjunction with the exercise of other rights. One can, for example, think of rights to take part in cultural life, minority rights and economic, social and cultural rights generally.[91] The International Convention on the Elimination of All Racial Discrimination (ICERD) also aims to combat racial discrimination in a broad way.[92]

Equality has been called one of the core principles of contemporary indigenous rights[93] or the very foundation of minority and indigenous rights.[94] The Committee on the Elimination of Racial Discrimination (CERD) is particularly active in the context of discrimination and indigenous peoples. In General Recommendation No. 23, and in many Concluding Observations on state reports, the CERD expresses its concern about indigenous peoples' marginalised position and lack of equal enjoyment, and essentially denial, of their rights. According to the CERD, discrimination of indigenous peoples has resulted in land loss and significant risks to the safeguarding of their cultures and historical identities.[95] Therefore, equality and non-discrimination are particularly acute principles and rights, interwoven with many of the struggles that indigenous peoples face.

Contemporary understandings of intellectual property exclude indigenous peoples from equal protection of their rights to their intangible heritage due to their specific cultural characteristics and 'modes' of production.[96] This lack of protection results in indigenous heritage being perceived as in the public

88 Glendon (n 80), 178.

89 M Nowak, *U.N. Covenant on Civil and Political Rights. CCPR Commentary* (NP Engel Publisher 2005), 29.

90 M Craven, *The International Covenant on Economic, Social, and Cultural Rights. A Perspective on its Development* (Oxford University Press 1995), 154. See also Craven, 192–193.

91 See CESCR, 'General Comment No. 20 on Non-Discrimination in Economic, Social and Cultural Rights' UN Doc E/C.12/GC/20 para 1.

92 See Article 1(1) ICERD.

93 Anaya, 'Intellectual Property and Genetic Resources' (n 78) 2.

94 J Castellino, 'The Protection of Minorities and Indigenous Peoples in International Law: A Comparative Temporal Analysis' (2010) 17 *International Journal on Minority and Group Rights* 393, 420.

95 CERD, 'General Recommendation No 23' (n 82) para 3.

96 See the comment on discrimination of indigenous peoples due to their specific cultures and modes of production, which justifies protection of their rights, in African Commission's Working Group of Experts on Indigenous Populations/Communities, 'Report of the African Commission's Working Group of Experts on Indigenous Populations/Communities', Adopted by The African Commission on Human and Peoples' Rights at its 28th ordinary session (2005), 88.

domain. In the same way, historical understandings of sovereignty and property excluded indigenous peoples in that they were neither considered as states nor as having property rights over their lands. According to the *terra nullius* doctrine, indigenous peoples were considered unable to hold property rights over their lands, which rendered the lands as belonging to no one. Non-discrimination has played a central role to abolish this regime that negatively affected indigenous peoples' territorial and land rights due to the unsuitability of the property concept.

Anaya has likened the *terra nullius* doctrine to the public domain: both concepts fail to protect indigenous peoples from discrimination, due to the differences between indigenous and non-indigenous cultures and understandings.[97] In this context, Anaya has discussed indigenous peoples' rights to genetic resources and traditional knowledge in conjunction with the core indigenous rights principle of equality.[98] Non-discrimination towards indigenous peoples would require that indigenous peoples are not (automatically) excluded from effective protection of the rights in their (intangible) heritage, knowledge and TCEs due to their specific cultural characteristics, such as their ways of artistic production and collective focus.[99]

3.1.3. Self-determination

Self-determination is a crucial principle for indigenous peoples, one that resonates with many – if not all – of their concerns. From lands and education to resources and culture, the ability to exercise control over all these elements is vital to their existence as distinct peoples.

Anaya has called the principle of self-determination one of the pillars on which the contemporary indigenous rights regime draws to ensure that indigenous peoples themselves can maintain and develop their community bonds and institutions. To this end, indigenous peoples should be able to determine and control "the future development of all those aspects of collective human interaction that define and constitute their distinct societies."[100] TCEs could very well be placed under this umbrella of 'all those aspects,' as they are closely connected to indigenous peoples' identities, distinctive cultures and communal, social and spiritual relationships.

The right to self-determination of all peoples is recognised in common Article 1 of the ICCPR and the ICESCR. With regard to indigenous peoples, self-determination is closely connected to the rights of Article 27 ICCPR protecting their ways of life. Also in UNDRIP self-determination is a central principle, despite initial resistance of states. Apart from the general provision of self-determination

97 Anaya, 'Intellectual Property and Genetic Resources' (n 78) 4–5; Anaya, 'Indigenous Peoples' Rights to Genetic Resources and Traditional Knowledge' (n 78) 2–3.

98 Anaya, 'Intellectual Property and Genetic Resources' (n 78) 2.

99 Anaya, 'Indigenous Peoples' Rights to Genetic Resources and Traditional Knowledge' (n 78) 5.

100 Anaya, 'Intellectual Property and Genetic Resources' (n 78) 2.

in Article 3, UNDRIP refers to matters of self-determination in many other provisions, including on cultural heritage.[101]

Self-determination plays a central role in the context of indigenous land and natural resources issues. Articles 1(2) of the ICCPR and the ICESCR state that "All people may, for their own ends, freely dispose of their natural wealth and resources (. . .). In no case may a people be deprived of its own means of subsistence." This people's right is also stressed in Articles 25 ICESCR and 47 ICCPR, respectively.[102] Something similar is laid down in Article 26(2) UNDRIP.[103] As indigenous peoples' cultures and societies tend to draw on their territories and natural resources, are dependent on these even, this underscores the principle of self-determination and the necessity of access to and control over these resources to guarantee cultural preservation and development.[104]

The foregoing can be analogously applied to indigenous peoples' 'cultural resources,' including their heritage and TCEs. In the same sense as self-determination is determinant for rights to lands and resources, the argumentation could also be considered applicable to other elements of indigenous peoples' heritage such as their traditional knowledge and TCEs. In fact, a right to autonomy and self-government over their intangible cultural heritage is laid down in Article 31(1) UNDRIP, which encompasses the right to maintain, control, protect and develop their cultural heritage, traditional knowledge and TCEs, as well as the manifestations thereof, and the right to the intellectual property over such material. Importantly, the Committee on Economic, Social and Cultural Rights has implicitly referenced the first part of this provision in its General Comment No. 21 on the right to take part in cultural life of Article 15(1)(a) ICESCR.[105]

To recap, self-determination has been called instrumental for the protection of indigenous cultural heritage. Several studies and statements have argued to fully take indigenous peoples' human rights into account in any approach to the protection of their traditional knowledge and TCEs, emphasised self-determination and stated that autonomy over the management and development of indigenous peoples' heritage should be recognised.[106] When accepting that indigenous peoples have rights of autonomy and self-governance over all matters that are relevant to

101 Articles 31 UNDRIP.

102 G Alfredsson, 'Article 17' in A Eide and others (eds), *The Universal Declaration of Human Rights. A Commentary* (Universitetsforlaget AS 1992) 260–261.

103 "Indigenous peoples have the right to own, use, develop and control the lands, territories and resources that they possess by reason of traditional ownership or other traditional occupation or use, as well as those which they have otherwise acquired."

104 Alfredsson (n 102) 261; Anaya, 'Intellectual Property and Genetic Resources (n 78) 2.

105 CESCR, 'General Comment No. 21 on the Right of Everyone to Take Part in Cultural Life (Article 15(1)(a) ICESCR)' (2009) UN Doc. E/C.12/GC/21 para 37.

106 See Anaya, 'Indigenous Peoples' Rights to Genetic Resources and Traditional Knowledge' (n 78) 3–6; Anaya, 'Intellectual Property and Genetic Resources' (n 78) 2–3 and 5–6. See further Kaska Dena Council, 'Opening Intervention', statement at WIPO IGC 2004 <www.wipo.int/export/sites/www/tk/en/igc/ngo/kdc_igc6_doc6_3.pdf> accessed 28 July 2017, point 8; Assembly

them, one could argue that these rights extend to elements of indigenous heritage such as genetic resources, traditional knowledge and TCEs, these being "integral elements of indigenous peoples' societies and cultures."[107] Following the self-determination principle, indigenous peoples should be able to exercise control over all matters that are relevant to their heritage, including its development, use, management and regulation.

3.1.4. Participation

Participation, consultation and free, prior and informed consent[108] are crucial notions in indigenous rights discourse and law. The procedural dimension of participation rights mostly lies in the sphere of public affairs and decision-making. In the context of indigenous peoples, these rights are particularly visible, and necessary, in decision-making processes regarding the use of land, territories and natural resources, in order to protect their cultures.[109] The participation right contributes to the effective enjoyment of many other rights,[110] including the right to self-determination,[111] the minority rights of Article 27 ICCPR,[112] economic, social and cultural rights and the specific indigenous rights of ILO Convention No. 169[113] and UNDRIP.[114]

of First Nations and others, 'Objectives, Principles and Elements of an International Instrument, or Instruments, on Intellectual Property in Relation to Genetic Resources and on the Protection of Traditional Knowledge and Traditional Cultural Expressions', submission to WIPO IGC 2004 <www.wipo.int/export/sites/www/tk/en/igc/ngo/afn_igc6.pdf> accessed 28 July 2017, principle 1 and 4; Centre for International Environmental Law, 'The Gap Between Indigenous Peoples' Demands and WIPO's Framework on Traditional Knowledge', study for WIPO 2007 <www.wipo.int/export/sites/www/tk/en/igc/ngo/ciel_gap.pdf> accessed 28 July 2017, 5, point ii, iii.

107 Anaya, 'Indigenous Peoples' Rights to Genetic Resources and Traditional Knowledge' (n 78) 5–6.

108 See leading decisions on free, prior and informed consent: *Saramaka People v Suriname* IACHR Series C no 172 (IACtHR, 28 November 2007) and *Ángela Poma Poma v Peru* Communication No 1457/2006, UN Doc CCPR/C/95/D/1457/2006 (HRC, 27 March 2009).

109 Expert Mechanism on the Rights of Indigenous Peoples, 'Final Report of the Study on Indigenous Peoples and the Right to Participate in Decision-making', including Expert Mechanism advice No 2 (2011): indigenous peoples and the right to participate in decision-making, Human Rights Council 2011, A/HRC/18/42, 22.

110 ibid., 25.

111 ibid., 26.

112 HRC, 'General Comment No. 23 on Article 27 on the Rights of Minorities' (1994) UN Doc. CCPR/C/21/Rev.1/Add.5 para 3(2) and para 7: "effective participation in decisions relating to land and resources may be integral to protecting the right to a 'way of life' under Article 27 ICCPR." See also: *Länsmän et al. v. Finland* Communication No. 511/1992, CCPR/C/52/D/511/1992 (HRC, 8 November 1994) para 9.5; *Mahuika et al. v. New Zealand* Communication No 547/1993, UN Doc CCPR/C/70/D/547/1993 (HRC, 27 October 2000) para 9.5, 9.6 and 9.8.

113 Articles 2(1), 6(1) and (2), 7(1), (2) and (3), 15(1), and (2), 16(2), 17(2), 22(2) and (3), 23(1), 27(3), 28(1) ILO Convention No. 169. The rights of participation and consultation have been described as the "basic pillars" of the Convention, E Desmet, *Indigenous Rights Entwined with Nature Conservation* (Intersentia 2011), 311.

114 Articles 3, 4, 5, 10, 11(2), 12(2), 14(1), 15(2), 17(2), 18, 19, 20(1), 22(2), 23, 26(3), 27, 28(1), 29(2), 30(1), 31(2), 32(2), 36(2), 38 and 41 UNDRIP.

As to the cultural dimension of participation rights, the right to take part in cultural life of Article 27 UDHR and Article 15(1)(a) ICESCR is of direct relevance to TCEs. The Committee on Economic, Social and Cultural Rights' General Comment No. 21 on Article 15(1)(a) and No. 17 on Article 15(1)(c) also highlight this.

For Article 15(1)(a) ICESCR, 'everyone's' right to take part in cultural life may mean the individual's or the collective's.[115] For 'cultural life,' culture should be understood as "a broad, inclusive concept encompassing all manifestations of human existence," which highlights in particular its living, dynamic and interactive nature.[116] Indigenous peoples are recognised as vulnerable communities requiring special protection. In particular, the cultural values underlying indigenous peoples' communal life, such as the emphasis on the collective when enjoying their culture, should be protected, including the right to the lands, territories and resources which they have traditionally owned, occupied or otherwise used or acquired.[117]

According to the UNCESCR, state parties should take measures to guarantee that the exercise of the right to take part in cultural life takes account of these specific cultural values. These values would be essential for indigenous peoples' existence and development.[118] Furthermore, indigenous peoples' rights in their cultural heritage, traditional knowledge and TCEs are underlined, and the importance of the principle of free, prior and informed consent is stressed.[119] In this sense, land rights and rights in their heritage are connected to safeguarding the enjoyment of rights to the particular ways of life of indigenous peoples. The emphasis on the collective interests of indigenous peoples in protection and respect of both their lands and heritage provides a basis for TCE protection arguments.

Article 15(1)(c) ICESCR contains another dimension of the right to take part in cultural life, namely, the right of everyone to benefit from the protection of the moral and material interests resulting from any scientific, literary or artistic production of which he or she is the author. The CESCR has described this as "a human right, which derives from the inherent dignity and worth of all persons" in its General Comment No. 17 on this provision.[120] The Committee further explains the difference between the very nature of this human right and intellectual property regimes. Whereas intellectual property systems would be mainly concerned with protecting business and corporate interests and investments, this human right would safeguard the personal link between authors and creations or

115 "[I]n other words, cultural rights may be exercised by a person (a) as an individual, (b) in association with others, or (c) within a community or group, as such"; see CESCR, 'General Comment No 21' (n 105) para 9.

116 ibid., para 11.

117 ibid., para 36–37.

118 ibid., para 36.

119 ibid., para 36–37.

120 CESCR, 'General Comment No 17 on the Right of Everyone to Benefit From the Protection of the Moral and Material Interests Resulting from Any Scientific, Literary or Artistic Production of Which He or She is the Author (Article 15(1)(c) ICESCR)' (2005) UN Doc E/C.12/GC/17 para 1.

between peoples, communities or groups and their collective heritage.[121] 'Any scientific, literary or artistic production' also includes the knowledge, innovations and practices of indigenous peoples.[122]

The Committee specifically mentions indigenous peoples under the obligation to protect the right of Article 15(1)(c): "States parties should adopt measures to ensure the effective protection of the interests of indigenous peoples relating to their productions, which are often expressions of their cultural heritage and traditional knowledge." State parties should take the preferences of indigenous peoples into account when adopting these measures. In particular, free, prior informed consent and oral or other customary forms of transmission should be respected.[123] Indigenous authors are also mentioned specifically in the section on violations of the obligation to protect. This includes cases where states fail to guarantee adequate compensation by "third parties for any unreasonable prejudice suffered as a consequence of the unauthorized use of their scientific, literary and artistic productions."[124]

The principle of participation is also reflected in many rights included in UNDRIP that are especially relevant for the maintenance, development, control over and expression of TCEs. These rights include the right to practise and revitalise cultural traditions and customs, including designs and performing arts and literature, the right to the dignity and diversity of their cultures, the right to establish their own media in their own languages and, particularly relevant for TCEs, the aforementioned right to maintain, control, protect and develop their cultural heritage, traditional knowledge and TCEs, as well as the manifestations thereof, and the right to the intellectual property over such cultural heritage.[125]

In sum, the main concern that the participation principle reflects seems to be autonomy over any cultural development and existence, or generally stated, the ability of indigenous peoples to determine themselves what happens with their culture as regards access, use, regulation and continuation. In the specific case of TCE protection, the central issue would be the ability to continue with these practices and transmit these to future generations according to own terms and conditions, following indigenous worldviews and customary rules of sharing, using and creating. TCE protection arguments can thus draw on the principle of participation.

121 ibid., para 2, [italics added].
122 ibid., para 8–9.
123 ibid., para 32.
124 ibid., para 45.
125 See Articles 3, 8, 11 and 13, 15, 16 and 31 UNDRIP. See also P Bird, 'Intellectual Property Rights and the Inuit Amauti. A Case Study,' prepared for The World Summit on Sustainable Development by Pauktuutit Women's Association, July 2012, presented to the IGC of WIPO <www.wipo.int/export/sites/www/tk/en/igc/ngo/wssd_amauti.pdf> accessed 30 July 2017, 2–3.

4. Conclusion

This chapter has shown that the existing copyright regime presents multiple challenges to TCE protection. How could these tensions be addressed? By expanding and adapting the existing copyright regime towards inclusion of TCEs and indigenous peoples' concerns and specific characteristics? This does not seem likely. As debates at the international level and in scholarly literature demonstrate, that stage has already been passed.

Constructing a *sui generis* or stand-alone regime – that is independent of existing intellectual property or copyright rules – could be an option. This is what WIPO's IGC has been working on for many years now at the international level. The 'pro' of this option would be its potential of being shaped according to indigenous peoples' particular needs, with their participation and input. But in practice, the question could be raised whether the whole process does not still draw largely on intellectual property and copyright considerations, if only because it is conducted in an international intellectual property forum. Also, despite an indigenous panel and related inclusive efforts at WIPO's IGC,[126] the negotiations on the actual text and instrument still take place between states. In fact, a 2016 study for the UN Permanent Forum on Indigenous Issues signals that member states "have undertaken action within WIPO to diminish indigenous peoples' human rights."[127] The study finds that (disobedience of) procedural rules enable this and that indigenous peoples and organisations are excluded from the existing WIPO framework. For example, they have to seek Member State approval to be accredited to participate.[128] A lack of resources is another hurdle for participation.[129]

Furthermore, the idea of protecting what has previously been unprotected is also criticised: one concern is that the public domain would be limited, which has negative consequences for creative industries, freedom of expression, and so on.[130] The main question is therefore how a balance can be found between non-indigenous and indigenous views on protecting creative works. In addition, to formulate indigenous concerns in a suitable way for an international treaty inevitably seems to cause a 'translation' of such needs, especially when indigenous peoples do not actually participate in the negotiations themselves. Legal wordings and categories could prove to be too static to cover their wide-ranged interests and specific worldviews. Clearly, even on a *sui generis* level, differences

126 See on this Expert Mechanism on the Rights of Indigenous Peoples, 'Promotion and Protection of the Rights of Indigenous Peoples with Respect to their Cultural Heritage', Human Rights Council 2015, A/HRC/EMRIP/2015/2, 13.

127 E John and D Sambo Dorough, 'Study on how States exploit weak procedural rules in international organizations to devalue the United Nations Declaration on the Rights of Indigenous Peoples and other international human rights law. Note by the Secretariat', Study for the Permanent Forum on Indigenous Issues, E/C/.19/2016/4 (United Nations Economic and Social Council 2016), 11 para 39.

128 ibid., 11 para 39.

129 ibid., 12 para 41.

130 Band (n 36).

in indigenous and non-indigenous worldviews can still cause disconnects in progressing towards an actual legal protection regime.

So, what are the opportunities of a human rights perspective? One of the most useful contributions of such a viewpoint is that it helps to show and highlight the actual concerns regarding TCE protection as part of broader (human rights) struggles and issues for indigenous peoples. This perspective could help formulate and understand the existing needs and concerns within a broader context and therefore inform arguments to protect TCEs *beyond* dominant intellectual property(-like) approaches and rationales. Relevant human rights principles to inform any protection approach are dignity, equality and non-discrimination, self-determination and participation. What ultimately seems to be at stake for indigenous peoples is to have a say over their own culturally distinctive existence and to control and safeguard the development of their cultures on their own 'terms and conditions.' The ability to transmit cultural heritage to future generations, and to safeguard distinctive cultural dignity and integrity in the process, is instrumental in this regard. These are not issues that intellectual property laws, such as copyright law, primarily aim to address.

The application of human rights principles can fill this conceptual gap and provide better understanding of the 'why' of TCE protection in order to advance the 'how to' of constructing a protection regime. To this end, cultural sensitivity by way of including customary laws and practices in protection initiatives can for example shape protection approaches that are guided by – and operationalise – principles of dignity, non-discrimination and self-determination. To operationalise the principle of participation, any protection approach should guarantee participation in matters that affect indigenous communities as the absolute bottom line, whether in negotiations and law making, generally in the management of their heritage or in the establishment of an administrative competent authority that can manage indigenous rights and enforcement, for example, with regard to access- and benefit-sharing licences.

There are, of course, also tensions and limitations to a human rights perspective of TCE protection, both substantively and more fundamentally. Substantive tensions can occur between human rights that provide a basis for TCE protection and related cultural practices and rights of individuals, 'minorities within minorities' or rights of women within communities, a risk that is especially observed with regard to (collective) cultural rights.[131] Another intrinsic tension is likely to occur with the right to freedom of (artistic) expression of third parties: rights of protection, control and exclusion over TCEs inevitably have the potential to thwart freedom of expression rights. This is also inherent to public domain arguments. A fundamental limitation of a human rights perspective is that difficulties with respect to enforcement and implementation of indigenous rights tend to be a hurdle

131 A Eide, 'Cultural Rights as Individual Human Rights' in A Eide, C Krause and A Rosas (eds), *Economic, Social and Cultural Rights. A Textbook* (Martinus Nijhoff Publishers 1995) 238–239.

Part II.B Creating space for counter-narratives within international law

7 Indigenous peoples' involvement in the REDD+ global debate

Case study from the Amazon basin

Liliana Lozano

Introduction

The climate change regime has emerged with a set of principles, norms, and actors with diverse interests in order to look for solutions, mostly market oriented, to combat this common problem. REDD+ (Reducing Emissions from Deforestation and Degradation)[1] is an example of this market-oriented approach and of the depoliticization of the climate regime, since its framing has simplified the complex forestry agenda into a carbon debate and has displaced contentious issues such as land tenure. As such, it seems that REDD+, which might be implemented in forestry-rich countries, has arrived as a new form of governmentality[2] in the forestry sector.

The chapter builds on the intersection between hegemonic neoliberal discourses in the new scenery of climate change and the historical indigenous resistance to such discourses. The question of whether it is possible to challenge the structural factors that both legitimize and boost 'the subordination of the environment' to socio-political and economic interests and goals becomes a main aspect for this project.[3] This chapter argues that in the process of REDD+ framing, subaltern groups such as indigenous organizations challenge this new form of governmentality by using a counter-narrative that strategically makes use of indigenous rights language and draws attention towards an alternative narrative. By doing so, indigenous groups take distance from a historically marginalized position in society to become relevant political actors in the climate regime.

The chapter analyses the experience of an Amazonian indigenous organization, the Coordinator of Indigenous Organizations from the Amazon Basin (COICA), building its strategy to challenge the REDD+ global framing. Its main questions are how do indigenous networks respond and take part in the global REDD+ framing process, and what alternative framing do they bring?

1 The + sign refers to more than just carbon.

2 A Agrawal, *Environmentality: Technologies of Government and the Making of Subjects (New Ecologies for the Twenty-First Century)* (Duke University Press 2005).

3 K O'Brien, B Hayward, and F Berkes, 'Rethinking Social Contracts: Building Resilience in a Changing Climate' (2009) 14 *Ecology and Society* 12.

The material presented here rests on primary data collected during a three-month fieldwork period in 2014 through participant observation and in-depth semi-structured interviews. It also relies on secondary data, including United Nations (UN) documents and negotiation texts, interventions of states and indigenous leaders during UN conferences, Amazonian networks' statements, planning documents, and reports, as well as an extensive revision of policy documents.

The first section of the chapter introduces the topic of study, REDD+, and presents the actor, COICA. It aims to explain the origins of the conceptualization of REDD+ and puts emphasis on the risks and opportunities for indigenous peoples in the international environmental policy. The second section presents the analysis of indigenous network strategies along three lines: narrative, interactions, and agency. In the conclusion, the chapter argues that COICA has become an active member in the REDD+ regime as a strategy to make progress in its political agenda concerning land rights and participation. This has been essential in the framing and implementation of REDD+, as well as in transforming COICA into a more legitimate and representative actor, both locally and globally. COICA has done so by self-representing the roles and responsibilities appointed by the normative regime. Nevertheless, it has also done so by building a counter-narrative, the Amazon Indigenous REDD+ (AIR), by building inter-institutional networks and by committing to diverse stakeholder engagement at different levels. This AIR narrative represents a counter-hegemony to the global framing of REDD+, since its development aims to shape people's thoughts and conduct based on COICA's subjectivities around REDD+.

1. The climate change debate

1.1. The climate change discourse

The climate regime is part of the sustainable development discourse and was institutionalized in 1992 with the creation of the United Nations Framework Convention on Climate Change (UNFCCC). It was created with the objective of stabilizing the discharge of greenhouse gas (GHG) emissions in the atmosphere to reach levels that are not dangerous for the natural and human system (UNFCCC, 1992 Art 2). The climate narrative has built ideologies and discourses on problems, causes, and solutions to climate change. It has done so by creating environmental subjectivities through the construction of environmental subjects that has changed the ways of understanding and operating the human–nature relation.[4]

The climate change narrative agrees with and reinforces the neoliberal discourse of market for conservation and poverty alleviation: framing the problem is mainly science-based while the solution narrative is mostly market oriented.

4 Agrawal (n 2) 89–100.

The Intergovernmental Panel on Climate Change (IPCC)[5] argues that climate change is a natural problem caused by human activity.[6] In opposition to this narrative, anthropologists, based on the Anthropocene perspective, argue that climate change is a human problem rather than a natural problem, which is caused by political decisions.[7]

The solution-framing narrative includes some market-based mechanisms such as carbon trading, carbon offsets, adaptation funds, clean development mechanisms, food miles, cap-and-trade policies, and other non-market mechanisms. These instruments have come with rules that are written and rewritten at fast speed by all state members of the UNFCCC.[8] However, to what extent does 'neoliberal environmentalism' that is based on market-based approaches represent the only possible solution for tackling climate change problems? Or is it just the most popular one because it employs the best-known mechanism, which is easy to implement and accept by all countries?

1.2. The role and representation of indigenous peoples in the climate change debate

In the climate discourse, indigenous peoples are portrayed as an exceptional group that are menaced by the impacts of climate change.[9] They are considered an important vulnerable group for two reasons. The first reason is due to their condition of historical marginalization that resulted in inequalities in terms of climate exposure, as well as socioeconomic status and income.[10] The second reason is due to the impact of climate change on their lives and cultures in terms of livelihoods, means of production, and housing.[11] At the same

5 The Intergovernmental Panel on Climate Change (IPCC), established in 1998 under the auspices of the United Nations (UN), is a scientific body that provides a 'clear scientific view on the current state of knowledge in climate change and its potential environmental and socio-economic impacts'. Several scientists from 195 members of the UN contribute with IPCC work which is globally recognized for being 'policy-relevant and yet policy-neutral, never policy-prescriptive' <www.ipcc.ch/organization/organization.shtml> accessed 5 September 2017.

6 IPCC 'Summary for Policymakers' in *Climate Change 2013: The Physical Science Basis*. Contribution of Working Group I to the Fifth Assessment Report of the Intergovernmental Panel on Climate Change (2013); IPCC 'Summary for Policymakers' in *Climate Change 2014: Impacts, Adaptation, and Vulnerability*. Part A: Global and Sectoral Aspects. Contribution of Working Group II to the Fifth Assessment Report of the Intergovernmental Panel on Climate Change (2014).

7 Fiske and others, *Changing the Atmosphere Anthropology and Climate Change* (2014), <www.aaanet.org/cmtes/commissions/upload/ GCCTF-Changing-the-Atmosphere.pdf> accessed 5 September 2017; <www.futureearth.org/news/anthropologists-see-climate-change-human-problem-not-natural-problem> accessed 5 September 2017.

8 K O'Brien, B Hayward and F Berke (2009) (n 3) 4.

9 M Lindroth 'Indigenous Rights as Tactics of Neoliberal Governance: Practices of Expertise in the United Nations' (2014) 23 *Social & Legal Studies* 341.

10 P Wade, 'Racial Identity and Nationalism: A Theoretical View from Latin America' (2001) 24 *Ethnic and Racial Studies* 845; P Wade, *Race and Ethnicity in Latin America* (Pluto 2010); IPCC 2014 (n 6) 6.

11 ibid. 30–32.

time, indigenous peoples are also represented as environmental agents, who can significantly contribute with their knowledge and traditional practices to tackle climate change.[12] Indigenous lifestyles and local knowledge, the so-called 'indigenous intelligence',[13] are considered key elements to increase effectiveness of adaptation actions.[14]

In the climate discourse, indigenous peoples are formally recognized as political actors where they play three roles[15]: knowledge holders, stakeholders since they live in the areas affected by climate change and forest keepers due to its close relationship with nature. According to Lindroth and Sinevaara-Niskanen, these three roles constitute the place and agency of indigenous peoples in the climate debate. These roles are attached to specific requirements and expectations that indigenous peoples might play. In the first role, indigenous peoples are appealed to constantly expand their understanding, cultivate themselves and harmonize their traditional knowledge with western science. In the second role, indigenous peoples are urged to adapt, persist and change in relation to the changing environment. In the third role, indigenous peoples are exhorted to sustain the indigenous–nature relationship.

From all previously mentioned considerations, it has been suggested that there is an idealization in the global political context of the meaning of being indigenous and of the role they play in the climate change regime. The descriptions of indigenous peoples are founded on fixed representations around well-established conceptions of indigeneity. Moreover, indigenous peoples put themselves in that role and mask this idealization in order to be heard and recognized in the climate debate.[16] To some extent, this idealization emphasizes the responsibility of indigenous peoples of taking care of the survival and well-being of their communities.[17]

During the UNFCCC Conference of Parties 16 (COP16), held in 2010 in Cancun, state parties undertook important steps towards the recognition of indigenous rights.[18] For instance, the preamble of the UNFCCC COP16 agreement introduces the narrative on indigenous vulnerability, saying,

> Noting resolution 10/4 of the United Nations Human Rights Council on human rights and climate change, which recognizes that the adverse effects of climate change have a range of direct and indirect implications for the effective enjoyment of human rights and that the effects of climate change

12 United Nations, Rio Declaration on Environment and Development (1992) Principle 22. 4.

13 L Rival, *The Resilience of Indigenous Intelligence* (2009) ch 14, 106.

14 IPCC 2014 (n 6) 16.

15 M Lindroth and H Sinevaara-Niskanen, 'At the Crossroads of Autonomy and Essentialism: Indigenous Peoples in International Environmental Politics'. (2013) 7 *International Political Sociology* 279–287.

16 Lindroth and Sinevaara-Niskanen (n 15) 275–276.

17 ibid. 288

18 L Wallbott, 'Indigenous Peoples in UN REDD+ Negotiations: 'Importing Power' and Lobbying for Rights through Discursive Interplay Management" (2014) 19 *Ecology and Society* 2.

> will be felt most acutely by those segments of the population that are already vulnerable owing to geography, gender, age, indigenous or minority status and disability.
>
> (Preamble of UNFCCC/COP16 agreement, 2010)

Article 7 of the UNFCCC COP16 agreement places the mandate for indigenous peoples' involvement in all climate change actions:

> The UNFCCC (. . .) recognizes the need to engage a broad range of stakeholders at global, regional, national and local levels, be they government, including subnational and local government, private business or civil society, including youth and persons with disability, and that gender equality and the effective participation of women and indigenous peoples are important for effective action on all aspects of climate change.
>
> (Article 7 of the UNFCCC/COP16 agreement, 2010)

Finally, article 12 of the UNFCCC COP16 agreement reinforces its role as environmental agents and knowledge holders:

> The UNFCCC (. . .) affirms that enhanced action on adaptation should be undertaken in accordance with the Convention; follow a country-driven, gender-sensitive, participatory and fully transparent approach, taking into consideration vulnerable groups, communities and ecosystems; and be based on and guided by the best available science and, as appropriate, traditional and indigenous knowledge; with a view to integrating adaptation into relevant social, economic and environmental policies and actions, where appropriate.
>
> (Article 12 of the UNFCCC/COP16 agreement, 2010)

1.3. REDD+

The REDD+ mechanism is an international policy instrument that aims to induce forestry-oriented countries to perform actions to keep forest standing and reduce global GHG emissions that derive from deforestation and degradation. These actions include among others the implementation of sustainable management practices. It also includes the implementation of the necessary measures, the so-called 'enabling conditions', in the regulatory, institutional and governance frameworks in order to ensure deforestation control. At country level, REDD+ might follow a gradual implementation, which encompasses three phases: readiness, implementation, and result-based payment.[19] Its operationalization implies conditional transfers or payments against the delivery of carbon outcomes. In its early stages of implementation, payments or transfers could be also performed against the delivery of policy outcomes.

19 Article 73 of UNFCCC/COP16 agreement, 2010.

1.3.1. Conceptualization and background of REDD+

Tropical forests are an important sink and source of carbon. In 2007, as a result of pressure from some member states to integrate forests in the negotiations of the new climate agreement,[20] the international climate community created the REDD+ mechanism aiming to compensate countries that are willing to reduce emissions from deforestation and degradation. After several years of negotiations, a consensus on its methodological framework was achieved in 2013. Since then onwards, the national authorities/institutions have the mandate to move forward in the design and implementation of REDD+ at national, subnational and project levels. Up to now, the Forest Carbon Partnership Facility (FPCP) has revealed that almost 47 states have become a 'REDD+ Country Participant' and are currently benefiting from the diverse REDD+ funding schemes.[21] Furthermore, by 2016, UNDP affirmed its support to 64 countries to become 'REDD+ ready'; 25 count already with REDD+ national programmes.[22]

The basic premises of REDD+ are the following: first, REDD+ acknowledges that at least 17% of the global GHG emissions come from deforestation.[23] Second, the policy instrument follows principle 7 of the 1992 Rio Declaration related to 'common but differentiated responsibilities' and a common agreement. This implies that developed countries might be able to compensate developing countries for emission reduction on forests as part of their pledges to climate action.[24] Last, REDD+ relies on the idea that direct-payment approaches represent an incentive to private landowners to stop deforestation and to implement actions to protect ecosystems and biodiversity. By doing so, an improvement of landowners and local people's economy is also expected. Consequently, REDD+ is claimed to be the most cost effective or cheapest way of resource allocation in terms of social and conservation outcomes. Hence, it is expected that through the implementation of REDD+, it could be possible to reach a triple win – biodiversity, ecosystem, and development – at low cost.[25]

1.3.2. Towards a new form of governmentality?

The understanding of REDD+ has generated much debate among scholars and many other actors.[26] Some authors embrace the idea that REDD+ represents an

20 A Angelsen, 'REDD + as Result-Based Aid : General Lessons and Bilateral Agreements of Norway' (2017) 21 *Review of Development Economics* 237.

21 <www.forestcarbonpartnership.org/redd-countries-1> accessed 26 November 2017.

22 <http://web.unep.org/annualreport/2016/index.php?page=2&lang=en> accessed 26 November 2017.

23 R Hiraldo and T Tanner, 'Forest Voices: Competing Narratives over REDD+' (2011) 42 *IDS Bulletin* 43; R Lyster, 'REDD+, Transparency, Participation and Resource Rights: The Role of Law' (2011) 14 *Environmental Science & Policy* 118.

24 CL McDermott, 'REDDuced: From Sustainability to Legality to Units of Carbon: The Search for Common Interests in International Forest Governance' (2014) 35 *Environmental Science and Policy* 12.

25 Hiraldo and Tanner (n 23) 42.

26 S Milne and E Niesten, 'Direct Payments for Biodiversity Conservation in Developing Countries: Practical Insights for Design and Implementation' (2009) 43 *Fauna & Flora International* 530.

example of a balanced trade-off, since it perfectly covers both economic means and ecosystem benefits. This approach is different from other climate issues policies, such as biodiversity conservation, watershed protection, and pollination.[27] Others criticize REDD+ for aiming to confirm and legitimize certain discourses[28], tools, and actors while disregarding others.[29] According to its critics, REDD+ has become a new technology of governance that aims to follow a process of 'environmentalization on REDD+' (adapted from Agrawal, 2005). This governance project aims to reinforce the discourse of the commodification of ecosystems' carbon storage and sequestration functions on a global scale in order to solve both environmental and development problems. The main critiques to REDD+ include the following. To begin with, it proposes a mercantilism vision of nature[30] founded on a simple logic of commodification, which offers a win–win solution at a low cost.[31] Second, the technical manner in which the problem is framed oversimplifies the causality of deforestation and degradation. Moreover, it omits the political and structural causes, by avoiding other contentious topics, such as land tenure and rights, decentralization, benefit sharing, and safeguards. The final main critique argues that REDD+ has created a perverse incentive for developed countries by creating a 'right to pollute'.[32]

The development of the REDD+ mechanism has created not only a new and intangible commodity, the so-called forest carbon, but also a carbon market.[33] This process has come along with social and material entanglements[34] in the different stages of the commodity chain of forest carbon. Among them is the crucial question of how the rights of indigenous peoples regarding land tenure, participation, benefit sharing, and knowledge production could be protected.[35]

27 Y Malhi and others, 'Climate Change, Deforestation and the Fate of the Amazon' (2008) 319 *Science* 169.
28 A Larson and others, 'Land Tenure and REDD+: The Good, the Bad and the Ugly' (2013) 23 *Global Environmental Change* 678.
29 E Corbera, 'Problematizing REDD+ as an Experiment in Payments for Ecosystem Services' (2012) 4 *Current Opinion in Environmental Sustainability* 612; R Hiraldo and T Tanner (n 23) 47–48; A Shankland and L Hasenclever, 'Indigenous Peoples and the Regulation of REDD+ in Brazil: Beyond the War of the Worlds?' (2012) 42 *IDS Bulletin* 80. <doi:10.1111/j.1759-5436.2011.00225.x> accessed 27 November 2017; M Thompson, C Baruah and E Carr, 'Seeing REDD Plus as a Project of Environmental Governance' (2011) 14 *Environmental Science & Policy* 100.
30 Corbera (n 29) 612.
31 Mc Dermott (n 24) 12.
32 RB Norgaard, 'Ecosystem Services: From Eye-Opening Metaphor to Complexity Blinder' (2010) 69 *Ecological Economics* 1219.
33 S Mahanty and others, 'Unravelling Property Relations around Forest Carbon' (2013) 34 *Singapore Journal of Tropical Geography* 188; S Mahanty and others, 'The Social Life of Forest Carbon: Property and Politics in the Production of a New Commodity' (2012) 40 *Human Ecology* 661; S Milne 'Rounding Forest Carbon: Property Relations and Avoided Deforestation in Cambodia' (2012) 40 *Human Ecology* 693.
34 S Mahanty and others (n 33) 661.
35 R Lyster (n 23) 118.

1.3.3. REDD+: *Opportunities and risks for indigenous peoples?*

Scholars' analyses of how REDD+ could affect indigenous peoples' livelihoods reflect contrasting ideas. Some authors underscore the risk that REDD+ could bring to indigenous peoples. To begin with, REDD+ projects have put land tenure at risk by increasing land speculation, land grabbing, and land conflicts.[36] Second, REDD+ could potentially bring negative effects in non-modern societies that depend on natural resources,[37] for instance, the imposition of a restricted use of forest resources for indigenous peoples.[38] Last, there is a perception that REDD+ could fail in terms of indigenous participation. According to Larson, REDD+ has excluded indigenous participation in its design and implementation at all stages and levels of discussion.[39] On this particular point, Shankland and Hasenclever affirm that REDD+ could boost the existing power configurations, failing in the effort to link local realities with political decision-making. In general, there is the perception that REDD+ repeats the colonial notion of indigenous exploitation in a modern global context that is embedded in international agreements. This is done by reinforcing top-down approaches on forest conservation from which indigenous peoples are excluded as decision-makers.[40]

Other scholars have seen opportunities in the REDD+ scheme. For instance, some scholars see REDD+ as an innovative tool to engage local community and resource users in conservation actions or as a mechanism to conduct global investment in environmental services.[41] Others state that REDD+ allows questioning the foundation for effective stewardship of land and resources. For example, it makes possible to discuss the role of traditional knowledge and practices. Furthermore, several authors argue that REDD+ could increase efforts to clarify and decentralize forest tenure that are relevant to REDD+ objectives.[42] Moreover, some authors have also seen opportunities in terms of the renegotiation of power relationships with the state because it creates space for local actors to be involved in the design and implementation of REDD+ (sub)national agendas. Last, as expressed by Wendland and colleagues and Duchelle and others, REDD+ could make possible to clarify and strengthen

36 AM Larson, 'Forest Tenure Reform in the Age of Climate Change: Lessons for REDD+' (2011) 21 *Global Environmental Change* 540; R Lyster (n 23) 118; D Roe, 'The Origins and Evolution of the Conservation-Poverty Debate: A Review of Key Literature, Events and Policy Processes' (2008) 42 *Oryx* 491.

37 S Milne and B Adams, 'Market Masquerades: Uncovering the Politics of Community-Level Payments for Environmental Services in Cambodia' (2012) 43 *Development and Change* 133.

38 R Lyster (n 23) 118.

39 AM Larson (n 36) 540.

40 Roe (n 36) 491; Wallbott (n 18) 6.

41 Milne and Niesten (n 26) 530.

42 Larson and others (n 28) 678; Milne (n 33) 693; W Sunderlin and others, 'How Are REDD+ Proponents Addressing Tenure Problems? Evidence from Brazil, Cameroon, Tanzania, Indonesia, and Vietnam' (2014) 55 *World Development* 37.

indigenous rights.[43] For instance, it could bring concrete funding for securing the borders of indigenous territories.[44] For this group of scholars, REDD+ has brought new challenges in 'citizen–state relationships' by putting at risk both state power and legitimacy.[45]

1.4. Amazonian indigenous peoples

1.4.1. The actor: COICA as a social system

Amazonian indigenous peoples consist of 5000 indigenous communities, 400 indigenous organizations, and 390 indigenous groups.[46] Over the past decades, the indigenous peoples in the Amazon region have organized themselves in communities as well as in representative federations and organizations with the specific purpose of securing their territories. In every country, indigenous peoples have established local representative federations under the protection of national federations. These national federations are the United and Organized Confederation of Bolivian Indigenous People (CIDOB) in Bolivia, the Coordination of the Indigenous Organizations of the Brazilian Amazon (COIAB) in Brazil, the Organization of Colombian Amazon Indigenous People (OPIAC) in Colombia, the Confederation of Indigenous Nationalities of Ecuador (CONFENIAE) in Ecuador, the Amerindian Peoples Association (APA) in Guyana, the Federation of Amerindian Organizations of French Guiana (FOAG) in French Guiana, the Interethnic Association for the Development of the Peruvian Rainforest (AIDESEP) in Peru, the Organization of Indigenous People (OIS) in Suriname, and the Organization of Amazon Indigenous People (ORPIA) in Venezuela. In 1984, these national organizations came together to establish a pan-Amazonian indigenous organization, COICA. As members of COICA, these nine organizations select the steering committee.

In the literature, COICA is categorized as a transnational social indigenous movement due to two factors:[47] on the one hand, the existence of shared interests, identities, and values among its members, and on the other hand, the continued interaction among all its members across national boundaries.[48] As such, it has

43 K Wendland and others, 'Rewards for Environmental Services and Collective Land Tenure: Lessons from Ecuador and Indonesia' (2010), *Mountain Forum Bulletin*; A Duchelle and others, 'Linking Forest Tenure Reform, Environmental Compliance and Incentives: Lessons from REDD+ Initiatives in the Brazilian Amazon' (2014) 55 *World Development* 53.
44 Larson and others (n 28) 678.
45 O'Brien (n 3) 12.
46 COICA, *Agenda Indigena Amazonica* (2004).
47 A Brysk, *From Tribal Village to Global Village: Indian Rights and International Relations in Latin America* (Stanford University Press 2000) 97; P Martin, *The Globalization of Contentious Politics: The Amazonian Indigenous Rights Movement* (Routledge 2003) 95.
48 Martin (n 47) 105.

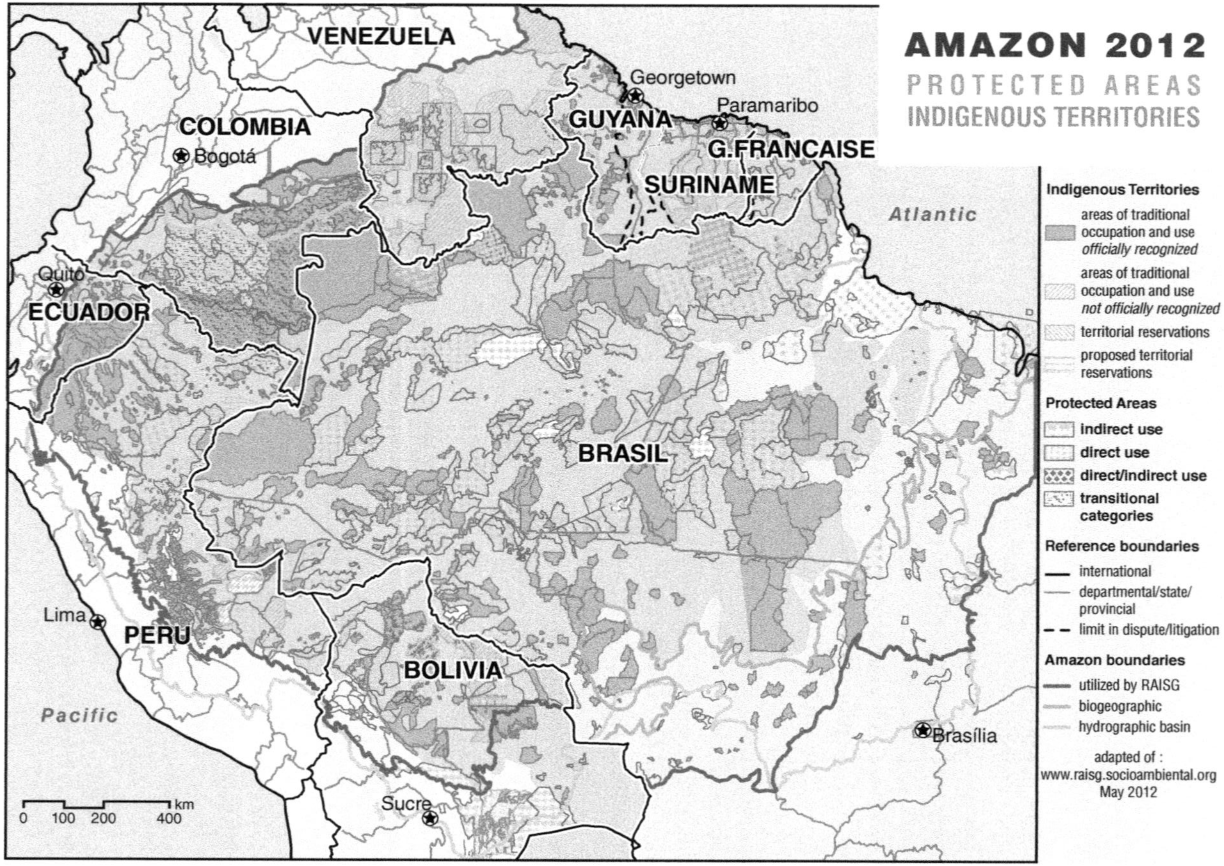

Figure 7.1 Map of Amazonian indigenous territories

Source: (RAISG 2012)

obtained the legitimacy to represent the Amazonian indigenous identity across the Amazon borders.[49] Consequently, COICA is a well-respected body that has become a 'definitive representative' of the Amazonian indigenous peoples, being present in most of the relevant international fora. In addition, it has received political and financial support of funders and international organizations.[50]

1.4.2. Land tensions related to REDD+

Indigenous relationship with land and forest is the building block of their culture, spiritual life, integrity, and livelihoods.[51] Land possession is crucial for the survival of the Amazonian indigenous peoples. The nexus between indigenous peoples and forest is different from what it is assumed by the REDD+ promoters.[52] Indigenous people have a holistic vision in which the forest reflects different meanings that are highly interconnected to their culture: forest as synonymous of life itself, forest as a supplier, making no difference on ecological functions or ecosystem services such as water production, carbon stock, biodiversity. The latter are concepts that Latour calls 'western scientific mononaturalism'.[53] Consequently, the fact that the REDD+ discourse simplifies the meaning of forest to a tradable commodity (carbon), and put on risk land tenure, endangers a broader indigenous understanding and validation.

REDD+ will be implemented in forest-rich developing countries within areas that are traditionally occupied by indigenous peoples and local communities. The possibility that the future implementation of REDD+ could have an impact on the livelihoods and land accessibility of indigenous peoples has made indigenous groups become aware of the need to safeguard their rights in the REDD+ negotiation.[54]

Indigenous peoples' officially recognized territories cover 25.3% of the total Amazonian territory.[55] The relevance of indigenous territories in the Amazon basin has led to the emergence of several specific land tenure systems based on collective property of land and forests.[56] This situation has created a particular complex geopolitical context in terms of conservation and development strategies, putting indigenous lands constantly under threat, mainly due to the following reasons.

49 ibid. 94.

50 Brysk (n 47) 97–98.

51 B Rojas Garzon, '*REDD+ En Territorios Indigenas de La Cuenca Amazonica: Seran Los Pueblos Indigenas Los Directos Benficiarios?*' (EDF 2009).

52 A Shankland and L Hasenclever, 'Indigenous Peoples and the Regulation of REDD+ in Brazil: Beyond the War of the Worlds?' (2011) 42 *IDS Bulletin* 80.

53 B Latour cited in A Shankland and L Hasenclever, 'Indigenous Peoples and the Regulation of REDD+ in Brazil: Beyond the War of the Worlds?' (2011) 42 *IDS Bulletin* 80.

54 Wallbott (n 18) 6.

55 Rojas Garzon (n 51) 24.

56 Rojas Garzon (n 51) 25.

The first reason is the overlapping of several forms of land tenure and rights systems, such as state and indigenous ones.[57] The second reason refers to the aggressive exploitation of natural resources and the development of infrastructure projects in the Amazon that undermine land and livelihood rights of indigenous peoples.[58] This complex context has created continuous conflicts among states and indigenous groups for access to land and the use of natural resources.

COICA has argued against the REDD+ mechanism, stating that it represents a direct violation of those elements on which Amazonian indigenous peoples base their existence as a group, land, resources, and culture. Some of the critiques expressed by COICA are the following. First, while at global and national level, the REDD+ debate has developed slowly; at local level, communities were promptly confronted with small-scale REDD+ private initiatives. The early implementation of small-scale private REDD+ initiatives among the Amazonian indigenous communities allowed the presence of so-called carbon cowboys. These carbon entrepreneurs attempted to obtain the rights to trade carbon credits by the establishment of unfair contracts.[59] For instance, the contract between an Australian carbon cowboy and the Matses community in the Peruvian jungle implied a full transfer of forest and carbon rights to the carbon cowboy. As a consequence, land tenure and forest use were put at risk, and it created a division among the community members.[60] Second, COICA also criticized the fact that REDD+ goes against the traditional cultural aspect of indigenous peoples because it mainly focuses on a carbon-narrow approach rather than a holistic view of the forest.[61]

Notwithstanding its critiques to REDD+, COICA could not avoid taking part in the REDD+ debate and its implementation in the Amazon. Furthermore, COICA, which represents several indigenous organizations, has taken part in the REDD+ debate by bringing their demands and claims and aiming to challenge and influence the system from within. To do so, it has developed a strategy that will be explained in the next section.

2. Discussion: COICA's resistance strategy to REDD+

2.1. The theoretical framework

To analyse COICA's response to REDD+, this chapter makes use of the concepts of hegemony, counter-hegemony, ideology, and resistance from Gramsci and Scott.

57 ibid. 33.

58 C Nobre and others, 'Land-Use and Climate Change Risks in the Amazon and the Need of a Novel Sustainable Development Paradigm' (2016) 39 *Proceedings of the National Academy of Sciences* 10759.

59 W De Jong and D Del Castillo 'Carbon Cowboys in Peru and the Prospects of Local REdd Governance' (2014) 8 *Portes, revista mexicana de Estudios sobre la Cuenca del Pacífico* 61.

60 <www.redd-monitor.org/wp-content/uploads/2011/05/1371.pdf> accessed 27 November 2017.

61 <unfccc.int/resource/docs/2014/smsn/ngo/412.pdf> accessed 27 November 2017.

Gramsci's concept of hegemony denotes a situation of rationalization of power in which people make use of a 'false consciousness' to appropriate the rules that recognize an institutionalized structure of lasting power.[62] For instance, citizens rationalize the situation of power that is exercised by the state when setting the rules to govern a country; furthermore, they embrace those rules. However, different from Marxism that recognizes the hegemony power as unique and invariable, Gramsci also discusses the concept of cultural power, which is based on an ideology that is characterized by a system of ideas that is expressed through a 'living and habitual social practice'.[63] This cultural hegemony, expressed in a form of resistance, could extend new boundaries to create counter-hegemony. Gramsci argues that this counter-movement could undermine different forms of faith that aim to perpetuate the status quo. It could also bring other more 'progressive forms of faith' infused of 'progressive values and beliefs'.[64]

Scott disagrees with Gramsci's concept on hegemony based on 'false consciousness'. As expressed by Sivaramakrishnan, Scott argues in favour of the agency of the subaltern groups.[65] For Scott, these subaltern groups constantly challenge hegemonic power through a process of 'everyday resistance'. The latter is characterized by a behaviour that is expressed in two ways, through a public transcript and/or a hidden transcript.

2.2. *The strategy: REDD+ as an opportunity to realize indigenous peoples rights?*

This chapter argues that COICA's reaction to the REDD+ global mechanism represents a counter-hegemony, which has made use of cultural power to build trust among its members and allies. This cultural hegemony is expressed through COICA's everyday discourse and praxis. Through the expression of these narratives and practices, indigenous groups aim to reach a common agreement on the foundations of indigenous struggles and to create space for a collective revolution. For instance, this process has allowed them to develop an alternative framing on the REDD+ debate.

According to Sivaramakrishnan, the expression of resistance would depend on the characteristics of the dominant power.[66] For the purposes of this chapter, the dominant power is represented by the REDD+ regime. Taking into account the variety of actors, spaces, and discourses in the REDD+ regime, COICA's strategy consists of two main components. The first element is the construction of a particular narrative, the AIR, that makes use of the indigeneity narrative. The second

62 K Sivaramakrishnan, 'Some Intellectual Genealogies for the Concept of Everyday Resistance' (2005) 107 *American Anthropologist* 346.

63 S Buckel and A Fisher-Lescano, 'Gramsci Reconsidered: Hegemony in Global Law ' (2009) 22 *Leiden Journal of International Law* 437.

64 J Swanson, 'Gramsci as Theorist of Politics' (2009) 21 *Rethinking Marxism* 336.

65 Sivaramakrishnan (n 62) 346.

66 ibid. 351.

element is the development of an inter-institutional activist strategy. This strategy is performed in a contentious space by using diverse tools including networking, diplomacy work, building alliances, and the articulation of the local reality with the global debate.

This counter-narrative and praxis on REDD+ aims to make COICA's ideas available through an everyday social practice both in public and/or hidden transcripts. For instance, COICA makes use of scientific data and concrete examples of indigenous capacity to conserve the forest as a way to get support for their political speech. Indigenous leaders make use of a 'language of discontent' to both inform and motivate their audience, as well as to build a collective understanding of their fragile situation and the arguments to join indigenous collective action.[67] By using this narrative, COICA aims to shape people's perspectives on what is acceptable or not acceptable for the implementation of REDD+ within the Amazonian indigenous territories.

2.2.1. The reinforcement of the hegemonic discourse

COICA aims to incorporate its own agenda in the REDD+ pan-Amazonian debate by redirecting the REDD+ discussion towards the debate on the compliance of enabling conditions that must be fulfilled in order to achieve REDD+ outcomes. To do so, COICA has made use of a 'false consciousness' by tailoring its self-representation to the expectations of the UNFCCC's discourse. This has entailed the reproduction of the development, commodification of nature, and indigeneity discourses. For instance, COICA's lexicon continuously highlights the distinctions between the 'native' and 'settler', making constructions that reinforce dichotomies of 'traditional ecological knowledge vs. Western science' and 'peoples living on the land vs. industrialized world'. Furthermore, COICA's lexicon embraces the indigenous rights discourse by drawing attention to the language of remedy and recognition. This implies that indigenous peoples need to be compensated, and their rights need to be clarified. COICA's narrative and cultural elements, such as body language, also deploy the language of exceptionality to self-portray as both vulnerable and as agents of change. COICA's ideology for resistance reflects the vision of its ancestral culture, in which land and forest constituted the foundations of the Amazonian indigenous identity. This narrative has also played a critical role to build unity around a single discourse on REDD+. Finally, as expressed by some indigenous leaders, the contextualization of the REDD+ scheme in a historical backdrop of indigenous exclusion and resistance has allowed them to use the momentum created by this debate in order to advocate for the Amazonian indigenous agenda.

67 R Guha (1989) in P Routledge, 'Critical Geopolitics and Terrains of Resistance' (1996) 15 *Political Geography* 505.

2.2.2. Framing a counter-narrative on REDD+: Amazonian Indigenous REDD+

Along the REDD+ debate, COICA aims to both create and change what Florini called 'norms': 'A norm is a legitimate behavioural claim; norms are obeyed because they are considered legitimate'.[68] COICA has done so by introducing an alternative framework, the so-called AIR narrative. The AIR represents an innovative approach to REDD+ that has been co-produced since 2009 by the Amazonian indigenous networks and their allies.[69] It is the result of indigenous peoples' and their networks' discontent with the market-oriented REDD+ framing. The AIR framework has taken into account what Swanson has called 'deep-seated beliefs and norms'.[70] These beliefs and norms are related to the indigenous rights discourse, the current REDD+ framing, the UN Declaration on the Rights of Indigenous Peoples, as well as the indigenous vision of how REDD+ may be implemented within Amazonian indigenous territories.

The strategic framework of the AIR proposal is founded upon three main pillars.[71] The first one is a holistic vision of indigenous territories. It focuses on the design and implementation of indigenous life plans[72], in which REDD+ activities are to be incorporated as part of the resource management strategy. Therefore, the AIR discourse draws attention to concrete actions to protect indigenous peoples and their lands. These actions might take into account the following elements among others: (i) the provision of legal security through the recognition, demarcation, and titling of indigenous territories; (ii) setting regulatory reforms to offer solutions to the overlapping of rights; (iii) enhancing the implementation of 'full life plans' for indigenous communities; and (iv) indigenous self-determination. The second pillar requires a major commitment from the developed countries as potential carbon buyers to take actions to reduce GHG omissions in their own countries by emphasizing their own commitments, which are part of a carbon contract. The third pillar draws attention to the drivers of deforestation. It emphasizes the need to focus on the political and structural causes of deforestation and degradation in the Amazon forest. It does so by pleading for the design and implementation of national and regional strategies

68 A Florini (1996) in M Lindroth, 'Indigenous-State Relations in the UN: Establishing the Indigenous Forum' (2006) 42 *Polar Record* 239.

69 S Hvalkof, 'Imperatives to REDD+ Sustainability: Non-Carbon Benefits, Local and Indigenous Peoples' (2013) *IWGIA* <www.iwgia.org/iwgia_files_publications_files/0639_REED_Final_solved_eb.pdf> accessed 27 November 2017.

70 Swanson (n 64) 340.

71 AIDESEP, 'Construyendo REDD+ Indigena' (2013) <www.forestpeoples.org/sites/fpp/files/publication/2011/03/aidesepreddindigenasp.pdf> accessed 27 November 2017; COICA, 'Territorios de Vida Plena para enfriar el planeta' (2011) <www.bankinformationcenter.org/wp-content/uploads/2014/02/COICA-Alternativa-de-REDD+-Indigena.pdf> accessed 27 November 2017.

72 Indigenous life plans contain the vision of indigenous peoples about their culture and territory.

to reduce and control the pressure on forests by all those industries that are also affecting indigenous territories.

AIR's discursive narrative as expressed in the three pillars has also brought to discussion other relevant topics that are not part of the Warsaw REDD+ methodological package[73] approved in 2013. For instance, the AIR has called for the incorporation of non-carbon benefits (first pillar) and non-market-based approaches[74] (second pillar). It has also requested the inclusion of specific land tenure indicators in the safeguards systems[75] (first pillar). Moreover, the AIR proposal demands concrete agreements to tackle the political and structural causes of deforestation and degradation in the Amazon as well as the formal recognition that an extractive-based economy has caused the climate crisis (third pillar). Finally, COICA has brought new topics to the REDD+. This includes two specific demands: on the one hand, an appeal for an equal commitment to reduce GHG omissions from the carbon buyers as part of the carbon contract agreement (second pillar), and on the other hand, a demand that donors commit themselves to establish direct funding sources for indigenous peoples. For instance, COICA requests the establishment of a specific fund, the so-called Amazon Indigenous Fund for Humanity[76], through which REDD+ funding for indigenous issues could be allocated. Progressing in setting the basis of this funding mechanism was the priority of COICA's advocacy agenda during COP20.

COICA argues that the UNFCCC's definition of REDD+ is not an acceptable solution for controlling deforestation in indigenous territories. For that reason, the AIR proposal, which brings the local voice into global discussions, represents what Gupta and Ringuis called a 'morally adequate solution' for implementing REDD+ over indigenous territories.[77]

In view of this, it can be argued that COICA has created an interpretive framework for AIR according to which REDD+ related events are deemed problematic and illegitimate. This interpretation creates the boundaries of what is acceptable or not, and by doing so, it aims to exercise social pressure. For instance, COICA gives meaning to the conceptual foundations of REDD+ by arguing that deforestation and degradation are not the root cause of forest loss. Rather it is the neoliberal economic model that is followed by developed

73 The Warsaw REDD+ methodological framework approved in 2013 defines the elements to operationalize REDD+. These elements are a REDD+ strategy or action plan, a forest reference emission level and/or forest reference level, a robust and transparent forest monitoring and reporting system, and a safeguards information system.

74 See COICA's submission to UNFCCC on non-carbon benefits and non-market-based approaches. <http://unfccc.int/resource/docs/2014/smsn/ngo/412.pdf> accessed 27 November 2017.

75 See COICA's submission to UNFCCC on safeguards. <http://unfccc.int/resource/docs/2014/smsn/ngo/469.pdf> accessed 27 November 2017.

76 See COICA's proposal on the creation of a specific funding for indigenous peoples in the Amazon, which is called Fondo Amazonia Indigena para la Humanidad <http://earthinnovation.org/wp-content/uploads/2014/09/10-COICA-Fondo-Indigena.pdf> accessed 27 November 2017.

77 J Gupta and L Ringuis (2001) in Wallbott (n 18) 2.

countries and emerging economies that increases the pressure on the forest. Furthermore, COICA claims that focusing on threatened areas[78] without looking at surrounding areas does not entail a coherent solution to tackle the direct causes[79] of deforestation and degradation. In both cases, COICA presents the REDD+ framing as problematic.[80] By doing so, it creates a boundary between the acceptable and the non-acceptable, by making people endorse COICA's subjective meaning.[81] This illustrates how the AIR creates what Gibson-Graham has called 'identifications and affective attachments'.[82]

2.2.3. Norm socialization

COICA, as a pan-Amazonian regional organization, performs its advocacy work in a specific area, the Amazonian territory, and in a geopolitical space of international development. This geopolitical space is characterized by the mobility of ideas, people, products, and information across worldwide borders. COICA's members participate in different international events representing the voice of their people. Their workspace is hybrid. Each of the members belongs to a specific community and group, such as the Huitoto indigenous group. Each member also belongs to a subnational and a national organization. In this process, indigenous leaders have learned to speak locally and globally on behalf of their people in order to translate local needs on a global platform, as well as to translate global policies into local actions.

According to Martin, transnational social movements aim to employ diverse tools to maintain their networks and boost their effectiveness.[83] In addition to norm framing, COICA has also performed what Lindroth called 'norm socialization'.[84] This has been done by engaging different actors and gaining their political, technical, and financial support for COICA's norm framing. To do so, COICA has applied the following tools: networking among other indigenous groups, conducting diplomacy work, building convenient alliances, and connecting the local to the global discussion. For COICA members, this has meant a process of learning the politics of the climate change and REDD+ regime, while tailoring their self-representation and strategies in order to be heard by the international community.

78 REDD+ is applicable in deforested areas or those with potential risk for deforestation. Indigenous peoples also argue, 'What happened with the areas that are not threatened? Why must they be "punished" by not participating in the REDD+ mechanism?'.

79 In the Amazon, the main drivers of deforestation are related to land-use change policies promoting agricultural industries (biofuels, plantations), cattle ranching expansion, mega projects (hydroelectric plants, highways) and extractive industries (hydrocarbons, mining) (WWF 2010).

80 COICA, 'Territorios de Vida Plena para Enfriar el Planeta' (2011) <www.bankinformationcenter.org/wp-content/uploads/2014/02/COICA-Alternativa-de-REDD+-Indigena.pdf> accessed 27 November 2017.

81 Adapted from Wallbott (n 18) 9.

82 JK Gibson-Graham (2006) in Swanson (n 64) 336.

83 Martin (n 47) 92.

84 Lindroth (n 68) 241.

COICA's advocacy work on the AIR has been done with two different groups: on the one hand, with other indigenous groups, and on the other, with states party to the Convention, as well as multilateral and non-state actors. At the level of indigenous networking, one of COICA's objectives has been to encourage collaborative network among all indigenous peoples worldwide (COICA 2004). Then, COICA has joined diverse mobilization strategies against REDD+ including protests, campaigns such as 'no rights, no REDD+', and the formulation of political statements. In this geopolitical space, COICA has aimed to engage other indigenous networks, such as the Abya Yala network of representatives of Latin American indigenous groups, to back up the AIR proposal. In 2014, the Abya Yala members made a statement supporting COICA's AIR proposal.

As for diplomacy work, the call for agency for indigenous peoples in the global climate and REDD+ debate has had an impact on the relationship between indigenous groups and state actors. In this context, COICA has performed diplomacy[85] by directly engaging diverse actors in search of thematic sponsorships and ambassadors.[86] Among these are states party to the Convention, including Amazonian states such as Peru and Colombia and indigenous-friendly countries like Germany and Norway. COICA has also engaged REDD+ negotiators as well as representatives of multilateral funds, such as the Forest Carbon Partnership Facility and UN REDD programme. At the same time, states have taken advantage of COICA's skills for issue linkage and bridge building in the indigenous-states interplay. During one of the interviews, an indigenous leader stated that indigenous networks are aware of the fact that the Convention is a state decision-making platform, and that indigenous peoples' duty is to provide state parties with timely and accurate information.

With regard to non-government organization (NGO) alliances, historically, indigenous struggles for land and rights have involved the intervention of actors at the international level including international environmentalism. The alliances among these actors and the indigenous groups have been embedded in inequalities.[87] COICA's relationship with its allies has reproduced this paternalist model. Allies have engaged the 'technical' narrative, for instance, by estimating carbon stocks and developing legal statements, while COICA's role has been the deployment of the political indigeneity discourse. Along the REDD+ debate, COICA has established new forms of donor–recipient relationship with these environmental groups, shifting its role from being the passive 'beneficiary' towards becoming an active protagonist. It has done so by establishing convenient and robust transnational alliances for policy advocacy on a common agenda, knowledge sharing, and project funding development with diverse actors.

85 As expressed by some authors, diplomacy implies to 'make use of diplomatic and political skills like issue-linkage, integrative structuration, bridge-building, and mobilizing networks and coalitions of allies' (Young 1991, Underdal 1994, Andresen and Agrawal 2002 in Wallbott 2014, 2).

86 M Betsill and E Corell (2008) in Wallbott (n 18) 2.

87 D Lewis and D Mosse, *Development Brokers and Translators: The Ethnography of Aid and Agencies* (Bloomfield Kumarian Press 2006).

Finally, at the level of articulating the local and the global, COICA has performed a strategic role in negotiations by positioning the local community within the global REDD+ debate. This has been done by using both top-down and bottom-up approaches to spread COICA's narrative on REDD+ and receive financial support. COICA translates local discourses and praxis into the global debate through the introduction of alternative narratives on REDD+ and through the creation of a scene of indigeneity at global events. COP20 is an example of this. During this two-week event, COICA brought the local reality into the global debate through guaranteeing a representative participation of indigenous leaders[88] (measured on number of people) and exposition[89] of indigenous topics (measured on access to slots and number of events). COICA also brings the global message to local spaces through increased participation of its local leaders in global events. The indigenous leaders that took part in the COP20 came back to their local communities with critical reflections and ideas. Moreover, COICA is doing strategic translations by converting indigenous demands into the AIR and REDD+ jargon, and vice versa, by translating COICA's subjective interpretation of the REDD+ technical discourse into community language.

2.3. Impact on indigenous agency

To analyse COICA's strategies, this chapter relies on Campbell's concept of agency. To this author, agency refers to the 'ability to initiate and maintain a progress of action' and the 'ability to display a conduct that possesses subjective meaning'.[90] In this sense, Finnemore and Sikkink's concept of norm entrepreneur, which refers to the agentic properties of an actor to create and promote new norms and strengthen their validity, is also useful. By introducing its own agenda in the debate and influencing it as a collective group, COICA has engaged in what these authors called 'norm framing'[91] and 'norm socialization'.[92] The concepts of

88 During COP20, there were 100 indigenous leaders coming from the nine Amazon countries and 200 Peruvian indigenous leaders. Among them, there were women, young, and the 'sabios'.

89 Regarding indigenous exposition, COICA negotiated with the Convention and the Peruvian government/presidency to have access to the different slots available within the COP20 venue. After negotiations with the Convention, COICA got one daily slot for press conferences (of 30 minutes each), two slots in the official area of side events (of 1.5 hours each), and two daily slots in the non-official area of side events. After negotiations with the Peruvian government in its role of COP20 presidency, COICA got two daily side events in the Peru pavilion in the COP20 venue (of 45 minutes each) and a whole pavilion for indigenous people in the Voces del Clima venue (for two weeks). Most of the slots were mainly used by Amazon indigenous people (each of the nine Amazon countries was allocated one slot, and some subnational organizations as well; the one who represented an AIR pilot has also another slot). This caused internal problems within the indigenous groups that participated in the conference.

90 C Campbell (2009) in Wallbott (n 18) 2.

91 M Finnemore and K Sikkink, 'International Norm Dynamics and Political Change' (1998) 52 *International Organization* 887.

92 Lindroth (n 68) 241.

norm socialization and norm framing have made it possible for COICA to become a norm entrepreneur. COICA's capacity to perform as a norm entrepreneur has been influenced by the following factors. First, COICA possesses strong credibility since it is considered to represent the Amazon indigenous voice legitimately. Second, it counts with 'moral superiority' since indigenous peoples are the most affected by climate change and their cause is widely perceived as just. Finally, the general perception of an indigenous–nature special connection attributes expertise to indigenous peoples as knowledge brokers.

Based on this analysis, COICA has increased the agency of the Amazonian indigenous organization and of the Amazon indigenous members since it has shown its ability to propose a legitimate alternative framing of REDD+ and to engage the international community in it. It is likely that COICA's increased agency – just as the increased agency of its members – has not only been the result of its own conduct but also of the perception of its capacity as a norm entrepreneur. As stated by McAdam and colleagues, the understanding of agency emphasizes 'motivation, intention, and goal-orientation and a strong strategic self-consciousness on the part of the actors'.[93] COICA has displayed these characteristics when developing the counter-narrative to REDD+. For instance, its motivation resulted from the opportunity to clarify land rights, gain access to funding, and incorporate the Amazonian indigenous agenda in the forestry debate at all scales. COICA's goal orientation was its firm commitment to 'no rights, no REDD+', to progress on indigenous historical fights and to increase Amazonian indigenous peoples' credibility as the biggest indigenous territorial group in the Amazon. At the same time, COICA also possesses a strong strategic self-consciousness of the expected roles and responsibilities of indigenous groups in the global environmental debate. These roles refer to being knowledge holders, stakeholders, and custodians of nature.

This increased agency has affected COICA in several ways. First, COICA reinforces and self-represents the UN discourse of indigenous exceptionality, both as vulnerable and as an agent group. Second, COICA's unity as a group has been strengthened, by highlighting the differences among diverse ethnics. Third, it has been possible to progress the Amazonian indigenous agenda since REDD+ put the discussion on land rights back in the debate. Finally, COICA's internal and external legitimacy has increased.

The call for participation as expressed in several UN documents has created various channels, both globally and nationally, to enhance indigenous peoples' agency,[94] for instance, by giving them the position of stakeholders (with attached responsibilities) and providing them with a political status in global meetings. Through this, indigenous peoples could see themselves as taking part of the 'planned solution'. This has created room for indigenous organizations such as COICA to effectively contribute to the global debate. However, it is necessary to reflect on the extent to which participation mechanisms genuinely

93 JD McAdam and others (1996) 16 in Wallbott (n 18) 2.

94 Among the United Nations documents that call for indigenous participation are Article 7 of the UNFCCC/COP16 and Decision 135 of the Paris agreement.

create agency for indigenous movements. There are two contrasting positions regarding indigenous environmental agency in UN events. Some authors argue that the indigenous contentious agenda has opened the way for re-negotiating power relations.[95] Others state that improving indigenous agency has become a practice of biopower.[96] To these authors, biopower refers to a power that operates under a façade of an active agency and participation and that makes use of a 'biopolitics discourse' by which indigenous people participation reinforces the hegemonic power.

3. Conclusion

The process of translating the global REDD+ discourse into local practice has created room to make progress on the indigenous agenda. Despite its critiques on the REDD+ mechanism, COICA has become an active participant in the REDD+ regime as a strategic manoeuvre. The strategy comprises the development of an alternative framing as well as the deployment of multiple mechanisms to influence REDD+ as a collective group in an inter-institutional space. This tactic has made it possible to introduce their own political agenda – improved land rights and increased participation – as these elements are key in the framing and implementation of REDD+.

COICA's AIR represents a counterproposal to the REDD+ mechanism. COICA has adhered to the REDD+ regime by bringing a counter-narrative and praxis. The AIR discourse has made use of COICA's cultural power to formulate and set boundaries on what is acceptable or non-acceptable. It aims to shape people's thoughts and conduct in accordance with the indigenous peoples' subjectivities around REDD+.

The REDD+ debate has had a positive impact on COICA's agency. By strategically playing the roles and responsibilities of a vulnerable environmental agent, COICA has become a norm entrepreneur in the REDD+ debate. Moreover, it has made use of this new scenery, not only to advance its political agenda, but also to transform the indigenous organization into a more desired state of legitimacy and representation among its people and other stakeholders within the REDD+ debate. This has made this Amazonian indigenous network stronger. Furthermore, it has contributed to confirming its cultural identity, increasing its unity despite the differences, and increasing its credibility as a respectable authority among territorial-based organizations within the climate change debate in the Amazon region.

To conclude, COICA's experience in this new scenery of climate change could represent an example of collective agency. Future research should analyse how the global climate change narrative on adaptation and mitigation strategies could bring new venues in terms of empowering the agency of indigenous peoples.

95 O'Brien (n 3) 12.

96 Lindroth (n 68) 341; Lindroth and Sinevaara-Niskanen (n 15) 275.

8 The rights of indigenous peoples in the jurisprudence of the Inter-American Court of Human Rights

A 'Third World Approaches to International Law' assessment to advance their protection in the Inter-American Human Rights System

Salvador Herencia Carrasco

1. Introduction

The framework to achieve the protection of indigenous peoples in Latin America has been mostly developed by the Inter-American Human Rights System (hereinafter, "IAHRS"). This regional human rights body was created under the American Convention on Human Rights (hereinafter, "ACHR").[1] The standards set by the IAHRS, mainly through the jurisprudence of the Inter-American Court of Human Rights (hereinafter, "IACtHR"), has contributed to fostering legal and institutional change[2] in the States Parties of the ACHR. This includes the adoption of specific laws regarding indigenous rights, the creation of specialized governmental ministries or agencies on indigenous rights, as well as the adoption of national policies.

The jurisprudence of the IACtHR on the rights of indigenous peoples has addressed different types of violation to the ACHR, including cases regarding forced disappearances,[3] sexual violence,[4] freedom of expression, and lack of due process,[5] among others. However, it is on cases related to territory and

1 *American Convention on Human Rights*, 22 November 1969, 1144 UNTS 123, 9 ILM 99 (entered into force 7 July 1978).

2 See TM Antkowiak and A Gonza, *The American Convention on Human Rights: Essential Rights* (Oxford University Press 2017) 263–284; Inter-American Commission on Human Rights, Indigenous Peoples, *Afro-Descendent Communities, and Natural Resources: Human Rights Protection in the Context of Extraction, Exploitation, and Development Activities* (IACHR 2015); K Quintana and R Flores (eds), *Los Derechos de los Pueblos Indígenas: Una Visión Desde el Sistema Interamericano de Derechos Humanos* (Instituto de Estudios Constitucionales de Queretaro 2017).

3 IACtHR, *Case of the Río Negro Massacres* (Guatemala) (2012) Inter-AmCtHR (Ser C) No 250.

4 IACtHR, *Case of Rosendo Cantú et al.* (Mexico) (2010) Inter-AmCtHR (Ser C) No 216.

5 IACtHR, *Case of Norín Catrimán et al.* (Leaders, members and activist of the Mapuche Indigenous People) (Chile) (2010) Inter-AmCtHR (Ser C) No 2014.

consultation that the IACtHR has made a broader impact in the field of indigenous rights. In the 2001 landmark decision on the *Awas Tingni* case,[6] the IACtHR expanded the notion of Article 21 of the ACHR[7] in order to include the right to collective property.

Since then, and despite some progress achieved,[8] the IAHRS has acknowledged the historic discrimination that indigenous peoples continue to face in the Americas and has used International Human Rights Law to address some of these discriminations, mainly ILO Convention 169[9] and the United Nations Declaration on the Rights of Indigenous Peoples[10] as interpretive instruments. In addition, the Court has adopted a framework to fulfill the right to consultation and the establishment of situations when it is required a free, prior and informed consent.[11]

As important as these decisions have been to the advancement of indigenous rights, this jurisprudence has been framed under civil and political rights, particularly the right to property. This does not reflect nor adequately respond to other violations or claims from indigenous peoples, particularly those that could be deemed of an economic, cultural, social or environmental nature. In recent years, the IACtHR has determined that indigenous peoples are collective subjects under international law, and that due to their particular nature, they can exercise the rights established in the ACHR in a collective manner.[12] However, the Court has not fully explained the contents or limitations of this determination.

This opens up the possibility of not only expanding the protection of indigenous rights, particularly in the context of extractive projects operating in their territory, but also of reexamining how human rights can be understood under the IAHRS. The use of Third World Approaches to International Law (hereinafter, "TWAIL") scholarship is an important tool for exploring the feasibility of an international institution like the IACtHR in contributing to the development of an emancipatory human rights framework for indigenous peoples in Latin America.

6 IACtHR, *Case of the Mayagna (Sumo) Awas Tingni Community* (Nicaragua) (2001) Inter-AmCtHR (Ser C) No 79.

7 Art 21.1 of the ACHR states the following: "Article 21. Right to Property. 1. Everyone has the right to the use and enjoyment of his property. The law may subordinate such use and enjoyment to the interest of society".

8 See Economic Commission for Latin America and the Caribbean, *Guaranteeing Indigenous People's Rights in Latin America: Summary* (ECLAC 2014).

9 Convention No 169, Convention concerning Indigenous and Tribal Peoples in Independent Countries, June 27, 1989, 28 ILM 1382 (entered into force 5 September 1991).

10 *Declaration on the Rights of Indigenous Peoples*, 13 September 2007, GA Res 61/295, UN Doc A/RES/47/1 (2007).

11 See IACtHR, *Case of the Saramaka People (Suriname)* (2007), Inter-AmCtHR (Ser C) No 172.

12 IACtHR, *Case of the Kichwa Indigenous People of Sarayaku (Ecuador)* (2012) Inter-AmCtHR (Ser C) No. 245. IACtHR, Entitlement of Legal Entities to hold rights under the Inter-American Human Rights System (Panama) (2016), Advisory Opinion, Inter-AmCtHR (Ser AC) No 22.

This chapter will be divided into three parts. The first section will analyze TWAIL with the purpose of identifying the main criticisms of the dominant paradigm of human rights and how this affects the international protection of indigenous peoples. The second part of the chapter will analyze some of the leading cases from the IACtHR regarding indigenous rights from a TWAIL perspective. The third part will analyze the recently adopted American Declaration on the Rights of Indigenous Peoples[13] to explore whether this resolution could open up a possibility to advance indigenous rights.

1.1. Positioning of the research in the context of indigenous peoples in the Americas

There is a rich international framework regarding the rights of indigenous peoples. The American Declaration on the Rights of Indigenous Peoples is the newest addition of instruments that build on the efforts of the 169 ILO Convention and the United Nations Declaration on the Rights of Indigenous Peoples, among others. There are specialized bodies and rapporteurships at the United Nations and the Organization of American States that seek to advance indigenous rights.

In Latin America, the decisions of the IACtHR and the reports of the IACHR have triggered legal and institutional change.[14] However, indigenous peoples continue to be marginalized and suffer systemic discrimination. My idea is not to mirror Eric A. Posner's critique of the International Human Rights Law regime,[15] but to highlight the need to expand the current paradigm of this field so that groups like indigenous peoples are able to use the system to protect their rights. The recent adoption of the decision of the IACtHR in the *Lagos del Campo* case,[16] where the Court determined the responsibility of a state for violation of an economic, social and cultural right, may contribute to how human right lawyers and victims frame their cases before the IAHRS.

This also represents a challenge for lawyers, particularly those working on public interest litigation. We need to start using other forms of evidence[17] and consider more deeply the limitations that dominant human right narratives impose on collective groups such as indigenous peoples. Interdisciplinary studies may allow progress in this respect. If we are to advance the field of human rights law within the IAHRS, we must think beyond existing treaties and increasingly turn to socially based evidence to expand our notions of law—to progress towards systems of law that have indigenous peoples at the forefront and not only at the receiving end.

13 American Declaration on the Rights of Indigenous Peoples, 15 June 2016, OEA/Ser.P, AG/doc 5537/16 (2016).

14 See Due Process of Law Foundation, OXFAM, Derecho a la Consulta y al consentimiento previo, libre e informado en América Latina: Avances y desafíos para su implementación en Bolivia, Brasil, Chile, Colombia, Guatemala y Perú (Due Process of Law Foundation 2015).

15 See E Posner, *The Twilight of Human Rights* (Oxford University Press 2014).

16 IACtHR, *Case of Lagos del Campo (Peru)* (2017) Inter-AmCtHR (Ser C) No 340.

17 See A Huneeus, 'Human Rights between Jurisprudence and Social Science' (2015) 28:2 *Leiden Journal of International Law* 255.

Therefore, this chapter will assess the recently adopted American Declaration on the Rights of Indigenous Peoples as well as decisions of the IACtHR that acknowledge that indigenous peoples are collective subjects under international law.

2. TWAIL as a critique to dominant narratives of international law and international human rights

TWAIL scholarship[18] offers a valid critique that helps explain the domination of international law by Western states.[19] By tracing international law to its origins and subsequent practice,[20] TWAIL argues, convincingly, that the Third World has become a recipient rather than a maker of these norms that shape the economy, international relations and human rights. This unequal situation affects power relations and the understanding of international law as a universal law of nations.

Generally, the first generation of TWAIL scholars focused on the role of Third World states (1960s and 1970s), while the second (1990s) focused on how international law affected vulnerable groups.[21] Regardless of the focus of research, the purpose of TWAIL scholarship is to decolonize international law. As leading scholars Antony Anghie and BS Chimni have argued, the purpose of this school of thought is:[22]

> (. . .) to transform international law from being a language of oppression to a language of emancipation—a body of rules and practices that reflect and embody the struggles and aspirations of Third World peoples and which, thereby, promotes truly global justice.

TWAIL scholars advocate for the need to move from a state-driven international law to a "post-colonial international law".[23] How this process of transformation should ideally take place is up for debate.[24] Some authors, like BS

18 It is important to highlight that TWAIL agglomerates different critical scholars. In no way this chapter seeks to suggest that this is a uniform school of thought. However, the foundations of TWAIL are a common ground, despite the specificities and scope of individual scholars.

19 See OC Okafor, 'Critical Third World Approaches to International Law (TWAIL): Theory, Methodology, or Both?' (2008) 10 *International Community Law Review* 371.

20 See A Anghie, *Imperialism, Sovereignty and the Making of International Law* (Cambridge University Press 2005).

21 See OA Badaru, 'Examining the Utility of Third World Approaches to International Law for International Human Rights Law' (2008) 10:4 *International Community Law Review* 379.

22 A Anghie and BS Chimni, 'Third World Approaches to International Law and Individual Responsibility in Internal Conflict' (2003) 2, 1 *Chinese Journal of International Law* 77, 79.

23 See A Anghie, 'Towards a Postcolonial International Law' in P Singh and B Mayer (eds), *Critical International Law: Postrealism, Postcolonialism, and Transnationalism* (Oxford University Press 2014), 123–142.

24 See L Eslava and S Pahuja, 'Between Resistance and Reform: TWAIL and the Universality of International Law' (2011) 3, 1 *Trade, Law and Development* 103–130.

Chimni[25] and Sundhya Pahuja,[26] have written manifestos and calls for resistance, particularly against economic institutions and a development discourse dominated by global financial institutions. However, other scholars like Rajagopal[27] and Sornarajah[28] have called for the need to reform the international legal system in order to decolonize international law, with human rights as a field of primary concern.

The main contribution of TWAIL scholarship is to identify the limitations and imperialistic aspirations[29] of international law, disguised as universal and rational values. By posing a direct challenge to the structure and foundations of international law, TWAIL opens up the possibility for Third World states to better identify and propose alternatives in the notion and application of an international law regime. This would lead to the possibility of "(. . .) fashioning a more humane type of global civilization by self-confidently entering the dialogic space between entrenched political power and transnational social forces, acknowledging the relevance of both, but subordinating their autonomy to neither".[30]

Regarding the study of human rights, TWAIL scholarship contributes to provide a better understanding on how the limitations in the protection and adjudication of rights are based in historical and cultural imperatives, transformed into law. This poses a challenge to the Third World and its peoples to create norms and institutions that can fully address their problems and aspirations. Most of the academic work has focused on the functioning of global institutions. However, a closer look at existing regional systems and how these mirror constraints set by dominant international law could also represent an opportunity to expand our understanding of human rights.

2.1. TWAIL and human rights: A review for a constructive reassessment of the Inter-American Human Rights System

Human rights have become the accepted dominant discourse around the pursuit of indigenous peoples[31] for emancipation and liberalization.[32] This discourse has

25 See BS Chimni, 'Third World Approaches to International Law: A manifesto' in A Anghie and others (eds), *The Third World and International Order: Law Politics and Globalization* (Martinus Nijhoff Publishers 2003), 47–74.

26 See S Pahuja, *Decolonizing International Law: Development, Economic Growth and the Politics of Universality* (Cambridge University Press 2013).

27 See B Rajagopal, *International Law from Below: Development, Social Movements and Third World Resistance* (Cambridge University Press 2003), 165–170.

28 See M Sornarajah, 'On Fighting for Global Justice: The Role of a Third World International Lawyer' (2016) 37, 11 *Third World Quarterly* 1972–1989.

29 See Chimni, 'A Manifesto' (n 25) 47–74.

30 R Falk, 'The Coming Global Civilization: Neo-Liberal or Humanist?' in A Anghie and G Sturgess (eds), *Legal Visions of the 21st Century: Essays in Honour of Judge Christopher Weeramantry* (Kluwer Law international 1998), 32.

31 TWAIL scholars working on human rights address the importance of indigenous peoples and social movements. The present chapter will focus just on the situation of indigenous peoples while acknowledging that there is further research to be done in the international protection of social movements in Latin America.

32 See Rajagopal (n 27) 165–170.

arguably displaced other narratives due to its universal approach and "common language of humanity".[33] However, the human rights approach imposes a world view and perspective common to Western states. This imposition will have certain impacts in Third World countries and among indigenous peoples who challenge the market-oriented view of development and modernity embedded in the dominant human rights discourse.

The dominant human rights discourse is state centered and state driven, privileging individual liberties and a market-based economy over social, cultural and economic rights.[34] In this context, private property rights play a pivotal role,[35] and much of the international institutional framework, including human rights, has been built to protect these rights.[36] This limited view poses obstacles to the goal of converting human rights into a true emancipatory and liberating discourse.

For example, TWAIL scholars argue that in practice, the dominant human rights discourse results in suppressing any alternatives that challenge dominant views on development and modernity, especially those of indigenous peoples. An example of this can be seen in Latin America in the case of social conflicts created by extractive industries.[37] The efforts of indigenous peoples to oppose mining activities in their territories[38] could be seen as a victory of human rights,[39] as it would imply that these groups are increasingly exercising their civil liberties, including freedom of association, freedom of speech or their right to consultation. However, in practice, the exercise of these rights is curtailed by the state,[40] resulting in greater marginalization from their potential role to change dominant norms.

TWAIL scholars also highlight the limitations set by international law on the exercise of rights by vulnerable groups when the exercise of these rights contradicts the goals of the states themselves, particularly economic policies. A relevant example would be the right to prior, free and informed consultation and consent, something that most states in Latin America have acknowledged as a right of indigenous peoples. Although often seen as a victory for indigenous peoples, generally, the final decision on the approval or refusal of an economic project that will affect their lives mostly lies with the state.[41]

33 ibid. 171.

34 Chimni, 'A Manifesto' (n 25) 62–63.

35 ibid. 63.

36 See BS Chimni, 'International Institutions Today: An Imperial Global State in the Making' (2004) 15 *European Journal of International Law* 1, 1–37.

37 See A Bebbington, *Social Conflict, Economic Development and the Extractive Industry: Evidence from South America* (Routledge 2012).

38 See Grupo de Trabajo sobre Minería y Derechos Humanos en América Latina, *The Impact of Canadian Mining in Latin America and Canada's Responsibility: Executive Summary of the Report Submitted to the Inter-American Commission on Human Rights* (Due Process of Law Foundation 2014).

39 Rajagopal (n 27) 172.

40 See C Coumans, 'Alternative Accountability Mechanisms and Mining: The Problems of Effective Impunity, Human Rights and Agency' (2010) 30:1 *Canadian Journal of International Development Studies* 27.

41 See S Thériault, 'Justice Environnementale et Peuples Autochtones: les Possibilités et les Limites de la Jurisprudence de la Cour Interaméricaine des Droits de l'Homme' (2015) *Hors-série Revue Québécoise de Droit International* 129.

One could argue that international law has included in its agenda issues like prior consultation, governance, accountability and democratic participation as a form of control,[42] appeasing vulnerable groups with rights that in practice they cannot fully exercise, and thus avoiding substantial challenges and questionings of the current international law and human rights framework.[43]

Within this context, the dominant human rights discourse does not fully address the needs of indigenous peoples in Latin America, particularly when these have a communal experience that tends to prioritize the collectivity over the individual and see their culture and social aspects as fundamental to their own existence and wellbeing. As important as functionalism[44] might be to the advancement of human rights, TWAIL scholarship does not seek to enhance the participation of the Third World within the existing international law and human rights framework, but argues for fundamental changes to the framework itself. It proposes a change from an international law of the state to an international law of individuals,[45] and even considers constructing a new post-colonial international law.[46]

As indigenous peoples strive to challenge hegemony and domination, human rights could emerge as a bridge that could help balance the unequal relations of power. However, as seen in the case and limitations imposed on the right to consultation, the dominant human rights discourse, consciously or not, perpetuates forms of colonialism and dominance.[47] Human rights will only be able to fully address the struggles that indigenous peoples face in Latin America if substantial changes are made to international law.

For the purpose of this chapter, an element worth considering includes the direct participation of indigenous people in the reconstitution of the human rights paradigm. This would mean that their collective concerns—over issues regarding their identity, autonomy, territory and culture—would be at the forefront of new human rights discourse.[48] As stated before, human rights have prioritized civil and political rights over economic, social and cultural rights. This is a result of political rather than legal justifications,[49] based on the existing state-centred approach to human rights where elites determine the allocation of resources that could benefit marginalized groups.

42 See C Rodriguez-Garavito, 'Ethnicity.gov: Global Governance, Indigenous Peoples, and the Right to Prior Consultation in Social Minefields' (2011) 18 *Indiana Journal of Global Legal Studies* 263.

43 See Rajagopal (n 27) 168.

44 ibid. 167–168.

45 ibid. 156.

46 See Anghie, 'Towards a Postcolonial International Law' (n 23) 123–142.

47 An analysis of the hegemonic and counter-hegemonic nature of human rights can be seen at B Rajagopal, 'Counter-Hegemonic International Law: Rethinking Human Rights and Development as a Third World Strategy' in R Falk, B Rajagopal and J Stevens (eds), *International Law and the Third World: Reshaping Justice* (Routledge-Cavendish 2008) 63–80.

48 Rajagopal 'International Law from Below' (n 27) 165.

49 ibid. 191.

In the context of Latin America, the recent adoption of the American Declaration on the Rights of Indigenous Peoples could mean a small step forward. Although the final adoption of the Declaration was done by states, indigenous peoples actively participated in the almost seventeen years of deliberation. There are approximately 45 million indigenous peoples in Latin America, which represents approximately 8.3% of the population,[50] and it is encouraging to see that indigenous groups were not set aside in the discussions regarding their rights and interests.

In TWAIL, decolonization is an important notion to build an understanding of the *status quo* of international law.[51] In this chapter, this will be understood as a means not to create a new institution—in this case the IAHRS—but to go beyond the current limitations.[52] In the case of human rights, there are grounds to support the idea of change within the system, even in TWAIL scholarship. As Rajagopal has stated,[53]

> Current human rights discourse and practice has a choice (. . .): it can either insinuate itself within hegemonic international law or it can serve as an important tool in developing and strengthening a counter-hegemonic international law.

The next section will explore how the protection of the rights of indigenous peoples within the IAHRS can be expanded, going beyond current limitations set by the ACHR.

3. The Inter-American Human Rights System and the protection of indigenous peoples

The Organization of American States (hereinafter, "OAS") adopted the ACHR in 1969, and the Convention entered into force in 1978.[54] In order to assure compliance in the fulfilment of its object and purpose, a dual oversight mechanism

50 Economic Commission for Latin America and the Caribbean (n 8) 36–38.

51 Latin American scholarship has increasingly focused on the Decolonization of Law, particularly in countries with Constitutions that are open-ended in rights (Colombia) or have adopted new Constitutions to increase the participation of Indigenous Peoples and social movements (Bolivia or Ecuador). Their main criticism, which mirrors areas of concern from TWAIL and other critical socio-legal scholarships, is that the existing Constitutional and legal frameworks are full of restraints that protect the elite and a capitalist society. Among others, see O Correas, D Sandoval and A Melgarito (eds), *Movimientos Sociales y Procesos Constituyentes Contemporáneos en México y América Latina* (Ediciones Coyoacán & Universidad Nacional Autónoma de México 2015).

52 See A Noguera Fernández, *Los Derechos Sociales en las Nuevas Constituciones Latinoamericanas* (Tirant Lo Blanch 2010).

53 Rajagopal, 'Counter-hegemonic International Law' (n 47) 71.

54 As of October 2017, twenty-three states have ratified the American Convention, and twenty have accepted the jurisdiction of the IACtHR: Argentina, Barbados, Bolivia, Brazil, Chile, Colombia, Costa Rica, Dominican Republic, Ecuador, El Salvador, Guatemala, Haiti, Honduras, Mexico, Nicaragua, Panama, Paraguay, Peru, Suriname and Uruguay. See Corte Interamericana de Derechos Humanos, *Informe Anual 2016* (Corte Interamericana de Derechos Humanos 2017), 12.

was created, composed of the IACHR, created under the OAS Charter, and the IACtHR. The IACHR channels the communications from alleged victims that claim to have had their rights breached by a state party to the ACHR, and, if needed, the IACHR may take the case to the IACtHR. The IACHR also publishes thematic reports regarding the standards and interpretation of rights within the ACHR. Although not legally binding, these reports are academically authoritative and used by states and non-government organizations (NGOs) as a guiding tool to implement law and policy.

The IACtHR is an international human rights tribunal that can decide on Contentious Cases[55] or render Advisory Opinions.[56] The Court has its framework set by the ACHR and has the competence to exclusively determine the international responsibility of a state. The jurisdiction of the IACtHR is complementary to the one exercised by the state, and its judicial decisions are binding and final.[57] The Court has the capacity to order a broad range of reparations,[58] according to the terms established by Article 63 of the American Convention.[59]

3.1. The Inter-American Court of Human Rights and the jurisprudence on indigenous peoples

As stated in the introduction the IACtHR has developed a comprehensive jurisprudence regarding the protection of human rights of vulnerable groups. In the case of indigenous peoples, the jurisprudence has focused on the rights to property and consultation. A significant contribution by the Court was to set up the legal framework to protect indigenous rights, since the ACHR does not establish specific obligations to protect these rights.

55 See Articles 62 and 63 ACHR (n 1).

56 See Article 64 of the ACHR (n 1).

57 Article 67 of the ACHR states the following:

"The judgment of the Court shall be final and not subject to appeal. In case of disagreement as to the meaning or scope of the judgment, the Court shall interpret it at the request of any of the parties, provided the request is made within ninety days from the date of notification of the judgment".

58 See TM Antkowiak, 'Remedial Approaches to Human Rights Violations: The Inter-American Court of Human Rights and Beyond' (2008) 46 *Columbia Journal of Transnational Law* 351.

59 Article 63 of the ACHR states the following:

"1 If the Court finds that there has been a violation of a right or freedom protected by this Convention, the Court shall rule that the injured party be ensured the enjoyment of his right or freedom that was violated. It shall also rule, if appropriate, that the consequences of the measure or situation that constituted the breach of such right or freedom be remedied and that fair compensation be paid to the injured party".

"2 In cases of extreme gravity and urgency, and when necessary to avoid irreparable damage to persons, the Court shall adopt such provisional measures as it deems pertinent in matters it has under consideration. With respect to a case not yet submitted to the Court, it may act at the request of the Commission".

Article 29.2 of the ACHR grants the possibility of expanding "the enjoyment or exercise of any right or freedom recognized by virtue of the laws of any State Party or by virtue of another Convention to which one of the said states is a party".[60] On the basis of this disposition, ILO Convention 169 and the United Nations Declaration on the Rights of Indigenous Peoples have been used as guiding tools to determine state responsibility under the ACHR.

In recent years, the IAHRS has outlined and/or acknowledged the importance of protecting some of the collective concerns formulated by TWAIL scholars: the protection of economic, social and cultural rights; the protection of collective rights of indigenous peoples; the protection of collective territory; and, the protection of the environment. However, the IAHRS has made very little progress in putting forward how these collective rights could be put into practice and enforced. This presents an opportunity for TWAIL to contribute to a potential framework that effectively emancipates indigenous peoples, by challenging the "hegemony of the dominant narratives of international law".[61]

To this date, the IACtHR has decided over twenty cases regarding indigenous peoples. Some of these cases have expanded the understanding of rights within the ACHR, while others have become a standard tool for the assessment of legislation and policies on consultation. In the 2001 *Awas Tingni* case,[62] the IACtHR determined that collective property should be protected under Article 21 of the ACHR. In this case, the Court determined that

> Among indigenous peoples there is a communitarian tradition regarding a communal form of collective property of the land, in the sense that ownership of the land is not centered on an individual but rather on the group and its community. Indigenous groups, by the fact of their very existence, have the right to live freely in their own territory; the close ties of indigenous people with the land must be recognized and understood as the fundamental basis of their cultures, their spiritual life, their integrity, and their economic survival. For indigenous communities, relations to the land are not merely a matter of possession and production but a material and spiritual element which they must fully enjoy, even to preserve their cultural legacy and transmit it to future generations.[63]

Later, in the 2007 *Case of the Saramaka People*,[64] the IACtHR developed the jurisprudential framework for consultation processes of indigenous peoples and

60 See Article 29 of the ACHR (n 1).

61 See JT Gathii, 'TWAIL: A Brief History of Its Origins, Its Decentralized Network, and a Tentative Bibliography' (2011) 3, 1: *Trade, Law & Development* 26, 37.

62 See *Case of the Mayagna (Sumo) Awas Tingni Community (Honduras)* (n 6).

63 ibid. para 149.

64 See *Case of the Saramaka People (Suriname)* (2007) (n 11).

the exceptional situations under which these consultations imply a need for consent. Regarding the right to consultation, the Court stated,

> (. . .) in ensuring the effective participation of members of the Saramaka people in development or investment plans within their territory, the State has a duty to actively consult with said community according to their customs and traditions. This duty requires the State to both accept and disseminate information, and entails constant communication between the parties. These consultations must be in good faith, through culturally appropriate procedures and with the objective of reaching an agreement.[65]

In this same decision, the Court determined that this consultation becomes a free, prior and informed consent when a project would have a major impact[66] in the territory of an indigenous people. To this date, the *Saramaka* case is one of the most important decisions in the rights of indigenous peoples *vis-à-vis* extractive and development projects.

The 2012 *Case of the Kichwa Indigenous People of Sarayaku*[67] is relevant because the IACtHR acknowledges that indigenous peoples are collective subjects under international law. In addition, it states that the exercise and protection of some of their rights, including the right to culture and the right to territory, must be collectively protected, regardless of the accredited victims in a particular case. In this case, the Court stated,

> (. . .) international law on indigenous or tribal communities and peoples recognizes rights to the peoples as collective subjects of international law and not only as members of such communities or peoples. In view of the fact that indigenous or tribal communities and peoples, united by their particular ways of life and identity, exercise some rights recognized by the Convention on a collective basis, the Court points out that the legal considerations expressed or indicated in this Judgment should be understood from that collective perspective.[68]

The protection of the environment is a matter of recent concern in the jurisprudence of the IACtHR.[69] For example, in 2009, the *Case of the Kawas Fernández*[70] was important as it established that the protection of the environment is related

65 ibid. para 133.
66 ibid. para 134–137.
67 See *Case of the Kichwa Indigenous People of Sarayaku (Ecuador)* (n 12).
68 ibid. para 231.
69 See IACtHR, *Yakye Axa Indigenous Community (Paraguay)* (2005), Merits, Reparations and Costs, Inter-AmCtHR (Ser C) No 125; IACtHR, *Case of the Xákmok Kásek Indigenous Community (Paraguay)* (2010), Merits, Reparations and Costs, Inter-AmCtHR (Ser C) No 214.
70 See *Case of Kawas Fernández (Honduras)* (2009), Inter-AmCtHR (Ser C) No 196.

to the fulfilment of other rights within the ACHR.[71] The case related to the extrajudicial execution of an environmental defender in Honduras. However, this concept was later used in the *Kaliña and Lokono* case,[72] where the Court determined the following:

> The Court has established that the relationship with the land and the natural resources that the indigenous and tribal peoples have used traditionally, and which are necessary for their physical and cultural survival, as well as for the development and continuation of their world vision, must be protected under Article 21 of the Convention. The purpose of this protection is to ensure that the indigenous and tribal peoples may continue to enjoy their traditional way of life and that their cultural identity, social structure, economic system, customs, beliefs and distinctive traditions are respected, guaranteed and protected by the States. Hence, the indigenous peoples are entitled to the natural resources that they have traditionally used within their territory because, without them, their economic, social and cultural survival are at risk.[73]

In February 2018, the IACtHR published its Advisory Opinion regarding the relationship between human rights and the environment.[74] This Advisory Opinion focuses on the impact of infrastructure projects carried out by other states on the environment and the human rights of people located in the Caribbean Sea. The IACtHR takes the opportunity to precise the obligations of states regarding the environment *vis-à-vis* the ACHR,[75] focusing on the rights of indigenous peoples. The Court reaffirms the obligations to respect the right to consultation and to indigenous territory,[76] the importance of environmental studies[77] and the adoption of measures to protect indigenous land, customs and traditions. It will be important to see how this Advisory Opinion could change how the IACtHR decides cases regarding environmental damages and indigenous peoples, including the notion of collective rights.

The aforementioned cases demonstrate the important contributions of the Courts to the protection of the right to territory and consultation, as these have direct consequences on the life, culture and subsistence of indigenous peoples. However, this judicial construction seems to push the boundaries of the ACHR without focusing on creating a framework that can fully address their protection. In this sense, the criticism made by TWAIL scholars about the dominant narrative of human rights is applicable to the IAHRS.

71 ibid. para. 148.

72 IACtHR, *Case of the Kaliña and Lokono Peoples (Suriname)* (2015), Merits, Reparations and Costs, Inter-AmCtHR (Ser C) No 309.

73 ibid. para 164.

74 IACtHR, *Environment and Human Rights* (Colombia) (2017), Advisory Opinion, Inter-AmCtHR (Ser AC) No 23.

75 ibid. paras 46–70.

76 ibid. para 113.

77 ibid. paras 156–174.

3.2. Limitations of the jurisprudence of the IACtHR and changes needed

As important as the decisions described above have been to protect indigenous rights,[78] authors like Thomas Antkowiak[79] has criticized how the IAHRS has created a jurisprudential framework to protect the rights of indigenous peoples under the right to individual property. He has made a valid criticism of the jurisprudence of the IACtHR and its use of the right to property, proposing to replace it by a broader *vida digna*[80] approach. Although this criticism has validity, it tends to focus on how to extend—as opposed to reconstruct—the scope of protections established in the ACHR.

However, by proposing alternatives on how to interpret the ACHR, inadvertently one accepts the limitations imposed in the ACHR: the predominant focus on civil and political rights and the individual, relegating the protection of economic, social, cultural and environmental rights as well as those of collective nature. The Court has decided cases on economic, social and cultural issues,[81] but until December 2017, there had to be a connection with civil and political rights.[82] In these cases, the social dimensions of these claims did not receive the attention, protection and adjudication that they deserved.[83]

The limitations to the international protection of economic, social and cultural rights are not new. Article 26 of the ACHR declares the progressive nature of these rights,[84] in a similar way as other international

78 For a didactic tool on the jurisprudence of the IACtHR, see Corte Interamericana de Derechos Humanos, *Cuadernillo de Jurisprudencia de la Corte Interamericana de Derechos Humanos Nº 11: Pueblos Indígenas y Tribales* (Corte Interamericana de Derechos Humanos 2015).

79 TM Antkowiak, 'Rights, Resources and Rhetoric: Indigenous People and the Inter-American Court' (2013) 35 *University of Pennsylvania Journal of International Law* 113.

80 This term was first use in *Yakye Axa Indigenous Community* (n 69) para 176. The term has been later developed to include that the right to life must meet certain quality standards, including the right to dignity. This has been used to connect civil and political rights (e.g. right to life) to economic, social and cultural rights (e.g. right to a pension), particularly of members from vulnerable groups.

81 Among others, see IACtHR, *Case of the 'Five Pensioners' (Peru)* (2003), Merits, Reparations and Costs, Inter-AmCtHR (Ser C) No 98; IACtHR, *Case of the Dismissed Congressional Employees (Aguado - Alfaro et al.)* (Peru) (2006), Preliminary Objections, Merits, Reparations and Costs, Inter-AmCtHR (Ser C) No 158; IACtHR, *Case of Acevedo Buendía et al. ('Discharged and Retired Employees of the Comptroller') (Peru)* (2009), Preliminary Objections, Merits, Reparations, and Costs, Inter-AmCtHR (Ser C) No 198; IACtHR, *Case of Gonzales Lluy et al. (Ecuador)* (2015), Preliminary Objections, Merits, Reparations and Costs, Inter-AmCtHR (Ser C) No 298.

82 See JM Pasqualucci, 'The Right to a Dignified Life (Vida Digna): The Integration of Economic and Social Rights with Civil and Political Rights in the Inter-American Human Rights System' (2008) 31, 1 *Hastings International and Comparative Law Review* 1.

83 See C Courtis, 'Artículo 26: Desarrollo Progresivo' in C Steiner and P Uribe (eds), *Convención Americana sobre Derechos Humanos: Comentario* (Fundación Konrad Adenauer 2014) 654–676.

84 Art 26 of the ACHR states the following:

"Article 26. Progressive Development

The States Parties undertake to adopt measures, both internally and through international cooperation, especially those of an economic and technical nature, with a view to achieving progressively,

instruments.[85] For example, the 1988 San Salvador Protocol to the ACHR on Economic, Social and Cultural Rights[86] explicitly establishes in Article 19.6 that only cases regarding trade union rights and the right to education may be brought before the IAHRS.

Tara Melish has argued about the need to protect economic, social and cultural rights claiming that there is no need of an amendment to the ACHR to autonomously protect these tights.[87] As stated previously, this has been the practice of the IACtHR regarding the application and limitations of Article 26. However, in December 2017, the Court published its decisions on the *Lagos del Campo vs. Peru*[88] and on the *Case of Dismissed Employees of Petroperú vs. Peru.*[89] For the first time, the IACtHR determined the state responsibility under Article 26, focusing both cases on the right to work.[90]

These decisions have the potential to change how human rights are understood and protected under the IAHRS, with possible ramifications at the national level. For indigenous peoples, this could mean a greater protection and understanding of their collective rights but also a more nuanced understanding of what human rights could mean for indigenous peoples, particularly in the context of extractive industries.

This could open the possibility for indigenous peoples to see their economic, social, cultural and environmental rights protected and to include a new way of understanding the notions of development and collective rights.

4. Indigenous peoples as collective subjects of international law and the American Declaration on Indigenous Peoples: A possibility of emancipation?

As mentioned in the introduction, the purpose is not to expand conventional rights to cover indigenous claims (the property approach) or to create a *vida*

by legislation or other appropriate means, the full realization of the rights implicit in the economic, social, educational, scientific, and cultural standards set forth in the Charter of the Organization of American States as amended by the Protocol of Buenos Aires".

85 For example, see *International Covenant on Economic, Social and Cultural Rights,* 16 December 1966, 993 UNTS 3; 6 ILM 368 (entered into force 3 January 1976), Art 2.1.

86 *Additional Protocol to the American Convention on Human Rights in the Area of Economic, Social and Cultural Rights* (Protocol of San Salvador), 17 November 1988, OAS Treaty Series No. 69, 28 I.L.M. 156 (entered into force 16 November 1999).

87 TJ Melish, 'The Inter-American Court of Human Rights: Beyond Progressivity' in: M Langford (ed.), *Social Rights Jurisprudence Emerging Trends in International and Comparative Law* (Cambridge University Press, 2009), 372–408.

88 *Case of Lagos del Campo* (n 16) paras 133–163.

89 IACtHR, *Case of Dismissed Employees of Petroperú (Peru)* (2017), Preliminary Objections, Merits, Reparations and Costs, Inter-AmCtHR (Ser C) No 344.

90 See E Ferrer McGregor, M Moralres and R Flores (eds), *Inclusión, Ius Commune y Justiciabilidad de los DESCA en la Jurisprudencia Interamericana: El Caso Lagos del Campo y los Nuevos Desafíos* (Instituto de Estudios Constitucionales del Estado de Querétaro 2018).

digna approach to integrate economic, social and cultural rights under the sphere of civil and political rights. The challenge is to move beyond the legal constraints in order to meet the current needs of indigenous peoples. In the next section, the goal will be to determine if recent decisions from the IACtHR or recent decisions from the OAS can enable a change within the IAHRS without advocating the replacement of the system, as some TWAIL scholars would pose.

4.1. Advisory Opinion on the Entitlement of Legal Entities to hold victim status under the Inter-American Human Rights System

In April 2014, the Republic of Panama requested an Advisory Opinion of the IACtHR, to determine, among other things, if legal entities could be victims of violations of human rights under the ACHR and other international treaties within the IAHRS. The IACtHR rendered its Advisory Opinion[91] on February 20, 2016.[92]

The Advisory Opinion established that under Article 1.2 of the ACHR, legal persons, including corporations, cannot claim a victim status under the IAHRS. The system expressly states that only natural persons can be victims of human rights under the system. However, it acknowledged two important exceptions: (i) indigenous and tribal communities and (ii) trade unions, federations and confederations.[93]

The Court builds on the decision made in the *Case of the Kichwa Indigenous People of Sarayaku*[94] to determine that indigenous peoples are collective subjects of international law (*sujetos colectivos del Derecho Internacional*).[95] The Court determined that the breach of these rights also has a collective dimension and cannot be limited to an individual breach.[96]

Due to the specific nature of indigenous peoples, the IACtHR affirmed that indigenous peoples are entitled as a collective to some of the rights and protections covered by the ACHR.[97] The Court affirmed that indigenous communities not only have standing to bring claims on behalf of their members, but when the breaches of these rights affect an indigenous community as a whole, the community or indigenous organization representing such community could submit petitions against a state for alleged violations of these rights.[98]

The Advisory Opinion focuses on the entitlement of indigenous peoples to some of the rights acknowledged within the ACHR. However, the foundation

91 IACtHR, Entitlement of Legal Entities to hold rights under the Inter-American Human Rights System (Panama), supra note 12.

92 Until January 2018, the Advisory Opinion was only available in English.

93 In the case of trade unions, the IACtHR referred to the terms of Article 8.2 of the San Salvador Protocol, *supra* note 86.

94 *Case of the Kichwa Indigenous People of Sarayaku (Ecuador), supra* note 12.

95 Entitlement of Legal Entities to hold rights under the Inter-American Human Rights System (n 12) para 75.

96 ibid. para 82.

97 ibid. para 83.

98 ibid. paras 75 and 84.

to reach this conclusion is based on general principles of international law[99] and the right to self-determination.[100] This leaves the possibility for a broader interpretation of the term "collective subjects" under international law as a means to achieve the emancipatory promise. The individual and collective enjoyment of rights is also acknowledged in Article 1 of the United Nations Declaration on the Rights of Indigenous Peoples. However, the possibility in this case should open the possibility to push the IAHRS to expand its notion to other rights outside issues related to consultation, consent or communal property.

4.2. The American Declaration on the Rights of Indigenous Peoples

The American Declaration on the Rights of Indigenous Peoples[101] was adopted in June 2016, after seventeen years of negotiations and postponements. It reiterates many of the provisions stated in previous instruments regarding indigenous rights. However, as a soft law instrument from the OAS,[102] it gives ground for new litigation possibilities. The Declaration includes sections on the rights of indigenous peoples,[103] cultural identity,[104] organizational and political rights[105] and social rights,[106] among others.

In the case of collective rights, the Declaration states the following:[107]

> Article VI. Collective rights
>
> Indigenous peoples have collective rights that are indispensable for their existence, wellbeing, and integral development as peoples. In this regard, the states recognize and respect, the right of the indigenous peoples to their collective action; to their juridical, social, political, and economic systems or institutions; to their own cultures; to profess and practice their spiritual beliefs; to use their own tongues and languages; and to their lands, territories and resources. States shall promote with the full and effective participation of the indigenous peoples the harmonious coexistence of rights and systems of the different population, groups, and cultures.

The language of the Declaration is generic and open-ended. It provides more precision to what collective rights could mean in the Americas, becoming the

99 ibid. para 78.
100 ibid. para 82.
101 American Declaration on the Rights of indigenous peoples (n 13).
102 Regarding the importance of soft law for the advancement of the rights of indigenous peoples, see F Gómez Isa, 'The role of soft law in the progressive development of indigenous peoples' rights' in S Lagoutte, T Gammeltoft-Hansen and J Cerone (eds), *Tracing the Roles of Soft Law in Human Rights* (Cambridge University Press 2016) 185–211.
103 American Declaration on the Rights of Indigenous Peoples (n 13), Art V–Art XII.
104 ibid. Art XIII–Art XIX.
105 ibid. Art XX–Art XXIV.
106 ibid. Art XXV–Art XXX.
107 ibid. Art VI.

minimum standard that the IAHRS should use to advance collective rights of indigenous peoples. The final disposition of the Declaration states that this instrument, as well as the United Nations Declaration on the Rights of Indigenous Peoples constitute "(. . .) the minimum standards for the survival, dignity, and well-being of the indigenous peoples in the Americas".[108]

At first glance, this could be promising as it addresses many of the concerns of indigenous peoples, as well as some of the criticisms made by TWAIL scholarship. However, it is a non-binding instrument, and it remains to be seen how the enforcement of this Declaration will be ensured by states regarding indigenous peoples living in resource-rich areas. The pursuit of solutions on this topic is a brief example of further studies that are required in this field.

If we are to accept the TWAIL premise that the dominant human rights paradigm focuses on individual freedoms, is market oriented and state centred, this acknowledgement from the IACtHR should open the door for a new approach to the ACHR, where TWAIL scholarship could play a significant role. For this to happen, it is important to revisit the foundations of TWAIL and to assess the work of the IAHRS. A regional understanding of TWAIL and human rights focusing on the IAHRS could be a new developing field that could intertwine with decolonization studies taking place in different Latin American academic spheres.

Within the IAHRS, future cases could argue the need to move from collective entitlement and awarding of reparations, to law making and autonomy to determine their own concept of development. In this case, an alternative option could be to see the right to development established in different sections of the United Nations Declaration on the Rights of Indigenous Peoples or within the American Declaration on the Rights of Indigenous Peoples, not just as the possibilities of alternative development but also as alternatives to development.

If the IAHRS is to help indigenous peoples to fully exercise their human rights, the term collective subjects under international law must be advanced in order to move from procedural and entitlement aspects to substantive equality, which should also cover economic, social and cultural rights, as well as the environment.

5. Conclusion and areas of further research

The purpose of this chapter was to see how a TWAIL criticism of human rights could identify possible fields of expansion and improvement of the IAHRS. Although the debate regarding the international adjudication of economic, social and cultural rights is not new, I believe that the latest decisions of the IACtHR, including its recent Advisory Opinion, as well as the American Declaration on the Rights of Indigenous Peoples open the possibility to expand how we understand, protect and adjudicate rights within the IAHRS. The decision of the IACtHR on the *Lagos de Campo* case, although not related to indigenous rights, reaffirms this possibility.

108 ibid. Art XLI.

At a theoretical level, areas of further research should include the connection between TWAIL and decolonization studies taking place in Latin America. However, the most important area of further research should be a TWAIL approach to the IAHRS. In my view, the goal should not just be an acute criticism of the system but a study of alternatives on how to move beyond the current constraints established within the ACHR. As stated by Okafor, reflecting on the work of Baxi,

> (. . .) there is a sense in which enacting a form of TWAIL praxis beyond the academe by participating closely in the work of international institutions and on-the-ground groups can result in our helping give birth to aspects of international human rights itself. As Baxi teaches us, "human rights values, standards, and norms are created by people's praxes of resistance and struggle." In the same vein, he has also correctly noted that "the real birthplaces of human rights are far removed from the ornate norms of diplomatic conferences and are found, rather, in the actual sites (acts and feats) of resistance and struggle".[109]

My main concern is the increasing gap between legal victories and social change. In this case, critical socio-legal scholarships could focus on the decisions of the IACtHR and how these are implemented by the state. I will be the first one to admit that there are contradictions between the concern that motivated this chapter and the claim to expand the rights covered under the IAHRS for indigenous peoples. If human rights law and decisions are not fulfilled by the state, particularly in cases that have economic implications, why would you want to expand the legal protection to more complex issues like collective rights or economic, social, cultural and environmental rights?

I believe that these are two parallel fields, and the limitations of one cannot condition the other. The IAHRS has worked and has shaped how Latin American legal regimes have incorporated international human rights in their national systems. The implementation of the decisions of the IACtHR has implications, not only in law but also in public policies. The purpose of this chapter was to identify the work that needs to be done to achieve a full protection of human rights. There exists real potential to redefine what the IAHRS understands as human rights, not as a means to minimize it but as a tool to expand it and to deliver the promise of emancipation.

109 OC Okafor, 'Praxis and the International (Human Rights) Law Scholar: Towards the Intensification of TWAILian Dramaturgy' (2016) 33:3 *Windsor Yearbook of Access to Justice 1*, 24. Footnotes omitted.

Part II.C Designing new instruments

9 The 2005 Draft Nordic Sámi Convention and the implementation of the right of the Sámi people to self-determination

Dorothée Cambou

Introduction

During several centuries, the Sámi people, a group of indigenous Arctic people inhabiting the northern region of the three Nordic countries (Finland, Norway and Sweden) and the Kola Peninsula in Russia had a long history of colonisation, discrimination and assimilation policies. As a consequence, and similar to other indigenous peoples around the world, the Sámi people are currently striving for the recognition of their rights and entitlement to self-determination. Since the 1970s, the Sámi have mobilised to regain political status and reassert their rights, notably with the creation of a Sámi parliament in each of the Nordic states where the Sámi people live. Nonetheless, this institutional and legal development remains insufficient to guarantee the rights of the Sámi at the national level and does not adequately ensure the implementation of their rights at the transnational level, across the borders that separate them.

As a result, in 2005, an expert committee representing the governments of Finland, Norway and Sweden together with the Sámi parliaments adopted a Draft Nordic Sámi Convention.[1] The draft document recognises the right of the Sámi people to self-determination, including the right to determine their own economic, social and cultural development and the right to dispose of their natural resources for their own benefit. Importantly, the draft also describes how the right to Sámi self-determination can be implemented in the Nordic states. However, more than ten years after the proposal was filed, the finalised convention has not yet been adopted. The length of the process is certainly concomitant with the importance and controversial nature of the document. While the adoption of the Nordic Sámi Convention is justified

Note of acknowledgement. This research has been supported by the Finnish Academy research funding for the project HusArctic. The author is also grateful to Else Grete Broderstad and Øyvind Ravna at Tromso University for sharing their expertise and hosting the author during the time of this research.

1 For an official copy of the draft in Swedish, see the report of the Finnish government entitled "Pohjoismainen saamelaissopimus 13. marraskuuta 2002 nimitetyn suomalais-norjalais-ruotsalais-saamelaisen asiantuntijatyöryhmän 27. lokakuuta 2005 luovuttama luonnos", 2005, (hereafter the Report of the Draft Nordic Sámi Convention) 28–40. The report also contains a commentary of the draft provisions in Finnish language. An unofficial copy of the draft in English can also be found in M Åhrén, JB Henriksen and M Scheinin, *The Nordic Sámi Convention: International Human Rights, Self-Determination and Other Central Provisions* (Gáldu 2007) 98–108.

from a human rights perspective, it remains politically charged, and its content is contentious, especially concerning the recognition of the right of the Sámi people to self-determination. First, the question of self-determination is imbued with many uncertainties regarding its scope of application and its practical implications. Second, the recognition of the right of indigenous peoples to self-determination is a recent event that has yet not fully materialised at the domestic level and which therefore leaves some anxiety on the part of most governments as to what such recognition may entail. Finally, there are also several obstacles in each Nordic country that may limit the implementation of the draft convention. More precisely, the formal status granted to the (Sámi) parliament and the national policy and implementation of international law have been elsewhere acknowledged as current potential obstacles to safeguarding Sámi self-determination.[2] Thus, there are still clear tensions in the struggle of the Sámi people to exercise their right to self-determination.

In the light of these considerations, the purpose of this chapter is to study the relevance of the 2005 Draft Nordic Sámi Convention in implementing the right of the Sámi people to self-determination, and to examine whether the instrument provides an opportunity to operationalise the human rights of the Sámi people at the domestic level. In accordance with these objectives, the first section offers some preliminary remarks on the drafting process of the Draft Nordic Sámi Convention and its justification under human rights law. The second section focuses on the meaning of the right of self-determination under international law, more particularly in relation to the rights of indigenous peoples. The remainder of the chapter explains how the Draft Nordic Sámi Convention seeks to implement the right of the Sámi people to self-determination. The last section concludes with some remarks concerning the relevance of the adoption of the Draft Nordic Sámi Convention and its future.

1. The adoption of the 2005 Draft Nordic Sámi Convention

In 1986, the Sámi Council, a non-governmental organisation representing the interests of the Sámi people, proposed the adoption of a Nordic Sámi Convention to ensure the rights of the Sámi as an indigenous people across the borders separating them in the states of Norway, Finland, Sweden and Russia. Ten years later, the three Nordic states of Finland, Norway and Sweden agreed to investigate the need for such an instrument.[3] This eventually led to the appointment of an expert committee in 2002, consisting of one member appointed by each of the Nordic governments and one member appointed by each of the Sámi

2 U Mörkenstam, E Josefsen and R Nilsson, *The Nordic Sámediggis and the Limits of Indigenous Self-Determination* (1st edn, Gáldu 2016) 6.

3 For more information about the drafting process, see generally Åhrén, Henriksen and Scheinin (n 1). See also T Koivurova, 'The Draft Nordic Saami Convention: Nations Working Together' (2008) 10 *International Community Law Review* 279; T Koivurova, 'The Draft for Nordic Saami Convention' (2008) 6 *European Yearbook of Minority Issues* 103.

parliaments to elaborate a draft instrument.[4] For a period of three years, the group met regularly to draft a proposed convention that would establish a comprehensive framework for regulating the legal relationship between the Sámi people and the three Nordic states.[5] During the drafting process, several expert members were also consulted to investigate specific issues, such as the right to self-determination.[6] Ultimately, the expert committee agreed unanimously on a draft text that was submitted to the three Nordic governments and the three Sámi parliaments at the end of 2005.

After the adoption of the draft, discussions surrounding its content continued. However, in 2007, the expert committee could not proceed further with the negotiations. The alleged reason for this was that Finland had not been able to finalise the studies on the draft convention's impact on Finland's Constitution and on its implications for treaty making in general that were being prepared by the Ministry of Justice and the Ministry for Foreign Affairs.[7] However, and in contrast with the position of Finland, it is noteworthy that the adoption of the Draft Nordic Sámi Convention has been promoted by several of the human rights treaties bodies. For instance, the Committee on the Elimination of Racial Discrimination (CERD) has several times reiterated encouragement for Finland in its concluding observations to contribute to the timely negotiation and adoption of a Nordic Sámi Convention. In addition, the UN Special Rapporteur on the Rights of Indigenous Peoples at the time, James Anaya, endorsed the instrument and "commend(ed) the Sámi people and the Governments of Norway, Sweden and Finland for the significant work achieved to date to develop this important instrument".[8] Victoria Tauli-Corpuz, who was appointed as Special Rapporteur on the Rights of Indigenous Peoples in 2014, has also expressed her support for the draft and has indicated her hopes that the Nordic states will take advantage of the opportunity to adopt this instrument "to promote

4 During the drafting process, it was decided not to include the Russian Federation in the negotiations, essentially because the political situation in the three Nordic countries was simply too different. However, it was also said that negotiation should begin with the Russians as soon as the Draft Nordic Sámi Convention would enter into force in order to see how the spirit of the Convention may become a reality for the Sámi living on the Russian side of the border. Åhrén, Henriksen and Scheinin (n 1) 13.

5 "The Expert Committee convened altogether 15 times from the start of its work in January 2003 till the submission of the Report with a Draft text for a Nordic Saami Convention on 27 October 2005". Koivurova, 'The Draft Nordic Saami Convention' (n 3) 283.

6 Annika Tahvanainen was appointed to study the issue; for a copy of her work in Finnish, see Annex 1 of the 'Report on the Draft Nordic Sámi Convention', 90–96. In addition, Henriksen, Scheinin and Åhrén, members of the expert committee, have drafted a memo on self-determination. For a copy of their memo on this issue, see Åhrén, Henriksen and Scheinin (n 1) 52–96.

7 "The Ministry of Justice, the responsible ministry of Saami affairs in Finland, (together with the Finnish Saami Parliament), requested comments from altogether 88 authorities, bodies and associations to the draft Nordic Saami Convention on 2 March 2006". Koivurova, 'The Draft Nordic Saami Convention' (n 3) 292.

8 HRC, 'Report of the Special Rapporteur on the situation of human rights and fundamental freedoms of indigenous people' UN Doc A/HRC/18/35/Add 2, 2011, para 13.

respect for their obligations to indigenous people based on their human rights obligations, including the International Covenant on Civil and Political Rights and the International Convention on the Elimination of All Forms of Racial Discrimination".[9] Thus, despite some political controversy in the Nordic countries, UN human rights bodies generally support the adoption of the Nordic Sámi Convention.

Subsequently, an agreement to set negotiations for the adoption of the Convention was finally achieved in November 2010. In 2011, the negotiations resumed and fifteen meetings were organised between 2011 and 2016 to finalise the content of the instrument.[10] On 21–22 November 2016, the last negotiation meeting occurred in Rovaniemi with the aim of finalising the adoption of the Convention by 2017. At this stage, the delegation, which was composed of two representatives for each of the Sámi parliaments and two representatives for each Nordic government, tabled its final proposal for consideration by the respective Nordic ministries and Sámi parliaments.[11] At the time of this writing, the final proposal had still not been publicly released, although there is significant hope that the final convention could be adopted in 2017 to coincide with the 100-year anniversary celebrations of Sámi transnational cooperation taking place in Trondheim in February 2017.[12]

2. The right of the Sámi people to self-determination

Pending the possible adoption of the Convention, it is important to explain the relevance of the 2005 Draft Nordic Sámi Convention for the rights of the Sámi people, in particular the right to self-determination.

At the outset of the drafting process, the recognition of the right of Sámi to self-determination emerged as one of the most important issues to be included in the Draft Nordic Sámi Convention. Since the first meeting of the expert committee, it was made clear by the Sámi delegates that the right of Sámi to self-determination should be recognised in the Convention and that no instrument could be adopted without its recognition.[13] While the first year of meetings devoted a considerable time to discuss the issue, it was also noted that the representatives of the Nordic states were never really opposed to the

9 HRC, 'Report of the Special Rapporteur on the rights of indigenous peoples on the human rights situation of the Sámi people in the Sápmi region of Norway, Sweden and Finland' UN Doc A/HRC/33/42/Add.3, 2016, para 13.

10 Sweden 2011: Stockholm, Kiruna, Stockholm; Finland 2012: Helsinki, Inari, Helsinki; Norway 2013: Oslo, Guovdageaidnu/Kautokeino; Norway 2014: Oslo; Sweden 2015: Stockholm, Sigtuna; Finland 2016: Stockholm, Helsinki, Kirkonummi, Rovaniemi (Rovaniemi was the 15th meeting).

11 Johanna Suurpää, chair of the delegation of the drafting process of the Nordic Sámi Convention, Interview 22 November 2016, Rovaniemi.

12 The new proposed Nordic Sámi Convention was planned to be publicly released in January 2017.

13 Åhrén in Åhrén, Henriksen and Scheinin (n 1) 15.

recognition of the right.[14] Pursuant to the discussions that took place during this period, it was consequently agreed that the Convention should proclaim the right of the Sámi people to self-determination. Hence, article 3 of the Draft Nordic Sámi Convention was crafted and adopted by the equal number of representatives from the three Sámi parliaments and the three Nordic states. This article, entitled "The right of self-determination", articulates the right in the following way:

> As a people, the Sámi has the right of self-determination in accordance with the rules and provisions of international law and of this Convention. In so far as it follows from these rules and provisions, the Sámi People has the right to determine its own economic, social and cultural development and to dispose, to its own benefit, of its own natural resources.[15]

However, notwithstanding the unanimous support for the collective right of Sámi to self-determination,[16] it is still contested what the right entails in concrete terms.[17] The wording of article 3 of the draft convention is modelled after article 1 of the International Covenant on Civil and Political Rights (ICCPR) and the International Covenant on Economic, Social and Cultural Rights (ICESCR), which states the right of all peoples to self-determination, pursuant to which they freely determine their political status, freely pursue their economic, social and cultural development and may, for their own ends, freely dispose of their natural wealth and resources.[18] However, whether the right of Sámi to self-determination equates to that of other 'peoples' under international law remains a controversial issue. On the one hand, it is argued that indigenous peoples have the same rights as other peoples. In support of this argument, Mathias Åhrén, an appointee to the expert committee on the drafting process of the Convention, has emphasised

14 According to Åhrén, "the discussions on the issue of self-determination were never really heated. Without considerable debate, a consensus emerged within the Expert Group that it is evident that the Saami people indeed constitutes such a people that is entitled to the right to self-determination" in ibid.

15 Article 3 of the Draft Nordic Sámi Convention; unofficial translation produced in Åhrén, Henriksen and Scheinin (n 1).

16 Although the Draft Nordic Sámi Convention was adopted consensually, the government of Finland had nevertheless submitted a cover letter highlighting some difficulties with the text, among which the recognition of the right of Sámi to self-determination in article 3 of the Draft. Åhrén, Henriksen and Scheinin (n 1) 11.

17 In her report, Tahvanainen supports the view that indigenous peoples do not have the full right to self-determination. This interpretation conflicts with the position of some of the members of the expert committee, who argue that indigenous peoples have the same right to self-determination as other peoples. Annex 1 of the 'Report on the Draft Nordic Sámi Convention', 90–96. See also T Koivurova, 'From High Hopes to Disillusionment: Indigenous Peoples' Struggle to (re)Gain Their Right to Self-Determination' (2008) *International Journal on Minority and Group Rights* 1, 15, Åhrén, Henriksen and Scheinin (n 1) 54.

18 Åhrén, Henriksen and Scheinin (n 1) 67.

that the Sámi as a *people* are entitled to the general right to self-determination.[19] On the other hand, this statement contrasts with the position of the government of Finland, which has indicated that the Sámi, in spite of their status as an indigenous people,[20] are not a *people* entitled to claim the full benefit of the right to self-determination as proclaimed under the ICCPR and the ICESCR.[21] Finland bases its understanding of the concept of self-determination on the old, classic understanding, according to which the right to self-determination under the human rights covenants "is closely associated with the independence of colonies and the emergence of new national states, and thus does not apply to the Sámi".[22]

As it has been noted elsewhere, the view of the government of Finland is surprisingly traditional and does not in fact reflect adequately current developments of international law.[23] To begin with, the view that indigenous peoples are not entitled to claim the same right of self-determination as other peoples is highly questionable given the adoption of the United Nations Declaration on the Rights of Indigenous Peoples (UNDRIP). The UNDRIP, which was adopted by a majority of 144 states in favour, 4 votes against and 11 abstentions in 2007, recognises that indigenous peoples have the right to self-determination based on the same wording as article 1 of the human rights covenants. This can therefore be interpreted as conferring the same right to self-determination for indigenous peoples as other peoples, in the meaning of article of the ICCPR.[24] Furthermore, the argument claiming that the right of self-determination as proclaimed under the human rights covenants does not apply to indigenous peoples, or the Sámi, does not concur with the position of the Human Rights Committee (HRC), which

19 ibid. 15.

20 In 1995, the Constitution of Finland was amended to guarantee better protection for the rights of the Sámi. The new provisions recognise the status of the Sámi as an indigenous people and their right to maintain and develop their own language and culture. In addition, they acknowledge the Sámi cultural autonomy within the Sámi homeland. Sections 17 and 121 of the Constitution Act of Finland.

21 In her report, Tahvanainen supports the view that indigenous peoples do not have the full right to self-determination. Annex 1 of the 'Report on the Draft Nordic Sámi Convention', 90–96. See also Koivurova, 'From High Hopes to Disillusionment' (n 17) 15. An analysis of the position of Finland is also provided in L Heinämäki, 'The Nordic Saami Convention: The Right of a People to Control Issues of Importance to Them' in T Koivurova and N Bankes, *The Proposed Nordic Saami Convention: National and International Dimensions of Indigenous Property Rights* (Hart Publishing 2013) 130–131.

22 Heinämäki (n 21) 131.

23 On the contemporary interpretation of self-determination, see generally D Cambou, *The Legal Significance of the Right of Indigenous Peoples to Self-Determination and Its Implication for the Sámi People* (Vrije Univeristeit Brussel 2016). See also MC van Walt van Praag and O Seroo (eds), Report of the International Conference of Experts Held in Barcelona from 21 to 27 November 1998 'The Implementation of the Right to Self-Determination as a Contribution to Conflict Prevention' (UNESCO Division of Human Rights Democracy and Peace & Centre UNESCO de Catalunya 1999) 13.

24 The fact that all peoples have the right to self-determination does not mean that all of them will benefit from the same remedy. While indigenous peoples have the right to autonomy and participation in decision-making processes affecting them, colonised peoples have the right to independence. See J Anaya, 'Self-Determination as a Collective Human Right under Contemporary International Law', *Operationalizing the Right of Indigenous Peoples to Self-Determination* (Pekka Aikio and Martin Scheinin, Institute for Human Rights, Åbo Akademi University 2000).

has already applied the right to self-determination as expressed under article 1 of the ICCPR to indigenous peoples several times.[25] In the same respect, other human rights treaties bodies have also accepted the view considering the Sámi as a people with the right to self-determination.[26] Finally, the refusal to admit that indigenous peoples have the same right to self-determination as other peoples runs against the philosophy of international human rights law that seeks to ensure equality between all peoples. Today, indigenous peoples still suffer from the consequences of the vast human rights violations that have occurred historically and are facing new challenges which need to be urgently addressed. In this regard, self-determination constitutes a tool to ensure that the human rights of indigenous peoples are equally protected under domestic law, and it is this rationale that justifies the adoption of the Draft Nordic Sámi Convention.

Yet, to argue that indigenous peoples have the same right to self-determination as other peoples does not necessarily mean that they have a right to independent statehood. It also does not necessarily mean that they can resort to the same remedies as other peoples. The right to self-determination provides diverse remedies for different types of claims.[27] Whereas self-determination provides independence for colonised peoples, it provides democratic governance for the entire people of the state.[28] In relation to indigenous peoples, the right to self-determination is based on a relational conception of self-determination.[29] As specified under article 4 of the UNDRIP, in exercising their right to self-determination,

25 See in particular, HRC, 'Concluding Observations on Mexico' (1999) UN Doc CCPR/C/79/Add109; 'Concluding Observations on Norway' (1999) UN Doc CCPR/c/79/Add112; 'Concluding Observations on Australia' (2000) UN Doc CCPR/co/69/AUS; 'Concluding Observations on Sweden' (2002) UN Doc CCPR/CO/74/SWE.

26 For instance, the CERD commented the following in its conclusions on the state report of Finland in 2012: "While noting that the Supreme Administrative Court relied on the Committee's prior concluding observations in its decision of 26 September 2011 defining who is a 'Sámi' entitled to vote for Members of the Sámi Parliament, the Committee is concerned that the definition adopted by the Court gives insufficient weight to the Sámi people's rights, recognized in the United Nations Declaration on the Rights of Indigenous Peoples, to self-determination (art. 3), in particular their right to determine their own identity or membership in accordance with their customs and traditions (art 33), as well as their right not to be subjected to forced assimilation or destruction of their culture (art 8) (art 5 of the Convention). The Committee recommends that, in defining who is eligible to vote for Members of the Sámi Parliament, the State party accord due weight to the rights of the Sámi people to self-determination concerning their status within Finland, to determine their own membership, and not to be subjected to forced assimilation". 'Concluding Observations on Finland' (2012) CERD/C/FIN/CO/20-22 (CERD).

27 Anaya (n 24).

28 See generally Cambou, 'The Legal Significance' (n 23).

29 B Kingsbury, 'Reconstructing Self-Determination: A Relational Approach' in P Aiko and M Scheinin, *Operationalizing the Right of Indigenous Peoples to Self-Determination* (Abo Academy Press 2000) 19–38. Else Grete, in her analysis of the implementation of Sámi right to self-determination in Norway, has also endorsed the relational understanding of self-determination. EG Broderstad, 'Implementing Indigenous Self-Determination: The Case of the Sámi in Norway' (2014) E-International Relations <www.e-ir.info/2014/05/30/implementing-indigenous-self-determination-the-case-of-the-Sámi-in-norway/> accessed on 13 November 2016.

indigenous peoples have the right to autonomy or self-government in matters relating to internal and local affairs. In addition, article 5 of the UNDRIP stipulates that indigenous peoples also have the right "to maintain and strengthen their distinct political, legal, economic, social and cultural institutions, while retaining their right to participate fully, if they so choose, in the political, economic, social and cultural life of the State". Read together with articles 3 and 4 of the UNDRIP, this provision features a relational understanding of self-determination which relies upon the principle of equality between peoples. Similarly, Erica Daes, the former Chair of the Working Group on Indigenous Populations, indicated during the drafting process of the UNDRIP that

> the right of self-determination should ordinarily be interpreted as the right of these peoples to negotiate freely their political status and representation in the States in which they live. This process might best be described as a kind of belated State-building, through which indigenous peoples are able to join with all the other peoples that make up the State on mutually-agreed upon and just terms, after many years of isolation and exclusion. This process does not require the assimilation of individuals, as citizens like all others, but the recognition and incorporation of distinct peoples in the fabric of the State, on agreed terms.[30]

In accordance with this understanding, self-determination is conceived as a tool to reshape a new relationship between states and indigenous peoples in a spirit of partnership and mutual respect.[31] It is as an on-going process, which ensures the continuance of indigenous peoples' participation in decision-making and control over their own destinies.[32] In effect, the exercise of self-determination is focused on both indigenous "autonomous governance and participatory engagement" in the decision-making processes that affect them.[33] This conception of self-determination lies in the human rights understanding of the term, which defines self-determination as an on-going process of choice for the achievement of human security and fulfilment of human needs.[34]

In addition, indigenous peoples also have the right to control their traditional land and natural resources, which serves as the basis for their livelihoods. This constitutes the resource or economic dimension of their right to self-determination.

30 E Daes, 'Some Considerations on the Right of Indigenous Peoples to Self-Determination' (1993) 3 *Transnational Law & Contemporary Problems* 1, 9.

31 Preamble of the UNDRIP.

32 UN Expert Mechanism on the Rights of Indigenous Peoples, 'Progress Report on the Study on Indigenous Peoples and the Right to Participate in Decision-Making' UN Doc A/HRC/EMRIP/2010/2 para 31.

33 J Anaya, 'The Right of Indigenous Peoples to Self-Determination in the Post-Declaration Era' in C Charters and R Stavenhagen (eds), *Making Declaration Work: The United Nations Declaration on the Rights of Indigenous Peoples* (IWGA 2009) 193.

34 This is also the conception of self-determination that was highlighted in van Walt van Praag and Seroo (n 23).

Under the UNDRIP, several provisions consecrate the rights of indigenous peoples to land and natural resources, and the UN human rights treaty bodies have also increasingly emphasised those rights in their commentaries, decisions and conclusions on state reports.[35] Similarly, the draft convention recognises in its article 3 that the Sámi people have the right to dispose of, to their own benefit, their own natural resources pursuant to their right to self-determination. As discussed in the next section, the content of the right is also detailed in other parts of the convention.

Finally, even though the emphasis of the right of indigenous self-determination is on its internal aspects, human rights law does not confine the exercise of the right solely within state borders.[36] As mentioned in the UNDRIP, indigenous peoples, in particular those divided by international borders, have the right to maintain and develop contacts, relations and cooperation with their own members as well as other peoples across borders.[37] It is also stated under article 41 of the UNDRIP that the ways and means of ensuring the participation of indigenous peoples on issues affecting them shall be established at the international level. In effect, this means that indigenous peoples could claim either autonomous representation at the international level or special representation through their national delegation in decision-making processes affecting them beyond the domestic realm. These specific provisions can be characterised as external aspects of the right to self-determination to which indigenous peoples are also entitled. In this regard, indigenous peoples have the right to a political status at the international level, which does not incur the recognition of their status as a state.

Even if indigenous peoples' right to self-determination does not entail the right to secession, it has been argued elsewhere that in a domestic situation where the state would fail to uphold their right to self-determination and violate egregiously their human rights, the concerned people may be entitled to secede from its state as a last resort.[38] However, this interpretation is not formally recognised under international law,[39] and falls outside the framework of the rights of indigenous peoples as enshrined under the UNDRIP. Thus, as a general norm,

35 See in particular articles 26–32 of the UNDRIP.

36 According to the UNESCO report on the right to self-determination, the view according to which self-determination can be exercised externally only through secession or the creation of another state is based on the territorial conception of self-determination. This conception is, however, too narrow. There are other external aspects to the right to self-determination which are of considerable relevance for the exercise of the right but which do not entail the questioning of the territorial integrity of the states; van Praag and Seroo (n 23).

37 Article 36 of the UNDRIP.

38 Certain scholars have advocated for the theory of remedial secession; see, for instance, LC Buchheit, *Secession: The Legitimacy of Self-Determination* (2nd edn, Yale University Press 1978). However, we are far from arguing that this is the situation in the Nordic countries.

39 Outside the decolonisation context, whether the international law of self-determination confers upon part of the population of an existing state a right to separate from that state remains a controversial subject which does not allow the recognition of any right to remedial secession. See the ICJ *Kosovo Case,* Accordance with International Law of the Unilateral Declaration of Independence in Respect of Kosovo, Advisory Opinion, ICJ Reports 2010, para 82.

indigenous peoples, as other peoples, do not have the right to secession and must exercise their right to self-determination in a manner that is respectful of "the territorial integrity or political unity of sovereign and independent States", as enshrined under article 46 of the UNDRIP.[40] The right to self-determination must be operationalised on the basis of mutual respect and with a view to reinstituting equality between indigenous peoples and the rest of the population of the state. This is the philosophy underpinning the right to self-determination in the UNDRIP, and the Draft Nordic Sámi Convention must likewise be interpreted in accordance with these conceptions.

3. The implementation model of the right of Sámi to self-determination

The relevance of the Draft Nordic Sámi Convention lies in its recognition and description of the right of the Sámi people to self-determination. Although the Nordic governments have recognised the right of the Sámi people to self-determination by voting in favour of the UNDRIP in 2007, the Declaration does not specify how the right to self-determination can be implemented in the Nordic context. It also falls short from internalising the recognition of the right of the Sámi people to self-determination under domestic law. In this regard, the adoption of the Nordic Sámi Convention is important because it could supplement the UNDRIP and formalise a more specific recognition of the right of the Sámi people at the domestic level.

As embodied in the Draft Nordic Sámi Convention, the right of the Sámi to self-determination is based on the idea that the Sámi are an indivisible people who live in three Nordic states (and Russia).[41] In that regard, the draft convention aims to regulate the legal relations between four peoples, namely, the Norwegian, Swedish, Finnish and Sámi peoples. Thus, the document contrasts with the orthodox understanding of the nation state, which includes only one national population. It also diverts from previous interpretations of self-determination, which confine the right to its internal dimension: the application of the right at the domestic level through the right of individual citizens to choose their own government. By contrast, the draft convention seeks to establish a legal framework that could enable the Sámi people "to secure and develop its language, its culture, its livelihoods and society, with the smallest possible interference of the national borders", or in other words, to exercise its right to self-determination transnationally.[42] In addition, the Draft Nordic Sámi Convention also recognises that the Sámi have the right to determine their collective economic, social and cultural development and to dispose, to their own benefit, of their own natural

40 Article 46 of the UNDRIP.

41 The Russian Federation and the Sámi living on the Russian side are not party to the Convention. However, once the Convention is adopted, it is hoped that negotiations could begin for applying the Convention in Russia.

42 Article 1 of the Draft Nordic Sámi Convention.

resources, which corresponds to the resource dimension of the right of the Sámi people to self-determination. With this in mind, the implementation of the right of the Sámi people to self-determination therefore includes a political dimension, a resource dimension and a transnational dimension. Each dimension will be further examined in the following sections.

3.1. The political dimension of the right to self-determination

In order to understand what the right to self-determination implies under the Draft Nordic Sámi Convention, it is important to interpret this instrument in a holistic manner. As explained by Carsten Smith, chairperson of the expert committee, "the specific content of this right to self-determination will to a large extent be determined through other articles (other than article 3 of the draft convention) in the Nordic Sámi Convention, in particular those articles that apply to the relationship between the Sámi parliaments and the other authorities in the countries".[43] From this perspective, Chapter 2 of the draft convention (articles 14–22) is of particular relevance for the implementation of the right of the Sámi to self-determination because it focuses on Sámi governance. As a starting point, article 14 of the draft convention stipulates that the Sámi parliaments "shall have such a mandate that enables them to contribute effectively to the realisation of the Sámi People's right of self-determination pursuant to the rules and provisions of international law and of this Convention".[44] As such, the Sámi parliaments are considered as the self-governing entities through which the Sámi can exercise their collective right to self-determination.[45]

Then, articles 15 to 18 elaborate on the ways to exercise Sámi self-determination through what has been labelled a "sliding scale model of self-determination".[46] According to this model, the degree of self-determination and authority of the Sámi institutions varies in function, depending on the importance matters to the Sámi people. This means that the more significant an issue is to the Sámi people, the more influence the Sámi parliaments have over the matter.[47] For some matters, the Sámi parliaments shall have complete independence in the decision-making process, which would be complete authority over the issue, whereas for other matters, the draft convention provides rights to negotiation, consultation or participation, which would be exercised in relation to the rest of the population.

43 Carsten Smith, *Log og Rett* No 06/2006, 328.

44 Article 14 of the Draft Nordic Sámi Convention.

45 In spite of their leading role, it must be noted that the Sámi parliaments are not the only institutions through which self-determination can be operationalised. Article 21 additionally refers to other Sámi associations such as the Samebyar, siidas, the reindeer herder communities and the village assemblies of the Skolt Sámi as legitimate representatives of the Sámi people. Sámi. See article 21 of the draft.

46 JB Henriksen, *Sámi Self-Determination Land, Resources and Traditional Livelihoods Self-Determination and the Media* (Gáldu 2011) 50.

47 ibid.

Based on this division, the right of the Sámi to autonomy that corresponds to autonomous decision-making must primarily be defined. Under the Draft Nordic Sámi Convention, article 15 gives the Sámi parliaments independent authority on all matters for which they are responsible under national or international law.[48] However, there is a current discrepancy between what the Nordic states provide at the domestic level and what is required by international law. Today, the Sámi parliaments are granted various forms of decision-making power under national law, ranging from cultural autonomy in Finland to mere administrative authority in Sweden.[49] This is, however, considered insufficient to fulfil the requirements of international law, and more particularly article 4 of the UNDRIP, providing the rights of indigenous peoples to autonomy and self-government in matters relating to their internal and local affairs. While international law does not specifically define what local and internal affairs include,[50] there is little doubt that mere administrative authority does not meet the requirement of self-government and autonomy as provided under the UNDRIP.[51] In this regard, it is clear that the adoption of the Draft Nordic Sámi Convention would necessarily entail a revision of the mandate of the Sámi parliaments in each of the Nordic states to satisfy the right of autonomy and self-governance as currently recognised under international human rights law.

Beyond the scope of their right to autonomy, the right of the Sámi people to self-determination also entails the right to be included in external decision-making processes affecting them. In accordance with the Draft Nordic Sámi Convention, this aspect of self-determination ranges from the right to negotiation, which concerns matters of major importance to the Sámi (article 16) to the right of representation, which relates to other matters (article 17). More precisely, in matters where the Sámi parliaments do not hold independent decision-making power, but which are of 'major importance' to them, it is indicated under article 16 of the draft convention that

> negotiations shall be held with the Sámi parliaments before decisions on such matters are made by a public authority. These negotiations must take place early enough to sufficiently enable the Sámi parliaments to have a meaningful influence over the proceedings and outcomes.[52]

48 Article 15 of the Draft Nordic Sámi Convention.

49 For a recent analysis of the differences between the three Nordic Sámi parliaments concerning their respective status and mandates, see Mörkenstam, Josefsen and Nilsson (n 2).

50 In comparison, in the Declaration on the Rights of Indigenous Peoples, the scope of local and internal affairs was defined and included "culture, religion, education, information, media, health, housing, employment, social welfare, economic activities, land and resources management, environment and entry by non-members, as well as ways and means for financing these autonomous functions". Article 31 of the Declaration on the Rights of Indigenous Peoples.

51 Furthermore, it is also acknowledged that the differences between the three Sámi parliaments currently limit the possibility to speak about a unified model of Sámi self-determination. Mörkenstam, Josefsen and Nilsson (n 2) 6.

52 Article 16 of the Draft Nordic Sámi Convention.

In effect, article 16 of the Draft Nordic Sámi Convention reflects the logic and spirit of article 19 of the UNDRIP, which indicates that states shall consult and cooperate in good faith with the indigenous peoples concerned through their own representative institutions in order to obtain their free, prior and informed consent (FPIC) before adopting and implementing decisions that may affect them. In addition, the draft provision also stresses indirect emphasis on the principle of FPIC, as the provision prescribes that the states shall not adopt or permit measures that may significantly damage the basic conditions for Sámi culture, Sámi livelihoods or society unless consented to by the Sámi parliament concerned.[53] This also means that in certain cases, the Sámi parliament would have a limited right to veto certain decisions, more particularly those which could have a damaging impact on vulnerable Sámi areas.[54] The present provision is in line with the recent development of international law on the rights of indigenous peoples, which recognises the qualified right of indigenous peoples to veto certain projects when they have a significant impact on their traditional livelihoods.[55] This interpretation stems more specifically from the evolving interpretation of the principle of FPIC, which constitutes a cornerstone of the right to self-determination and is increasingly emphasised under international and regional human rights law.[56]

On other matters, article 17 of the Draft Nordic Sámi Convention stipulates that the Sámi have a right to representation, and that those matters shall be submitted to the Sámi parliaments before a public authority makes a decision.[57] While article 17 stipulates that the Sámi parliaments shall have the right to be represented on public councils and committees at the national level, it is also noteworthy that article 19 expands the right to intergovernmental matters. As a result, the right of the Sámi to participate in decision-making that concerns them is not limited to domestic matters. It also includes the right of the Sámi parliaments to represent the Sámi people in international affairs.[58] This is an aspect of the right

53 This provision can be interpreted as a reminder of the right of indigenous peoples to consultation based on the principle of free, prior and informed consent (FPIC) as recognised in several provisions of the UNDRIP.

54 See the 'Report on the Draft Nordic Sámi Convention', 179–185. See also Koivurova, 'The Draft for Nordic Saami Convention' (n 1) 120.

55 The topic of the right of indigenous peoples at the international level remains ambiguous. At the UN level, there is currently an on-going work concerning the way to promote the representation of indigenous peoples in UN bodies. See in particular, Human Rights Council, 'Ways and Means of Promoting Participation at the United Nations of Indigenous Peoples' Representatives on Issues Affecting Them', UN Doc A/HRC/21/24 (2012). More generally, see also D Cambou, 'Enhancing the Participation of Indigenous Peoples at the Intergovernmental Level to Strengthen Self-Determination: Lessons from the Arctic' *Nordic Journal of International Law* (forthcoming 2018).

56 See the following section on the resource dimension of the right to self-determination.

57 Article 17 of the Draft Nordic Sámi Convention.

58 However, it is not completely clear in the draft convention whether the Sámi parliaments shall have any sort of autonomous competences at the international level or whether they should only be allowed to participate as a member of the delegation representing the interests of the Nordic state at the international level.

of indigenous peoples that is not completely exemplified in the UNDRIP, but that does exist to a certain extent under article 41 of the Declaration recognising that the ways and means of ensuring the participation of indigenous peoples on issues affecting them shall be established at the international level. Today there is also increasing attention given to the representation of indigenous peoples at the international level, which has led the UN to investigate how to promote the participation of indigenous peoples' representatives at the UN on issues affecting them.[59] However, the specific representation of indigenous peoples at the international level remains a topic of controversy under international law insofar as it is not clear how to accommodate their specific status.[60] This is also an aspect of the rights of the Sámi people that is not completely clarified.

In sum, the draft convention seeks to guarantee the inclusion of the Sámi parliaments at all levels of the decision-making process that concern matters affecting the Sámi society, ranging from a right to autonomy and participation at the domestic level to a right to participation and representation at the international level. While all provisions do not specifically follow the letter of international legal instruments concerning the rights of indigenous peoples, the draft convention constitutes an adequate model to implement self-determination in the Nordic context.

3.2. The resource dimension of the right to self-determination

Another important aspect of the right of the Sámi people to self-determination concerns the right to freely dispose of the land and natural resources, which constitutes the resource dimension of the right. The resource dimension is further explained in Chapter IV of the draft convention (articles 34–40). In practice, the draft convention recognises in article 34 the right of the Sámi to occupy and use the traditional land or water areas that they have occupied or used before. In cases where those areas are used by the Sámi in association with other users, the draft indicates that "the exercise of their rights by the Sámi and the other users shall be subject to due regard for each other and for the nature of the competing rights". This chapter draws generally from the corresponding articles in the ILO Convention 169 and specifies the provisions in relation to the situation of the Sámi people.[61] It is also reflective of articles 26 to 32 of the UNDRIP. However, because of the difficulty and limited time in obtaining a compromise on the definition of the rights of the Sámi people to land and natural resources, it must be noted that the Convention does not clarify all issues. In particular, the draft convention does not provide any specification about the right of the Sámi people

59 Human Rights Council, 'Ways and Means of Promoting Participation at the United Nations of Indigenous Peoples' Representatives on Issues Affecting Them', UN Doc A/HRC/21/24 (2012).

60 See Cambou, 'Lessons from the Arctic Peoples' (n 55).

61 Åhrén, Henriksen and Scheinin (n 3) 27–28.

to territories that they have lost and the right to non-traditional resources. Those issues are left open for future discussions.

On a related note, the right of the Sámi people to their currently owned, occupied or used land and natural resources, article 35 recognises the duty of the state to identify the land and water areas that the Sámi have traditionally used. In practice, this means that the governments should establish procedures to investigate and clarify the right of the Sámi to land and natural resources at the local level in order to secure their property rights.[62] The provision is in compliance with article 14 of ILO Convention 169 and article 26 of the UNDRIP which recognise the duty of the state to establish adequate procedures within the national legal system to adjudicate the rights of indigenous peoples pertaining to their lands, territories and resources. If implemented, the latter provision could have important repercussions for the Sámi people, as it would allow the clarification of their rights to land and resources that are often not sufficiently protected under domestic law. Ultimately, such a clarification process would ensure the formal recognition of the Sámi rights to land and natural resources, the content of those rights, their scope of application and possibly provide the right of the Sámi communities to manage their traditional land and natural resource and eventually ensure protection from outside or unwanted intrusion.

Additionally of interest for the resource dimension of the right of the Sámi people to self-determination is article 36, which provides an obligation to secure the right of the Sámi to natural resources in the context of development projects taking place within their traditional land or water areas. More specifically, the provision states that

> before public authorities, based on law, grant a permit for prospecting or extraction of minerals or other sub-surface resources, (. . .), negotiations shall be held with the affected Sámi, as well as with the Sámi parliaments, when the matter is such that it falls within article 16.

The provision is also applicable to development projects such as forest logging, hydroelectric and wind power plants, construction of roads and recreational housing and military exercise activities. In effect, the latter provision to some extent reflects article 15 of ILO Convention 169 which indicates that governments shall establish or maintain procedures to consult with indigenous peoples, under the intention to ascertain whether and to what degree their interests would be prejudiced, before undertaking or permitting any programmes for the exploration or exploitation of resources pertaining to their lands. It is also in accordance with article 32 of the UNDRIP which acknowledges the obligation of states to

62 See, for instance, the example of the Finnmark Act adopted by the Government of Norway, which establishes a procedure through which the land rights of the Sámi who live in the Finnmark region are to be investigated and clarified. Finnmark Act, Act No 85 of 17 June 2005 relating to Legal Relations and Management of Land and Natural Resources in the County of Finnmark (2005).

> consult and cooperate in good faith with the indigenous peoples concerned (. . .) in order to obtain their free and informed consent prior to the approval of any project affecting their lands or territories and other resources, particularly in connection with the development, utilization or exploitation of mineral, water or other resources.

While article 36 of the draft convention does not make specific mention of the principle of FPIC, the draft provision is largely inspired from it. The draft convention notes more specifically that the state should not give permits for prospecting natural resources "if the activity makes it impossible or substantially more difficult for the Sámi to continue to utilise the areas concerned, and this utilisation is essential to the Sámi culture, unless so consented by the Sámi parliaments and the affected Sámi".[63] Thus, the latter provision suggests the recognition of the right of the Sámi parliaments to object to activities when those activities make it impossible or substantially more difficult for the Sámi to continue their traditional livelihoods. Although it is not completely clear how to define the right of the Sámi to object,[64] the spirit of this provision is consistent with international law and more precisely with article 32 of the UNDRIP insofar as it provides the Sámi with a qualified right to veto governmental decisions.[65] Under the UNDRIP, FPIC does not provide a unilateral veto right, and this interpretation stems from the drafting process of the Declaration.[66] Instead, the requirement of FPIC entitles indigenous people to effectively determine the outcome of decision-making that affects them, not merely a right to be involved.[67]

In certain circumstances, there is also a duty to obtain the consent of the indigenous peoples concerned, beyond the general obligation to have consent as the objective of consultations.[68] Both the HRC and the International American Court of Human Rights (IACtHR) have endorsed this position and emphasise that consultation is not sufficient in cases of large-scale development projects, and instead that FPIC is required.[69] In addition, the IACtHR stipulates that the state

63 Article 16 of the Draft Nordic Sámi Convention.

64 In particular, it is not clear what activities can be considered "impossible or substantially more difficult for the Sámi to continue their traditional livelihoods".

65 Article 32 of the UNDRIP states that "States shall consult and cooperate in good faith with the indigenous peoples concerned through their own representative institutions in order to obtain their free and informed consent prior to the approval of any project affecting their lands or territories and other resources, particularly in connection with the development, utilisation or exploitation of mineral, water or other resources".

66 Originally, article 32 explicitly recognised the right of veto of indigenous peoples. However, as a result of the contestation of numerous states, this interpretation was not retained in the final provision.

67 UN Human Rights Office of the High Commissioner, *Free Prior and Informed Consent*, 2016 <www.ohchr.org/Documents/Issues/IPeoples/FreePriorandInformedConsent.pdf> accessed on 8 January 2017.

68 ibid.

69 D Inman, S Smis and D Cambou, 'Evolving Legal Protections for Indigenous Peoples in Africa: Some Post-UNDRIP Reflections' (2017) *African Journal of International and Comparative Law.*

may be required to obtain full consent if a large-scale project affects the survival of a community.[70] In this regard, article 16 of the draft convention complies with the principle of FPIC as currently interpreted under human rights law, since it provides a limited right for the Sámi parliaments to object to activities that make it impossible or substantially more difficult for the Sámi to continue to utilise the areas concerned.

Finally, articles 39 and 40 underscore the right of the Sámi parliament to co-decisions in the public and environmental management of traditional Sámi areas. While it is not specified how such a governance model can be operated, the latter provisions seek to ensure that the Sámi parliaments are placed on an equal footing with public authorities in the governance of those issues. It is also in compliance with the rights of indigenous peoples to self-determination to the extent that the provision seeks to provide decision-making authority for the Sámi parliament in the governance of the traditional land and natural resources of the Sámi people.

Ultimately, the provisions of the draft convention on land and resources are therefore largely reflecting the developing state of international law on the rights of indigenous peoples and prove that the right to land and resources are a core component of the right of the Sámi people to self-determination.

3.3. The transnational dimension of the right to self-determination

A final interesting aspect of the Draft Nordic Sámi Convention concerns its transnational features. Since the Sámi people are living in four different states, their right to self-determination cannot be exercised within the boundaries of one state but must also include the right to maintain and develop contacts, relations and cooperation across the borders that separate them. In this regard, while the Draft Nordic Sámi Convention concerns the implementation of the right of the Sámi in each state, the draft also includes a number of provisions concerning the implementation of the rights of the Sámi at the cross-border level.

In the first chapter of the draft convention, article 11 discusses "cooperation on cultural and commercial arrangements", stipulating that "the states shall implement measures to render it easier for the Sámi to pursue economic activities across national borders and to provide for their cultural needs across these borders". The latter provision intends to ensure that the Sámi can pursue their traditional cultural and economic activities without being affected by transnational borders. In this regard, the draft convention further indicates that neither their citizenship nor their place of residence should be considered an obstacle for them to maintain and develop their livelihoods.[71] In addition, it is noteworthy that several issues that pertain to Sámi internal affairs, including media, research, cultural heritage or reindeer-herding activities are issues that need to be specifically or partly operationalised at the transnational level and which entail

70 IACtHR, *Saramaka People v Suriname*, 28 November 2007, IACtHR Series C, No 172, para 134.

71 Article 11 of the Draft Nordic Sámi Convention.

the duty of the state to implement measures for cooperation across national borders.[72] For instance, article 25 indicates that the states, in cooperation with the Sámi parliaments, have the duty to "promote cooperation across national borders between media institutions that provide programmes or articles in the Sámi language". Article 27 also indicates that "the states shall, in consultation with the Sámi parliaments, promote cooperation between Sámi and other research institutions in the various countries and across national borders". Finally, article 32 also stipulates that "the states shall implement measures for cooperation across national borders on documentation, protection and care of Sámi cultural heritage". Last but not least, article 46 recognises the right to reindeer husbandry across national borders. In effect, the provision clarifies that Sámi custom take precedent over any state treaty that has been adopted to regulate cross-border reindeer-herding activities.[73] This is of tremendous importance for the Sámi people, considering the impact that borders play in restricting Sámi reindeer-herding activities. Together, these provisions exemplify and clearly emphasise the goal of the Convention, which is to ensure that the Sámi can collectively develop as a people without interference from the borders that separate them. This objective is also in accordance with article 36 of the UNDRIP, which stipulates the duty of the states, in consultation and cooperation with indigenous peoples, to "take effective measures to facilitate the exercise and ensure the implementation of their right to maintain and develop relations across borders". The latter provision is clearly meant to recognise the right of indigenous peoples living on various sides of the border to maintain and develop relations and cooperation within their communities on the other sides of the border. It reflects the understanding that peoples divided by international borders should be entitled to exercise their right to self-determination in a way that is short of secession but which allows them to unite politically, cultural or economically, by way of cooperation.[74]

Ultimately, it is also salient to indicate that the Draft Nordic Sámi Convention recognises the right of the Sámi parliaments to create joint organisations, and that the states shall strive to transfer public authority to such organisations as needed. In this regard, the Draft Nordic Sámi Convention clearly envisions the possibility for the Sámi parliaments to exercise certain aspects of their right to

72 Articles 25, 27, 32 and 43 of the Draft Nordic Sámi Convention.

73 For more details about the significance of this provision, see Åhrén, Henriksen and Scheinin (n 2) 20–23.

74 By contrast, T Koivurova indicates that "[t]he UN Declaration does not attempt to bridge the gap between these segments of people divided by State borders to encourage them to unite; there is only the encouragement to develop contact between separate indigenous communities. This contrasts with the attempts made by the Saami Nordic states to build a more ambitious approach based on the whole people's self-determination". T Koivurova, 'Can Saami Transnational Indigenous Peoples Exercise Their Self-Determination in a World of Sovereign States?' in T Koivurova and N Bankes, *The Proposed Nordic Saami Convention : National and International Dimensions of Indigenous Property Rights* (Hart Publishing 2013) 119. However, it is the view of the present author that the institutionalisation of cooperation can be an instrument to strengthen the right of the Sámi people to self-determination.

self-determination transnationally, eventually leading towards the institutionalisation of a common Sámi parliament that would operate across the borders of the three states.[75] In this respect, it can be concluded that the Draft Nordic Sámi Convention discloses a vision of the right of the Sámi to self-determination that transcends state borders and exemplifies a model of self-determination that "represents the possibility to grow beyond the state-centred paradigm".[76]

4. Conclusion

As the Nordic states recognise in the preamble of the draft convention, "during the course of history the Sámi have not been treated as a people of equal value, and have thus been subjected to injustice". In this regard, the purpose of the draft convention is both to ensure equal respect for the rights of the Sámi and to secure its future as a people through the right to self-determination. Against this background, the main object of this analysis was to explain the relevance of this draft instrument for the Sámi people from the viewpoint of international human rights law. In addition, this analysis also explained how the draft convention intends to implement the right of the Sámi people to self-determination. As it has been noted previously, the model of self-determination enshrined in the draft is quite challenging. However, it is also realistic in the sense that it departs from the orthodox understanding prefiguring the existence of states with one single national people, and also because it underlines the possibility of exercising self-determination transnationally, without impairing the territorial integrity of sovereign states.

Thus, the draft convention represents a new framework for guaranteeing the rights of the Sámi people and for the development of new relationships between the Nordic peoples and the Sámi indigenous people. In this regard, the novelty of the Draft Nordic Sámi Convention lies in the opportunity it has created to fashion a framework capable of internalising the rights of the Sámi people at the domestic level. In addition, the draft document also represents an opportunity to set an example of good practices at the international level. While the situation of the Sámi people is certainly privileged vis-à-vis other indigenous peoples in the world, the adoption of the Convention could create an incentive for other groups of peoples to negotiate with their states on the formulation of a new framework to protect their rights. The recognition of the right of the Sámi people to self-determination in a binding treaty would also demonstrate that the recognition and implementation of the right of indigenous peoples to self-determination does not necessarily threaten state territorial integrity, a position that is still feared by many governments.

Yet, more than a decade after the adoption of the draft, the process has not come to completion. The value of the Convention for the advancement of the

75 Although this is not clearly stated in the Draft Nordic Sámi Convention, the implementation of the draft could in time lead to such a possibility.

76 T Koivurova, 'The Draft Nordic Saami Convention: Nations Working Together' (2008) 10 *International Community Law Review* 279, 293.

right of the Sámi to self-determination as well as for the fulfilment of the Nordic states' obligations under international human rights law thus remains untested. For the moment, the influence of the draft remains largely political with no obvious legal ramifications at the domestic level. Whether the draft convention can serve as an aspirational model for other indigenous peoples is also uncertain.

In this regard, several comments can be made about the future of the Nordic Sámi Convention. First, as it has been shown, there is solid ground to promote the adoption of the Nordic Sámi Convention from the vantage point of human rights. The 2005 draft is not only supported by human rights institutions but is also aligned with the contemporary understanding of the right to self-determination, which is based on relations rather than separation. To this end, it is argued that the adoption of the Nordic Sámi Convention must be encouraged.

The final negotiation meeting that occurred in November 2016 in Rovaniemi put an end to the process, and it is now the responsibility of the Nordic governments and Sámi parliaments to decide whether the proposal can be ratified. There will be no gain in accepting the adoption of an instrument that is inconsistent with the human rights of indigenous peoples. Conversely, it must also be stressed that no instrument can be perfect. The Convention will necessarily be the product of compromises.

To conclude, and in the event of its adoption, the Convention would certainly set the stage for important changes at the domestic level. It would also open a new avenue to operationalise the rights of indigenous peoples at the transnational level. However, the length of the adoption process of this instrument demonstrates that the internalisation of the right of indigenous peoples still constitutes a major struggle, even in the Nordic countries, which are among the most democratic countries in the world. Ultimately, it remains to be seen whether the promises of the Nordic Sámi Convention towards the right of the Sámi people to self-determination can really live up to expectations.

10 Legislating coordination and cooperation mechanisms between indigenous and ordinary jurisdictions

Reflections on progress and setbacks in Ecuador

Lieselotte Viaene and Guillermo Fernández-Maldonado

1. Introduction

While international human rights law increasingly recognizes indigenous peoples as legal subjects, one significant issue is how to close the implementation gap. Today, a global package of indigenous rights recognizes the right to ensure their preservation and development as unique cultures, with self-determination; land and territories; forms of social, political, legal and economic development; intercultural education; customs and legal systems; participation in state decision-making processes, amongst others. This package comprises Convention 169 on Indigenous and Tribal Peoples of the International Labour Organization (ILO) (1989), the United Nations (UN) Declaration on the Rights of Indigenous Peoples (2007) (henceforth UNDRIP), the recommendations of the UN Special Rapporteur on the Rights of Indigenous Peoples, the UN Expert Mechanism on the Rights of Indigenous Peoples, ILO monitoring mechanisms and regional human rights court jurisprudence, including the Inter-American Court of Human Rights and the African Court on Human and Peoples' Rights. International recognition has turned indigenous peoples into collective subjects of international human rights law and seeks to "put an end to the historical model of exclusion from the decision-making process".[1] Although states across the globe increasingly

This chapter is an abridged and updated version of L Viaene and G Fernández-Maldonado's 'Hacia una Ley de Coordinación y Cooperación Entre la Jurisdicción Indígena y la Jurisdicción Ordinaria en Ecuador. Un Análisis del Proceso y de los Nudos Críticos Desde los Estándares Internacionales de Derechos Humanos' (2016) 9 *Inter-American and European Human Rights Journal*, 1, 63–93.

Disclaimer: The views expressed herein are those of the authors and do not necessarily reflect the views of the United Nations.

1 Human Rights Council, 'Report of the Special Rapporteur on the Situation of Human Rights and Fundamental Freedoms of Indigenous People, James Anaya'. Addendum The situation of indigenous peoples in Chile: follow-up to the recommendations made by the previous Special Rapporteur, UN Doc A/HRC/12/34/Add.6 (2009), para 41.

accept international human rights obligations by ratifying international human rights treaties, compliance with these treaties is generally insufficient.[2] This has created an implementation gap in the case of indigenous peoples' rights, as identified by the first Special Rapporteur on the Rights of Indigenous Peoples, Rodolfo Stavenhagen, a decade ago.[3] In fact, indigenous peoples in the Global South continue to face political exclusion, extreme poverty, dispossession of their territories and threats to their natural resources. Thus, on the International Day of Indigenous Peoples, the UN system recently called upon states to "reduce" these implementation gaps.[4] Moreover, international debates increasingly focus on how governments can effectively fulfil their obligation to guarantee indigenous peoples' rights through, for example, formulation and application of domestic legislation, design and implementation of public policies and provision of the necessary funding.

This chapter addresses the dearth of human rights literature on the human rights and indigenous peoples' rights implementation gap. It specifically analyses possible causes of the gap between state obligations and effective compliance regarding the right of indigenous peoples to administer justice in Ecuador. Legislative powers to generate and administer indigenous justice in their territories are a substantial component of indigenous peoples' right to self-determination. When states constitutionally recognize indigenous justice, they formally accept the existence of legal pluralism or "of more than one legal order or mechanism in one single socio-political space, based on different sources of ultimate validity and maintained by forms of organization different from that of the State".[5] However, legal pluralism has triggered debate in international human rights law, as formal recognition by the state requires a critical revision of modern concepts of sovereignty, unity, autonomy and territoriality. There is limited research on why, how and under what conditions international human rights regulations are internalized in domestic practices.[6] Likewise, there is little empirical knowledge about the efforts, or lack thereof, of international human rights duty bearers to fulfil

2 X Dai, 'The "Compliance Gap" and the Efficacy of International Human Rights Institution', in T Risse, SC Ropp and K Sikkink (eds), *The Persistent Power of Human Rights. From Commitment to Compliance* (Cambridge University Press 2013) 85.

3 Commission on Human Rights, *Human Rights and Indigenous Issues,* Special Rapporteur report on the situation of human rights and fundamental freedoms of indigenous peoples, Sr Rodolfo Stavenhagen, E/CN.4/2006/78.

4 Message by United Nations High Commissioner for Human Rights Navi Pillay and ILO Director-General Guy Ryder on the occasion of the International Day of the World's Indigenous Peoples, 'Bridging the Gap: Implementing the Rights of Indigenous Peoples' (8 August 2014) <www.ilo.org/global/about-the-ilo/how-the-ilo-works/ilo-director-general/statements-and-speeches/WCMS_250837/lang--en/index.htm> accessed 20 November 2017.

5 F von Benda-Beckmann, 'Who's Afraid of Legal Pluralism?' (2002) 47 *Journal of Legal Pluralism* 37, 37.

6 HO Sano and H Thelle, 'The Need for Evidence-Based Human Rights Research', in F Coomans, F Grünfeld and M T Kamminga (eds), *Methods of Human Rights Research* (Intersentia 2009), 91–109 and T Risse, SC Ropp and K Kikkink (eds), *The Persistent Power of Human Rights. From Commitment to Compliance* (Cambridge University Press 2013).

their obligations or about the interaction between these international norms, specific socio-political contexts and domestic structures.[7] Moreover, in the case of indigenous peoples' rights, there is an empirical gap between these significant normative developments and the persistence of stagnation or regression in the practical implementation by states of international collective rights obligations.

Ecuador is an interesting case study for several reasons. Its 2008 constitution is a milestone in the Latin American constitutional reforms undertaken since the early 1990s, as it defines Ecuador as an intercultural and plurinational state, includes the indigenous principle of '*Buen Vivir*'[8] and is the first constitution in the world to recognize nature as a rights holder. This paradigmatic shift responds to the demand for the decolonization and reconfiguration of state–citizen relations.[9] This constitution, together with Bolivia's 2009 constitution, goes beyond previous constitutional transformations, opening a new cycle of "transformative constitutionalism".[10] It recognizes a number of collective rights for indigenous peoples and nationalities, including the right "to create, develop, apply and practice their own legal system or customary law, which cannot infringe constitutional rights, especially those of women, children and adolescents" (article 57.10). Moreover, in Chapter 4 "Judiciary and Indigenous Justice", article 171 formally recognizes legal pluralism: two jurisdictions, indigenous and ordinary, on equal footing governed by the principles of cooperation and coordination. This article is innovative in that legal pluralism is no longer based solely on the recognition of cultural diversity but on indigenous peoples' right to self-determination.[11] Furthermore, it stipulates the formulation of a law to establish mechanisms for coordination and cooperation between the indigenous and the ordinary jurisdictions.

This chapter analyses the drafting processes to develop such coordination and cooperation law by examining the interactions between human rights law, political powers and institutional interests to provide insight into progress and setbacks in this legal area. An extensive body of anthropological literature on legal pluralism in Ecuador and Latin America shows that there have been various degrees of coordination between state justice operators and indigenous authorities on specific cases at the local level.[12] However, the top-down coordination is controversial

7 T Risse, SC Ropp and YK Sikkink (eds), *The Power of Human Rights: International Norms and Domestic Change* (Cambridge University Press 2009).

8 The concept of good living is derived from the Quechua notion *sumak kawsay*, which refers to Andean indigenous ontology, where human beings are part of the *Pachamama* (Mother Earth).

9 B Santos, *Refundación del Estado en América Latina. Perspectivas Desde una Epistemología del Sur* (Ediciones Abya-Yala 2010) and R Avila Santamaría, *El Neoconstitucionalismo Transformador. El Estado y el Derecho en la Constitución de 2008* (Ediciones Abya-Yala 2011).

10 ibid. 103–118.

11 ibid. 150.

12 MT Sierra (ed.), *Haciendo Justicia: Interlegalidad, Derecho y Género en Regios Indígenas* (CIESAS and Miguel Ángel Porrúa 2004); R Huber (ed.), *Hacia Sistemas Jurídicos Plurales. Reflexiones y Experiencias de Coordinación Entre el Derecho Estatal y el Derecho Indígena* (Konrad Adenauer Stiftung 2008); B Santos and A Grijalva Jiménez, (eds), *Justicia Indígena, Plurinacionalidad e*

because discussion has centred on the limits of the personal, material and territorial jurisdictions of indigenous justice and its compatibility with human rights. Like the ordinary justice system, indigenous justice systems can also have norms and practices that violate human rights. In fact, indigenous leaders in Ecuador have recognized that their normative systems have been weakened due to historical processes of discrimination and exclusion and might sometimes violate certain human rights, such as in cases of gender-based violence.[13] However, in line with their right to self-determination, the indigenous movement has insisted that neither the ordinary justice system nor the state can impose its positivistic legal vision and limit indigenous jurisdiction.[14]

Several Andean countries have recently advanced in the legal regulation of coordination and cooperation mechanisms between ordinary and indigenous jurisdictions. In late 2010, Bolivia was the first country to adopt such a law, the Jurisdictional Demarcation Law.[15] However, the parliamentary approval process did not take into account the results of a broad pre-legislative consultation process organized by the Justice Ministry, in coordination with indigenous and peasant organizations.[16] The law was harshly criticized because it "reproduces legal colonialism"[17] by violating the constitutionally mandated hierarchical equality of indigenous justice and ordinary justice, and excludes crimes against the integrity of children, rape, murder and homicide from the indigenous justice jurisdiction. In Peru, there is a national debate about the need for and the content of a law on mechanisms for intercultural coordination between the two.[18] In contrast, in Guatemala, recent attempts to constitutionally recognize legal pluralism and coordination mechanisms have been met with strong opposition by the political and economic non-indigenous elite.[19]

Interculturalidad en Ecuador (Fundación Rosa Luxemburg/Abya-Yala 2012); M Thomas, *The Challenge of Legal Pluralism in Ecuador: Local Dispute Settlement and the Indian-State Relationship in Ecuador* (Routledge 2017).

13 Notes technical meeting CONAIE with UNWOMEN, OHCHR, UNDP regarding the results of the National Survey on Family Relationships and Gender Violence against Women (November 2011) July 2012.

14 Notes internal meetings OHCHR with indigenous representatives between 2009 and 2013. See also Editorial, 'Ecuador: Debaten Proyecto de ley Sobre Justicia Indígena' *Servindi* (26 May 2011) <https://www.servindi.org/actualidad/45546> accessed 20 November 2017.

15 Ley N° 073, Ley de Deslinde Jurisdiccional, 29 de diciembre 2010. *Gaceta Oficial de Bolivia*.

16 Ministerio de Justicia/Viceministerio de Justicia Indígena Originaria Campesina, FORDECAPI-Pueblos Indígenas y Empoderamiento (EMPODER), *Sistematización del Proceso de Consulta a los Pueblos Indígenas Originarios Campesinos. Anteproyecto de Ley de Deslinde Jurisdiccional* (Ministerio de Justicia 2010).

17 Z Quispe Colque, Bolivia. 'La Justicia Indígena y la Ley de Deslinde Jurisdiccional' *Servindi* (30 August 2011) <http://servindi.org/actualidad/50336> accessed 20 November 2017.

18 In November 2013, the Andean, Amazonian, Afro–Peruvian, Environment and Ecology Commission of the Congress of the Republic adopted an opinion that proposed the Law of Intercultural Coordination of Justice. This opinion is mainly based on a draft bill presented by the Supreme Court of the Republic (Law of Intercultural Coordination of the Justice of Peru, number 313/2011).

19 R Sieder, 'Indigenous Sovereignties in Guatemala: Between Criminalization and Revitalization', *NACLA Report on the Americas*, (2017) 49, 3, 370–372.

This chapter is based on two theoretical premises. First, law, understood as a wide range of legal phenomena, is a source of "constituting and legitimizing power"[20] and moral and ethical standards. At a legal institutional level, law defines the "relations and positions of power of persons or organizations, over persons, organizations and other resources in terms of general rights and obligations".[21] The second, related, premise is that changes triggered by law are determined by the interaction between power, political struggles and the instrumental interests of the main stakeholders.[22] The state "is not a black box"[23] but rather comprises different institutions and individuals, and the influence of international and national human rights standards on the behaviour of these state actors remains unclear. In addition, this state heterogeneity also comes into play in state relations with citizens and its control over them.[24]

This chapter first provides a brief description of Ecuador's domestic normative framework on legal pluralism. Next, it documents and critically analyses socio-political dynamics in Ecuador, in the executive and legislative branches, regarding the drafting processes begun in 2009 of a law to regulate coordination and cooperation between indigenous and ordinary justice. Thereafter, it discusses Ecuador's Constitutional Court landmark ruling on *La Cocha 2* in May 2014, a politically controversial case of indigenous justice that is intrinsically connected with the main legal and political issues underlying the drafting process. This chapter concludes by reinserting this empirical analysis into broader observations. The Ecuadorian experience highlights important challenges regarding the necessary conditions and most effective measures for states to address this implementation gap.

This analysis is based on academic and secondary sources as well as professional experience acquired by the authors during their work in Ecuador in the Office of the UN High Commissioner for Human Rights (OHCHR) during the Correa administration (2007–2017), especially in technical cooperation tasks related to human rights and indigenous peoples' rights, including the indigenous jurisdiction. Interviews were also conducted in September and October 2014 with the main official and opposition political actors and civil society on the aforementioned drafting process.[25]

20 F von Benda-Beckmann, K von Benda-Beckmann and A Griffiths, 'The Power of Law', in F von Benda-Beckmann, K von Benda-Beckmann and A Griffiths, *The Power of Law in a Transnational World: Anthropological Enquiries* (Berghan 2009) 1.
21 ibid. 4.
22 Risse and Sikkink (n 7) 9.
23 ibid. 7.
24 Von Benda-Beckmann (n 20) 3.
25 Interviews with (1) Carlos Poveda (litigating lawyer in cases of indigenous justice and former consultant of OHCHR), (2) Ramiro Avila Santamaría (university professor and former official of the Ministry of Justice, Human Rights and Cults), (3) María Paula Romo (President of the Commission of Justice and Structure of the State of the National Assembly from August 2009 to July 2011; she was Assembly Member in the constituent assembly and later in the National Assembly in the period 2009–2013, and (4) Mauro Andino (President) and members of the Commission of Justice and Structure of the National Assembly.

2. Ecuador's constitution (2008): indigenous jurisdiction on equal terms with ordinary jurisdiction

In line with the constitutional transformations in other Andean countries, in 1997 Ecuador recognized the cultural diversity of its society by granting several collective rights to both indigenous and Afro–Ecuadorian peoples, including the right of indigenous peoples to administer justice. This shift was clearly influenced by international norm-setting processes on indigenous peoples' rights, as that year Ecuador had ratified ILO Convention 169 and begun debate on the adoption of the UNDRIP.[26] However, the constitutional provisions were merely "a formal recognition"[27] of this cultural diversity, as they were never applied.

The 2008 constitution marked a new phase of Latin American constitutional transformations. It is considered to be amongst the most advanced constitutions in the world, as it recognizes a broad catalogue of human rights and stipulates that one of the state's main duties is to ensure their non-discriminatory respect, protection and fulfilment.[28] These constitutional guarantees are strengthened by the principles of direct application and justiciability of all rights recognized in the constitution and international instruments, including economic, social and cultural rights (article 11). Moreover, the new constitution recognizes indigenous peoples, Afro–Ecuadorian people and Montubio people as holders of 21 collective rights (articles 57–60), including the right to cultural identity, non-discrimination, prior, free and informed consultation, intercultural and bilingual education, and so on.

Furthermore, article 171 formally recognizes legal pluralism:

> The authorities of the indigenous communities, peoples, and nations shall perform jurisdictional duties, on the basis of their ancestral traditions and their own system of law, within their own territories, with a guarantee for the participation of, and decisionmaking by, women. The authorities shall apply their own standards and procedures for the settlement of internal disputes, as long as said procedures are not contrary to the Constitution, or to human rights enshrined in international instruments. The State shall guarantee that

26 ILO Convention 169 states that in applying national laws and regulations to the peoples concerned, "due regard shall be given to their customs or customary laws" and "procedures shall be established, wherever necessary, to resolve conflicts that may arise in the application of this principle" (Article 8). UNDRIP states that "indigenous peoples have the right to maintain and strengthen their distinct political, legal, economic, social and cultural institutions, while retaining their right to participate fully, if they so choose, in the political, economic, social and cultural life of the State" (Article 5), further pointing out in Article 34 the right to "promote, develop and maintain their institutional structures and their distinctive customs".

27 R Llasåg Fernández, 'Movimiento Indígena del Ecuador a Partir del Siglo XX: Visibilizando el Resurgir, Sus Avances y Retrocesos', in B Santos and A Grijalva Jiménez (eds), *Justicia Indígena, Plurinacionalidad e Enterculturalidad en Ecuador* (Fundación Rosa Luxemburg/Abya-Yala 2012) 134.

28 R Uprimmy, 'The Recent Transformation of Constitutional Law in Latin America: Trends and Challenges', (2011), *Texas Law Review* 1587.

> the decisions of indigenous jurisdiction are observed by public institutions and authorities. These decisions shall be subject to the monitoring of their constitutionality. The law shall establish mechanisms for coordination and cooperation between indigenous jurisdiction and ordinary jurisdiction.

Importantly, these two jurisdictions have the same limits, namely the constitutional principles and human rights recognized in international instruments. Furthermore, the inclusion of women, an initiative of indigenous women, distinguishes it from the previous constitution.[29]

In line with article 171, two laws on indigenous justice and legal pluralism were enacted. First, the Organic Code on the Judiciary (2009) regulates, inter alia, the relationship between indigenous and ordinary jurisdictions (articles 343–346) and establishes five principles of intercultural justice: diversity, equality, *non bis in idem* ("double jeopardy"), presumption in favour of indigenous jurisdiction and intercultural interpretation.[30] The second is the Jurisdictional Guarantees and Constitutional Control Law (2009), which ensures respect for the rights enshrined in the constitution and international human rights instruments. Chapter IX regulates the extraordinary protection from indigenous justice decisions. Article 65 establishes the right of anyone dissatisfied with the decisions of indigenous authorities that violate constitutional rights or discriminate against women to appeal to the Constitutional Court. Article 66 defines legal rules and procedures for the Court, including intercultural interpretation of the conflict, right to due process, orality, right to a second expert opinion and notification of judgment.

In line with the constitutional provisions, as of 2009, the Ministry of Justice, Human Rights and Cults (MJHR), in coordination with the Cultural Heritage Ministry, led a participatory process to draft a bill on coordination and cooperation between the indigenous and ordinary jurisdictions. However, this process was interrupted, and the final proposal, concluded in December 2010, was never presented to the Assembly for political consideration at the highest government levels. Meanwhile, in 2011, the Justice and State Structure Commission of the National Assembly (henceforth the Commission) analysed a draft bill on coordination and cooperation between the jurisdictions in a first debate in May 2012. However, the second and final debate on the bill is pending.

Between 2009 and 2014, OHCHR provided technical assistance to the draft processes and to civil society regarding this topic. This assistance focused on

29 A. Grijalva Jiménez, 'Del Presente se Inventa el Futuro: Justicias Indígenas y Estado en Ecuador', in B Santos and A Grijalva Jiménez (eds), *Justicia Indígena, Plurinacionalidad e Interculturalidad en Ecuador* (Fundación Rosa Luxemburg/Abya-Yala 2012) 66.

30 In addition, article 346 refers to the promotion of intercultural justice through three measures: the Judiciary Council is obliged to designate human and economic resources for coordination and cooperation between the two jurisdictions, training of Judiciary officials in "culture, language and customs, traditional practices, norms and procedures of indigenous or customary law" and last, that the "Judiciary Council shall not exercise any type of attribution, government or administration with respect to indigenous jurisdiction".

promotion of international human rights standards, with direct support from then Special Rapporteur on the Rights of Indigenous Peoples, James Anaya. Between 2009 and 2012, OHCHR activities were framed within the Development and Culture Program for Poverty Reduction and Social Inclusion (2009–2012), implemented by Ecuador's Cultural Heritage Ministry, with the support of the UN System and financed by the Spanish government's Millennium Development Goals Achievement Fund.[31]

The programme sought to strengthen the exercise of rights of communities, peoples and nationalities, increase their political participation, promote equal opportunities for groups excluded for reasons of ethnicity and generate information on cultural diversity to inform policy making.[32] After the programme closed, OHCHR continued to support these draft processes and activities to promote international human rights standards on indigenous justice. For example, workshops were conducted with the Confederation of Indigenous Nationalities of Ecuador (CONAIE) leaders, and debates were organized by non-governmental organizations (NGOs) and academics in Quito and the provinces.[33]

3. Creating coordination mechanisms between indigenous and ordinary justice: political controversies

After the new constitution came into force, several bills on coordination and cooperation mechanisms were drafted but none were approved by the National

31 To support the programme's implementation, the OHCHR established a team of national consultants, experts in legal pluralism: Fernando García (senior researcher of the Latin American Faculty of Social Sciences (FLACSO) and coordinator of the team), Carlos Poveda (litigation lawyer in several cases on indigenous justice; he was Criminal Judge in Cotopaxi where he became known for declining jurisdiction in favour of indigenous jurisdiction in the case of *La Cocha 1*) and Raúl Llasag (Quichua lawyer from the Panzaleo community, professor of the Simón Bolívar Andean University). OHCHR activities also included support for the book series *Justice and Human Rights Neoconstitutionalism and Society* from the MJDHC with two publications regarding legal considerations and comparative experiences in order to address the limited production of national legal doctrine and the very limited access to international doctrine on new constitutional developments; development of a socio-legal base line study 'Diagnóstico Socio Jurídico Para la Elaboración de la Ley de Coordinación y Cooperación Entre la Justicia Ordinaria y la Justicia Indígena' (2009–2010). During this research, two cases of the application of indigenous justice were documented by video which, together with the case of *La Cocha 1*, created a video documentary *Viviendo la Justicia. Case Studies on Indigenous Justice in Ecuador*, which proved especially useful in explaining the norms and practices of indigenous justices to different audiences, <https://vimeo.com/46993212>; and publication of the book *Viviendo la Justicia, Pluralismo Jurídico y Justicia Indígena en Ecuador* (2012).

32 See <http://mdgfund.org/en/program/ecuadorcultura> accessed 20 November 2017.

33 OHCHR supported and participated in seminars with local judges, local public prosecutors and indigenous authorities organized by the Regional Human Rights Advisory Foundation (INREDH), within the framework of the project entitled 'Access to Justice Systems and the Use of Constitutional Guarantees for the Protection of Human Rights on the Northern Border', supported by the European Union and with the participation of the Ecuadorian Ombudsman.

Assembly. What happened? What prevented approval of the law if the political movement that approved the new constitution remained in power and had a majority in the National Assembly? In this section, we analyse several intertwined obstacles that have prevented the adequate protection and promotion of the right of indigenous peoples to administer justice in general, and the adoption of this law in particular, namely, colonial and racist views, the theory–practice gap of the new constitutional provisions and the political implications of the indivisibility of indigenous peoples' rights.

3.1. Colonial and racist views

Research has revealed the lack of recognition of the validity of indigenous jurisdiction and the persistence of colonial attitudes and racism at multiple levels of the judiciary.[34] Along the same lines, the UN Special Rapporteurs on the Rights of Indigenous Peoples and on extrajudicial, summary or arbitrary executions observed during their visits to Ecuador that public officials and the media too often associate lynching and acts of tumultuous violence with indigenous justice practices.[35] Moreover, ignorance, prejudice and a profound lack of understanding of indigenous cultures create confusion and strengthen "racist stereotyping and reinforce anti-indigenous sentiment".[36] These attitudes, along with the treatment of indigenous justice in legal, political and media arenas, like the *La Cocha 2* case, analysed on pages 220–222, demonstrate the prevalence of "the demonization of culture".[37] In fact, a dominant belief in Ecuadoran society is that indigenous culture and its justice system are characterized by barbaric customs or traditions that violate basic human rights. Moreover, little relevant comparative legislative antecedents exist on indigenous normative systems and their ontological foundations and their relationship to ordinary justice and, despite their long-standing validity, these complex issues are rarely studied in law schools.

Thus, several fundamental concerns arise: how can cooperation and coordination between the two jurisdictions be regulated in the backdrop of colonial,

34 K Encalada, 'Racismo en la Justicia Ordinaria', in B Santos and A Grijalva Jiménez (eds), *Justicia Indígena, Plurinacionalidad e Interculturalidad en Ecuador* (Fundación Rosa Luxemburg/Abya-Yala 2012) 185–206 and FLACSO Ecuador/Oxfam América, *Los Pueblos Indígenas del Ecuador: Derechos y Bienestar: Alternative Report on Compliance with ILO Convention 169* (FLACSO Ecuador/Oxfam America 2007) 51.

35 Human Rights Council, *Report by the Special Rapporteur on the situation of human rights and fundamental freedoms of indigenous people, James Anaya. Addendum Observations on the progress made and challenges faced in the implementation of the constitutional guarantees of the rights of indigenous peoples in Ecuador*, UN Doc A/HRC/15/37/Add 7, 17 September 2010 and Human Rights Council, *Report of the Special Rapporteur on extrajudicial, summary or arbitrary executions, Philip Alston Addendum Mission to Ecuador*, UN Doc A/HRC/17/28/Add 2 (2011), para 15–16.

36 UN Doc A/HRC/17/28/ Add 2, para 17.

37 SE Merry, 'Human Rights Law and the Demonization of Culture (And Anthropology Along the Way' (2003) 26 *Political and Legal Anthropology Review PoLAR* 55, 55.

distorted and prejudiced views and profound lack of empirical understanding of at least one of them? Is legislation of this relationship possible when most politicians lack basic theoretical and empirical knowledge of indigenous peoples' rights and of the characteristics, scope and application of indigenous justice? In effect, legislators analysed this draft law through a Western-mestizo lens and with knowledge of and experience with only the ordinary justice system.[38] Although legal anthropologists, indigenous leaders and organizations, as well as Special Rapporteur James Anaya and OHCHR, helped to raise awareness during this years-long process, their efforts were insufficient to change deeply rooted visions and positions based on prejudice, stereotypes, discrimination and even racism against indigenous peoples. After five centuries of dominance of the nation state, legal monism and historical racism, understanding and promoting effective observance of the right of indigenous peoples to administer their justice has created significant challenges for political actors, justice administrators and Ecuadorian society that have not yet been overcome.

3.2. The theory–practice gap

The government and opposition political actors interviewed agreed that the obstacles to approving the bill are not legal or technical, but rather political and ideological in nature. To understand these obstacles, intrinsically intertwined with pre-existing racist attitudes, we briefly describe the broader political context surrounding these drafting processes.

Firstly, the position of President Correa's political party, the *Movimiento Alianza País,* changed over the years and became very critical of the progressive and protective human rights provisions of the Montecristi Constitution. The party even supported successive constitutional reforms in the opposite direction, like the indefinite presidential re-election. This alliance of political actors and social, academic and indigenous movements supported the Rafael Correa's candidacy in 2006 and formed a majority in the Montecristi constituent assembly (2007–2008), which approved the 2008 constitution. These actors introduced the protective tone of human rights, indigenous peoples' rights and the rights of nature in the new constitution, and many came to occupy prominent positions during the first years of government and in the National Assembly. However, over time they distanced themselves from Correa's political project and became prominent opposition leaders and organizations who criticized the government for abandoning the spirit of the constitution. In the words of former constituent assembly president, Alberto Acosta,

38 In fact, following his visit to the country in 2009, the Special Rapporteur on the Rights of Indigenous Peoples recommended, in view of this, "developing a process of information exchange and understanding between the state judicial authorities and the indigenous authorities on their respective justice systems". UN Doc A/HRC/15/37/Add 7 (n 33) 19.

> The ranks of government have reached a state of complacency, in which nobody, within 'the process', cares if the original principles, which were initially captured in the Government Plan of the *Movimiento País*, drawn up collectively in 2006, are betrayed. These are principles which were later enshrined in the Constitution of Montecristi.[39]

Meanwhile, another important faction of the party, despite not sharing many of President Correa's positions, remained in the *Movimiento Alianza País* or government positions because they believed that, despite the discrepancies, this was a historic opportunity to change Ecuador and that Rafael Correa's leadership was essential in this task.

Although the official discourse of Correa's government upheld human rights and indigenous peoples' rights, the interpretation of decisions, policies and laws increasingly diverged from the constitutional text and international human rights standards.[40] A symbolic example was the government's response to criticism from the Inter-American Commission on Human Rights (IACHR) and, in particular, from its Special Rapporteur on freedom of expression, regarding a domestic court ruling that sentenced a newspaper and a journalist to three years in prison for committing slander against President Correa and to pay $40 million in compensation.[41] In response, the government conducted a campaign to discredit the IACHR and those who appealed to it[42] and a campaign within the Organization of American States (OAS) to reform the regional protection system and create a parallel system.[43]

39 See foreword to F Muñoz Jaramillo (ed), *Balance Crítico del Gobierno de Rafael Correa* (Central University of Ecuador 2014), 15. See also M Becker, 'The Stormy Relations between Rafael Correa and Social Movements in Ecuador', (2013) 40 *Latin American Perspectives* 43. In an interview published in the government-owned newspaper, *El Telégrafo*, President Correa declared his worst political mistake in his seven years in power to be having trusted Alberto Acosta and having made him president in the constituent assembly, <www.eltelegrafo.com.ec/ noticias/politica/2/ aprobar-el-codigo-financiero-sera-una-lucha-politica-tenaz>.

40 For example, Ecuador went from receiving one or two UN Special Rapporteurs every year to receiving none. As response to the approval and application of laws violating international obligations, several Special Rapporteurs began to send the government various letters of allegation. For example, the Special Rapporteur on Freedom of Expression and Opinion regarding the Organic Law of Communication (UA G/SO 214 ECU 1/2012, of 19 of July of 2012), <https://spdb. ohchr .org/hrdb/22nd/public_~ UA_Ecuador_l 9.07.12_ %281.2012%29. pdf.>

41 'Office of the Special Rapporteur Expresses Profound Concern Regarding Conviction of Journalist, Directors and Media Outlet in Ecuador' (21 July 2011) <www.oas.org/en/iachr/expression/ showarticle.asp?artID=857&lID=1> accessed 20 November 2017.

42 Fundamedios, an NGO on freedom of expression, was publicly discredited by the government for having resorted to the IACHR. The IACHR issued a press release on 11 November 2011, expressing its deepest concern about the threats, reprisals and smear campaigns against some of the people attending their hearings such as on "Situation of the Right to Freedom of Expression in Ecuador" (25 October 2011), in some cases on the part of higher state authorities. Due to the seriousness of the facts, the Commission requested information from the state, <www.oas.org/en/cidh/prensa/comunicados/2011/116.asp>.

43 For example, during the 42nd OAS General Assembly (2012) in Cochabamba Bolivia, President Correa stated that IACHR was dominated by the interests of hegemonic countries, NGOs and the great capital, which endangered the democratic systems of the region <www.presidencia.gob.ec/ discursos/#search> accessed 20 November 2017.

This political shift and internal dynamics has been described as a fratricidal struggle, since many of these opposition leaders originally shared ideals and social struggles with academia and civil society organizations. Some denounced persecution by their former friends, now in power, whom they accuse of betraying their ideals, while officials accused former colleagues of behaviour ranging from "childishness" to participation in conspiracies by the traditional political machine, imperialism or transnational companies seeking to destabilize the government.[44] According to recent research, Rafael Correa first appeared as a social movement ally, particularly of the indigenous movement and CONAIE, but later sought to co-opt them through propaganda and clientelism, to eventually seriously weaken and dismantle them.[45]

During the coordination and cooperation law drafting process, these growing political differences within the *Movimiento Alianza País* surfaced within the executive branch and the National Assembly. María Paula Romo, member of the constituent assembly and president of the Commission (2009–2013), explained that during the constituent assembly, one of the main objections to indigenous jurisdiction, and indigenous rights in general, came from President Correa, who argued that recognizing indigenous justice on equal footing with ordinary justice would create a state within the state.[46] However, this view did not prevail in the new constitutional text. According to Romo,

> this line of thought initially came from the president but ended up as the official line of the party. During the constituent assembly and the first years of government certain agreements were reached because there were political counterweights to President Correa within the party, but today [during Correa's administration] they no longer exist.[47]

Moreover, officials and Assembly members who supported the constitution noted that President Correa and his immediate entourage distanced themselves from the

44 One example was the dissolution of the Pachamama Foundation on 4 December 2013 at the request of President Correa and pursuant to the Regulations for the Operation of the Unified Information System of Social and Citizens Organizations (Executive Decree No 16, of 20 June 2013). The Foundation, which had a strong track record in defending indigenous peoples' rights and the environment, participated and documented a protest of CONAIE leaders against the XI Oil Round of Concessions, where an indigenous leader mildly attacked two people who left the area and who turned out to be diplomats. The government dissolved the Foundation for deviating from its statutory objectives and interfering in public policies, according to the Ministry of Interior statement. One of the main drivers of the dissolution was the Minister for the Interior, José Serrano. Years earlier, José Serrano, along with Mario Melo, were prominent lawyers of the Pachamama Foundation leading the Sarayaku case before the Inter-American Court of Human Rights. The aforementioned regulation and its application to Pachamama were seriously questioned by several UN Special Rapporteurs in September and December 2013 for violating human rights standards, <https://spdb.ohchr.org/hrdb/24th/public_-_AL_Ecuador_16.09.13_%281.2013%29.pdf> and <https://spdb.ohchr.org/hrdb/24th/public_-_AL_ Ecuador_31.12.13_%284.2013%29.pdf>.

45 Muñez Jaramillo (n 39) 18.

46 Interview with María Paula Romo, September 2014.

47 ibid.

constitutional framework when inconvenient to them, and exercised ever-greater control over legal initiatives within the government and the Assembly. Young officials who sought to enforce the constitution had to maintain a low profile within their ministries to keep bills of law from the eyes of certain high-level authorities and especially the presidency, where the orders in favour or against these processes originated.[48] This was the case, as discussed in the next section, of the Justice and Human Rights Ministry.

3.3. The indivisibility of indigenous peoples' rights

A third, related obstacle is that effective enforcement of indigenous peoples' collective rights requires the critical revision of modern concepts of sovereignty, unity and autonomy as fundamental principles of the nation state. Although the new constitution reconfigures the Ecuadorian state paradigm, the country is undergoing a long complex process of profound transition. Like other Latin American countries, Ecuador is experiencing serious social conflict due to the exploitation of renewable and non-renewable natural resources in indigenous territories, without protecting constitutionally and internationally recognized indigenous peoples' rights.[49]

It is thus essential to understand that indigenous justice systems respond to their particular ontology, system of authority and management of territory. Due to this interconnectedness between the right of indigenous authorities to administer justice and the collective right to land, territory and natural resources, we argue that several political actors distanced themselves from the constitutional project to fully accept Ecuador's formal legal pluralism and enact a coordination and cooperation law. Effective enforcement of indigenous justice would constitute a serious obstacle to Correa's extractivist development model, because it

48 For example, an academic study on freedom of expression in Ecuador analysed from international human rights standards, prepared with the support of UNESCO and OHCHR, and with the participation of the Rapporteurs on freedom of expression from the inter-American system and the UN, was ready to be published as part of the collection on Justice and Human Rights promoted by the Secretariat of Normative Development at the Ministry of Justice and Human Rights. Following criticism from both Rapporteurs on the enacted communication law and taking note of the content of the study, senior officials ordered its publication to be suspended to avoid influencing the parliamentary debate. Many months later, they authorized the publication but only by the UNESCO/OHCHR and outside the aforementioned collection. See <http://unesdoc.unesco.org/images/0021/002156/215627s.pdf> accessed 20 November 2017.

49 In 2012, the Committee on the Elimination of Racial Discrimination (CERD) urged the Ecuadorian State to increase its efforts to establish constructive dialogue mechanisms and effective consultation processes with indigenous communities affected by projects that have an impact on their livelihoods. See CERD, *Concluding Observations of the Committee on the Elimination of Racial Discrimination, to Ecuador*, UN Doc. CERD/C/ECU/C0/20-22, para 17. The high level of social conflict continues in Ecuador. In August 2015, the current Special Rapporteur on the Rights of Indigenous Peoples, Victoria Tauli-Corpuz, called for calm and dialogue in the face of violent clashes that occurred in demonstrations convened by CONAIE against the government. <www.ohchr.org/EN/NewsEvents/Pages/DisplayNews.aspx?NewsID=16343&LangID=S> accessed 20 November 2017.

would imply the obligation of the state to ensure respect for territorial rights and use of the natural resources of indigenous peoples. Thus, in Ecuador, indigenous justice acquired new political significance, spearheading[50] the implementation of the Montecristi Constitution, which is "an important part of a decolonizing and anti-capitalist political project",[51] as constitutional recognition of formal legal pluralism requires a revision of hegemonic concepts of sovereignty, territoriality and autonomy.

Although Ecuador's constitutional provisions to effectively protect indigenous peoples' rights are very promising, compliance is taking place amid political controversies and deeply rooted misconceptions about indigenous justice practices. The following two sections analyse the legal and political dynamics of the coordination and cooperation law drafting process between 2009 and the first National Assembly debate of a bill in 2012.

4. Ecuadorian's executive power: a look from within

Between 2009 and 2012, the MJHR's Sub-Secretariat of Normative Development (henceforth the Sub-Secretariat) partnered with OHCHR to produce a draft bill on coordination between indigenous and ordinary justice. The Sub-Secretariat is responsible for preparing and revising executive bills and subsequently submitting them to the National Assembly. One of its duties is to improve the quality of bills, the participatory processes for their formulation and access to and dissemination of legal doctrine. From the outset, OHCHR and this state entity agreed that the legal basis should be the constitutional mandate, as well as ILO Convention 169, the International Convention on the Elimination of all forms of Racial Discrimination[52], UNDRIP and the recommendations of the Special Rapporteur on the Rights of Indigenous Peoples.

At this initial stage, the political and ideological differences within the government became evident. The participatory spirit and coherence with the constitution and international human rights standards that the Sub-Secretariat sought to introduce in the process clashed with the distrust and hierarchical control that characterized the attitude of Ministry of Cultural Heritage officials.

The Sub-Secretariat and OHCHR strategy sought to promote a technical and participatory process. It included support from national experts, lawyers and anthropologists with vast expertise in indigenous justice[53] and, building on prior research, an anthropological legal study to produce a participatory diagnosis on the viability and application of indigenous justice in various regions of Ecuador.[54]

50 B Santos, 'Cuando los Excluido Tienen Derecho: Justicia Indígena, Plurinacionalidad e Interculturalidad', in B Santos and A Grijalva Jiménez (eds), *Justicia Indígena, Plurinacionalidad e Interculturalidad en Ecuador* (Fundación Rosa Luxemburg/Abya-Yala, 2012) 17.

51 ibid. 15.

52 Ratified by Ecuador on 22 September 1966.

53 See n 31.

54 ibid.

Initially, the intention was to produce a first draft with the support of these experts and based on constitutional and international standards, the identification of obstacles and comparative law norms. It also sought the advice of then Special Rapporteur on the Rights of Indigenous Peoples James Anaya, who warned of the possible rejection by indigenous organizations of any proposal which did not include their participation from the beginning.

In December 2009, at the invitation of the Ecuadoran Ministry of Justice and Human Rights, Anaya visited Ecuador "to provide technical assistance in the development of mechanisms for coordination and cooperation between indigenous justice and ordinary jurisdiction and for dialogue on the situation of indigenous peoples in Ecuador".[55] Anaya met with government representatives, parliamentarians, indigenous organizations, the UN and other relevant actors to discuss progress and challenges in implementing indigenous peoples' rights as recognized by the new constitution.[56]

Following Anaya's recommendations, in January 2010 a new road map was elaborated by the Sub-Secretariat, including a methodology for participatory workshops with indigenous organizations. Due to tensions between the government and the indigenous movement about the content and lack of pre-legislative consultation on the water bill under discussion in the National Assembly, OHCHR was asked to invite the indigenous authorities. Seven national and regional indigenous organizations were invited to designate two persons, one man and one woman, in accordance with the constitutional mandate on gender equality with respect to collective rights. Representatives from the Commission and UN Women were also invited.

Two workshops were held to identify critical challenges regarding the content and scope of the draft bill, including identification of the indigenous authorities and the limit of their jurisdiction, personal, material and territorial competence, the scope of constitutional control, minimum due process criteria, decision-making effectiveness, definition of acts of torture, cooperation with state bodies and the prevalence of victims.[57]

However, this constructive and participatory process was interrupted in a surprising way. On 9 May 9 2010, an indigenous justice case took place in the community of La Cocha, Cotopaxi province, or *La Cocha 2*, discussed below. The media spread a biased, sensationalist version, taken out of context, while the government's reaction reflected a dramatic shift in its position on indigenous peoples' rights. In public statements on radio and television, the government severely criticized this indigenous trial, calling it savage. Days

55 'Relator Especial de la ONU Sobre los Pueblos Indígenas Visitará Ecuador' (Geneva 30 November 2009) <http://unsr.jamesanaya.org/statements/relator-especial-de-la-onu-sobre-los-pueblos-indigenas-visitara-ecuador> accessed 20 November 2017.

56 Anaya also participated in the Regional Forum on legal pluralism organized by Sub-Secretariat of the Ministry of Justice and Human Rights, which took place at the Universidad Andina Simón Bolívar. <www.uasb.edu.ec/contenido?la-andina-acogera-al-foro-regional-sobre-justicia-indigena>.

57 Notes of these workshops are in the archives of the authors.

later, the presidency instructed the Justice and Human Rights Ministry to cease meetings with indigenous organizations and finalize a draft bill independently and as soon as possible.

In a press release entitled "The key lies in dialogue", Special Rapporteur James Anaya expressed deep concern about this new polarization, which "go[es] beyond the reasonable and measured critique of a concrete case of indigenous justice implementation, and run[s] the risk of being perceived as encouraging racist and discriminatory views against all indigenous peoples of Ecuador".[58] Furthermore, he stated that the government's reaction was "counterproductive for the construction of an intercultural and plurinational State as declared in the new constitution of Ecuador".

As mentioned on pages 208–214, this new political controversy occurred in a very polarized climate provoked by the government's progressive distancing from the protective spirit of the constitution, the imposed extractive development model that affects indigenous territories, the omission of prior consultation on these extractive projects and on laws that affect indigenous peoples' rights, and protests against the proposed water law. Several interviewees shared the view that the government's offensive reaction to the *La Cocha 2* case and quest to reduce indigenous jurisdiction to a minimum sought to weaken the indigenous movement, which had brought down governments in the 1990s and had become one of the government's main political opponents.

In October 2010, Special Rapporteur Anaya submitted his comments on the draft bill to the sub-secretary. The bill was further revised in workshops with experts and the Justice and Human Rights Ministry' technical team. The final version, completed in late December 2010, was in line with international standards but not with the government's position following the politically sensitive *La Cocha 2* case.

Faced with the new political controversy, officials and experts from various ministries that supported this version of the bill met to discuss strategies for submitting this draft to the National Assembly. The first option was to convince the Presidential Legal Adviser, who President Correa fully trusted, during a private presentation and discussion of the draft law. The second strategy was to explain the project to *Movimiento Alianza País* parliamentarians so that they would present the bill. However, this second option was considered unrealistic, since these Assembly members knew that President Correa opposed the bill and therefore would be hard-pressed to present a draft on behalf of the presidential party but against the president's wishes. In this pessimistic setting, the group of state officials ultimately abandoned both strategies due to a new shift in the legislation process, discussed on pages 217–220.

58 'Ordinary and Indigenous Justice in Ecuador: "The Key Lies in Dialogue" Says UN Expert' (Geneva 8 June 2010) <http://unsr.jamesanaya.org/statements/ordinary-and-indigenous-justice-in-ecuador-the-key-lies-in-dialogue-says-un-expert> accessed 20 November 2017.

5. A new centre of gravity: National Assembly's Justice and State Structure Commission

On 4 January 2011, the drafting process moved to the National Assembly because the Council of Legislative Administration (CAL) submitted to the Commission a draft bill presented by Lourdes Tibán of the indigenous Pachakutik Party, which had the support of CONAIE.[59]

The Commission organized a series of meetings between indigenous representatives and academics from May to June 2011, to which OHCHR was invited. The previously identified critical issues included the personal, material and territorial jurisdiction of indigenous justice. Notwithstanding their membership in different political groups, the Commission members shared, to a greater or lesser extent, a restricted view on the scope and limits of indigenous justice: what crimes, in which territories, over which people and so on. By contrast, the indigenous leaders and other experts insisted that, according to the constitution, the coordination law should only regulate cooperation and coordination mechanisms between both jurisdictions. They believed that these mechanisms could not place additional limits on indigenous justice than those established in the constitution, namely, submission to the constitution and international human rights instruments (article 171 and article 172). Based on these discussions and Lourdes Tibán's proposal, the Commission prepared its own draft, which received written comments from the OHCHR expert team, indigenous leaders and the Planning and Development Secretariat (SENPLADES).

Once more, these debates showed that legislating the formal legal pluralism as established in the constitution was not a purely legal matter, but one of major power conflicts embedded in colonial and neo-extractivist assumptions. In the words of Carlos Poveda, "the existence of a law assumes the submission to mestizo norms. There is a mestizo-indigenous tension in which the latter is dominated".[60]

However, the position of the indigenous movement was clear: they would not accept a coordination law that limited the administration of indigenous justice. In fact, better to maintain the bottom-up coordination that had been operating up to that moment than a law that did not promote coordination and cooperation between both jurisdictions.

A key moment within this drafting process was a videoconference with Special Rapporteur Anaya, proposed and coordinated by OHCHR, during a National Assembly plenary session in June 2011 with parliamentarians, Constitutional Court members, academics and indigenous and social leaders.[61] This unprecedented and

59 Assembly member Lourdes Tibán submitted her proposal to the CAL on 1 February 2010 (Oficio No. AN-LTG-0043-10 4 February 2010). Draft laws under discussion at the National Assembly can be consulted at <http://leyes.asambleanacional.gob.ec/>.

60 Interview with Carlos Poveda (Quito August 2014).

61 The videoconference can be accessed at <http://unsr.jamesanaya.org/videos/video-conference-asamblea-nacional-ecuador> accessed 20 November 2017.

innovative direct dialogue with a UN Special Rapporteur, who as independent global expert has the mandate to support states in dealing with highly complex problems in a timely manner and in accordance with international human rights standards. During this virtual debate, Anaya clearly stated that the draft bill had to respect the indigenous peoples' right to self-determination and should therefore use indigenous justice as the basis for any discussion about personal, material and territorial jurisdiction.[62] Moreover, he asserted that as the scope of personal and material jurisdiction varies within indigenous communities, the state should not set limits.

However, it was not until May 2012 that the Commission, now presided by *Alianza País* parliamentarian Mauro Andino, submitted a draft law of only eleven articles and four chapters to the National Assembly for debate.[63] An explanatory memorandum on the draft law had already been released on 19 December 2011 containing, besides the bill, 21 pages of justification and explanation. The bill outlines, amongst others, coordination and cooperation principles, the competences of indigenous authorities, the effectiveness of indigenous decisions and principles of interinstitutional coordination. Regarding material competence, article 5 states that "Indigenous authorities have the competence to know and resolve, based on their ancestral traditions and own justice, all conflicts which undermine the harmony of the *comuna*, community, village or nationality to which they belong". The bill does not limit the competence of indigenous authorities regarding certain infractions or crimes; nor does the memorandum define "internal conflict". During this public debate, all of the interventions recommended limiting indigenous jurisdiction and the Assembly sent the draft back to the Commission for a second review.[64] Until the time of this publication, more than six years later, the draft law never returned to the National Assembly for a second debate and final vote, though the UN Committee on the Elimination of Racial Discrimination (CERD) had requested the state to ensure respect for and recognition of indigenous justice systems in compliance with international human rights and recommended speeding up the approval of a law to harmonize and regulate the functions, competencies, and responsibilities of both justice systems.[65]

The political debates about indigenous justice gained momentum in January 2013 when Gustavo Jalkh, first Minister of Justice and Human Rights, assumed

62 Press note: 'Bill on Indigenous Jurisdiction in Ecuador Must Take Indigenous Peoples' Laws, Customs, and Traditions as its Starting Point' (Geneva 22 June 2011) <http://unsr.jamesanaya.org/notes/bill-on-indigenous-jurisdiction-in-ecuador-must-take-indigenous-peoples-laws-customs-and-traditions-as-its-starting-point>.

63 This document was presented by the new Commission of Justice and Structure of the State under presidency of Mauro Andino, which resumed the work initiated by María Paulo Romo, but worked behind closed doors without the participation of indigenous leaders and other actors previously involved.

64 Notes of the authors, observation of the first debate in the National Assembly Ecuador 12 May 2012.

65 UN Doc CERD/C/ECU/CO/20-22 (n 49) para 19.

the Council of the Judiciary presidency. From this position, he began dialogue with CONAIE, and simultaneously and actively promoted limiting indigenous jurisdiction to minor and non-criminal issues by resorting to the media and advocating his position before the National Assembly.[66] Moreover, he suspended and removed judges who declined material competence in favour of indigenous jurisdiction.[67] Furthermore, he publicly stated that judges of the ordinary system should not decline jurisdiction in favour of indigenous jurisdiction in cases of sexual crimes, such as rape of children and adolescents, which he did not consider "internal conflicts".[68]

The Commission, with an *Alianza País* majority, realized that the call to limit the material jurisdiction of indigenous justice was driven by political rather than legal reasons. Therefore, in order to approve a non-restrictive bill on this matter in the Assembly and avoid a presidential veto – as was often the case with other laws of his own parliamentary majority – its members considered it necessary to first win the support of *Alianza País* and then try to convince President Correa.[69] However, an additional challenge faced by the Commission was the obligation to submit this draft bill to pre-legislative consultation with indigenous peoples, as per the constitution. The former and current presidents of the Commission, María Paula Romo and Mauro Andino, agreed that parliamentary regulations required both the Council of Legislative Administration and the National Assembly to speak on this consultation procedure. In fact, the Commission posed this request to the National Assembly during the presidencies

66 'CJ y Conaie Logran Consenso Sobre la Justicia Indígena' *El Telégrafo* (Ecuador 5 June 2013). <www.eltelegrafo.com.ec/noticias/judicial/13/cj-y-conaie-logran-consenso-sobre-la-justicia-indigena>. In May 2013, Jalkh met with the President of the National Assembly and handed over a document in which he based his position on the denaturing of indigenous justice and the need for the Assembly to limit its jurisdiction by a restrictive interpretation of the concept of indigenous internal conflict which does not cover criminal offences such as homicide, rape, etc. See "Gustavo Jalkh Pide Legislar Sobre la Justicia Indígena' *El Universo* (Ecuador 29 May 2013) <www.eluniverso.com/noticias/2013/05/29/nota/962856/jalkh-pide-legislar-sobre-justicia-indigena> accessed 20 November 2017.

67 In 2014, the Foundation for Due Process of Law (DPLF) published a study entitled 'Independencia Judicial en la Reforma de la Justicia Ecuatoriana', which analysed and documented different ways in which the government interfered in judicial activity, as well as the removal of judges ordered by the Council of the Judiciary when they did not agree with the views on specific cases expressed, in particular, by the President of the Republic. DPLF and the author of the study were subjected to attacks and public disqualifications, especially during President Correa's Saturday citizen liaisons, accused of being liars and agents financed by the oil company Chevron and the CIA to destabilize the government. (See <www.dplf.org/sites/default/files/ indjud_ecuador_informe_esp.pdf> and <http://dplf.org/en/news/indepéndencia-judicial-en-ecuador>).

68 Editorial, 'Consejo de la Judicatura Planteó Aclarar Reformas a la Justicia Indígena' *Consejo de la Judicatura* (Ecuador 30 May 2013) <www.funcionjudicial.gob.ec/index.php/saladeprensa/noticias/item/1350-consejo-de-la-judicatura-plante%C3%B3-reformas-a-la-justicia-ind%C3%ADgena.html> accessed 20 November 2017.

69 Notes of the meeting of one of the authors with the president and members of the Commission of Justice and Structure of the State, 3 September 2014.

of Fernando Cordero (2009–2013) and Gabriela Rivadeneira (2013–2017), as well as to *Alianza País*, but never received a response.

The Commission also wanted to postpone submission of a second and final draft bill until the Constitutional Court (henceforth the Court) ruled on *La Cocha 2*, under review since 2010. Both Jalkh and the Commission members noted the need for a Court interpretation of the term "internal conflict" as established in the constitution.[70] While the UN Special Rapporteur used international human rights standards to establish indigenous justice provisions from the perspective of the full respect for the right to self-determination, Jalkh's stance was very restrictive and limited it to minor issues and non-criminal matters. It was not surprising that the Court's ruling on *La Cocha 2*, on 30 July 2014, was essentially in line with the government's position. Although the Commission's bill for second and final debate sought to adhere to Anaya's broad and flexible interpretation, it was clear that the Court's judgment supported the government's and Council of the Judiciary's restrictive position. After the Court's decision, the members of the Commission met with academics and indigenous leaders to decide whether to follow the Court's interpretation or maintain the initial line of the bill, aware, however, that the possibility of acceptance by the CAL, the majority of *Alianza País* and President Correa was even more remote after this ruling.[71]

6. The Constitutional Court and the *La Cocha 2* case

Constitutional recognition of indigenous peoples' collective rights in several Latin American countries has attributed a new role to the judiciary in ensuring respect for these rights.[72] Both the Inter-American Court of Human Rights and the Colombian Constitutional Court have played a key role in creating "multicultural jurisprudence",[73] forging a multicultural concept of human rights that integrates indigenous visions of human dignity. For example, in the 1990s, the Colombian Court developed a doctrine of "minimum legal requirements" (*mínimos jurídicos*) for punishments that must be respected by both ordinary and indigenous justice, as well as on due process guarantees and intercultural dialogue mechanisms to interpret alleged human rights violations.[74]

The Ecuadorian Constitutional Court did not follow this progressive trend. *La Cocha 2* is a homicide case initially adjudicated by the indigenous authorities

70 Jalkh presented this problem before the President of the Constitutional Court during a meeting on 28 May 2013. See n 68.

71 See n 69.

72 R Sieder, 'The Judiciary and Indigenous Rights in Guatemala', (2007) 5 *International Journal of Constitutional Law* 211.

73 F Gómez, 'Cultural Diversity, Legal Pluralism, and Human Rights from an Indigenous Perspective: The Approach By The Colombian Constitutional Court and the Inter-American Court of Human Rights', (2014) 36 *Human Rights Quarterly* 722, 724.

74 Judgement ST-349/1996 and Judgement 523/1997. See also E Sánches Botero, *Justicia y Pueblos Indígenas en Colombia: La Tutela Como Medio Para la Construcción del Entendimiento Intercultural* (Universidad Nacional de Colombia 2004).

of the *La Cocha* community, Cotopaxi province, in which the "internal" aspect of the conflict became the central legal question, thereby touching the core of the ongoing legal and political debate about the limits of indigenous jurisdiction and boundaries of formal legal pluralism. An in-depth technical legal analysis of this judgement goes beyond the scope of this chapter; however, in light of the analysis of the coordination law drafting processes, some elements are highlighted on pages 214–216.

6.1. Background

In this murder case, five young men of the neighbouring Guantópolo community were accused of killing Marco Olivo on Mother's Day in 2010. Even though this case was settled locally, it was appealed before the provincial Court of Justice and subsequently the Constitutional Court. Importantly, in 2002 indigenous authorities in *La Cocha* had for the first time settled a murder case in accordance with the indigenous justice system. This case then passed to the ordinary justice system, through the action of one of the affected parties. However, provincial Third Criminal Court judge, Carlos Poveda, declared the investigation of the public prosecutor, who presented a criminal charge, null and void, arguing that according to the "double jeopardy rule", he was not competent to adjudicate the case. The indigenous authorities had already settled the case in accordance with the 1998 constitution and ILO Convention 169. Even though the public prosecutor appealed, and the case ended with a conviction by the ordinary justice system, *La Cocha 1* was until 2014 an emblematic example of formal recognition of indigenous law by the ordinary justice system. The outcome of *La Cocha 2* was totally different.[75]

As mentioned on pages 215–216, the national media covering *La Cocha 2* labelled the indigenous trial and punishments as savage, barbaric and in violation of basic human rights. In addition, after public statements by President Correa, the Justice and Human Rights Ministry and the Attorney General's Office intervened and asked that the five people judged by the indigenous authorities be transferred to the ordinary justice system. In the context of this case, three parties resorted to the Court: first, the Third Criminal Court of Cotopaxi, which consulted the constitutionality of articles 33 and 217 of the Criminal Procedure Code; second, the individuals sanctioned by *La Cocha* indigenous authorities, who presented an extraordinary writ of protection; and finally, the President of the Republic, who requested the interpretation of article 171 of the constitution, arguing that the indigenous authorities lacked jurisdiction to hear criminal cases.[76]

75 For an in-depth analysis of both cases, see Thomas (n 12), 185–211 and C Poveda, 'La Cocha: 2002–2010 Retrocesos en un Estado Constitucional de Derechos, Justicia, Social, Democrático, Soberanía, Independiente, Unitario, Intercultural Plurinacional y Laico', (2010) *Novedades Jurídicas* 6.

76 Llasag (n 31), ibid., 344–345.

Four years after the murder, the Court issued a sentence, and its president said that the decision "marks a before and after in the validity and application of the constitution of the Republic of Ecuador in the field of the collective rights of indigenous communities, peoples and nationalities and the administration of justice".[77] However, the long silence and omission of the Court to emit a judgement is described by analysts as "an insidious way of resolving constitutional conflicts".[78]

The pressure on the Court to define the scope of application and the principles of formal legal pluralism as established in article 171 increased substantially in 2013, following the massacre of Tagaeri-Taromenane indigenous people living in voluntary isolation and the abduction of two surviving girls by the Waorani indigenous people in the Orellana province. This case, which also received extensive media coverage for months, generated a fierce debate amongst anthropologists, lawyers and justice operators on how to deal with this kind of conflict when the authors are indigenous peoples in initial contact, and revenge is part of their warrior culture. Confronted with a new socio-political controversy about indigenous justice, OHCHR in Ecuador facilitated a dialogue on this case between UN Special Rapporteur Anaya, several government institutions and the Ecuadorian Attorney General. In a March 2013 press release, Anaya stated that the case could not remain in impunity and requested that the government conduct a thorough investigation in collaboration with the Waorani people and with the support of anthropological experts.[79] At the same time, he asserted that an intercultural human rights perspective should prevail during the prosecution, and that the Waorani indigenous justice system regulations and procedures should be examined. In March 2014, at the request of the Attorney General, the Orellana Criminal Court judge sent a query to the Court regarding the applicability of the punishment, which was 16 to 25 years in prison, as set out in article 441 of the Penal Code. At the time of the consultation, 17 Waoranis had been prosecuted and six were in pre-trial detention. The Attorney General stated that "With this consultation we want to send a clear message to the Waorani people that we seek to understand their culture and that this area would be one of peace."[80] Prison is not part of Waorani norms and legal procedures. In this politically sensitive context, a pronouncement in *La Cocha 2* was imperative. Political, legislative, legal and academic parties agreed on the urgent need for Court clarification of the grey area in the interpretation of the scope of constitutional norms.

77 Constitutional Court Ecuador, 'Corte Constitucional del Ecuador Emite Sentencia en el Caso La Cocha', (2014) 058 *Boletin de Prensa* 1.

78 Santos (n 50) 43.

79 'Relator Especial Para los Derechos de los Pueblos Indígenas, Experto de la ONU Pide el Fin de la Violencia Entre Indígenas Tagaeri-Taromeane y Waorani' *Ginebra* (16 May 2013). <http://unsr.jamesanaya.org/statements/ecuador-experto-de-la-onu-pide-el-fin-de-la-violencia-entre-indigenas-tagaeri-taromenane-y-waorani> accessed 20 November 2017.

80 'El Caso Tagaeri-Taromenane, a Consulta a la CC' *El Comercio* (Ecuador 25 March 2014) <www.elcomercio.com/actualidad/seguridad/caso-tagaeri-taromenane-a-consulta.html> accessed 20 November 2017.

6.2. Restrictive view on material jurisdiction

As previously described, the political climate in which the Court had to act was considered by defenders of indigenous peoples' rights to be unfavourable for a proactive judgement in line with the further establishment of multicultural jurisprudence. It was therefore unsurprising that the Court followed the position of President Correa and Gustavo Jalkh and stipulated mandatory norms saying that

> the jurisdiction and power to hear, resolve and punish cases that endanger the lives of every person, remains exclusive to and the exclusive power of the System of Ordinary Criminal Law, including cases where suspects involved and alleged perpetrators are citizens belonging to indigenous communities, peoples and nationalities, when the events occur within the territorial scope of a community, people or indigenous nationality.

Moreover, the Court stated that the indigenous justice jurisdiction is limited to "knowing and resolving internal conflicts that occur amongst its members within its territorial scope and that affect their community values".

6.3. International human rights standards?

The Montecristi Constitution is innovative in that it stipulates that the state's international human rights obligations are not limited to international treaties but extend to international instruments (soft law) (articles 11.3, 93 and 426). In fact, regarding the role of public servants, which includes judges, article 426, notes that

> the judges, administrative authorities, and public servants shall directly apply constitutional standards and those provided for in international human rights instruments, as long as the latter are more favorable than those set forth in the Constitution, although the parties do not invoke them expressly. The rights enshrined in the Constitution and international human rights instruments shall be for immediate observance and enforcement.

Despite these constitutional provisions, in *La Cocha 2* the Court did not apply international human rights standards regarding the right of indigenous peoples to administer justice. In fact, the Court ordered that "The ordinary criminal justice authorities, in the prosecution and resolution of criminal cases involving indigenous citizens, shall apply the provisions of ILO Convention 169", but did not elaborate on the practical scope of this obligation. Moreover, the Court omitted any reference to various provisions of international human rights instruments in UNDRIP or to observations and general comments of UN treaty bodies, such as CERD and the Human Rights Committee, as well as reports and recommendations arising from the pronouncements of the UN Expert Mechanism, whose contribution has been instrumental in creating a common understanding on the scope and understanding of the collective rights of indigenous peoples recognized by the UN universal system. Nor did the Court refer to relevant past recommendations of the UN Special Rapporteur on the Rights of Indigenous Peoples. It is also surprising that the Court did not incorporate a comparative perspective by discussing relevant jurisprudence in other countries, including Colombia.

As per the Jurisdictional Guarantees and Constitutional Control Law, the Court requested two anthropological reports; one was prepared by Colombian anthropologist, Esther Sánchez, the other by Pedro Torres, an Ecuadorian priest. However, it is striking that the Court has not incorporated the findings of the extensive body of legal anthropological studies on grassroots-level coordination experiences in Ecuador.

In addition, the composition of Constitutional Court judges is worrying, as at the time of the ruling there were no indigenous judges. This landmark judgement, which will guide the country's future judicial policies on indigenous peoples' rights, was enacted by Western-mestizo judges, with no involvement by indigenous judges or experts.

7. Concluding remarks

At first glance, Ecuador's 2008 constitution, one of the most advanced constitutions in the world regarding the recognition of human rights and collective indigenous peoples' rights, appears to have the necessary legal ingredients to become a successful case of compliance with these norms. Consistent with the "empirical turn" in international legal research, this chapter explored answers to why, how and under what conditions Ecuador did or did not make progress during the Presidency of Rafael Correa (2008–2017), whose political movement co-wrote the Montecristi Constitution, in guaranteeing the effective enforcement of the right of indigenous peoples to administer indigenous justice.[81] It focused on the drafting process of a law to regulate the coordination and collaboration between the indigenous and ordinary jurisdictions, within the executive and legal power. The analysis also sought to contribute to a better understanding of the complexities inherent to the interactions between the domestic law formulation process, political struggles and historical power asymmetries. On closer examination, we conclude that the balance is negative, due to significant setbacks in the phase of implementation of constitutional and international human rights standards regarding the rights of indigenous peoples. The implementation of human rights norms is a state-led process that, in the case of Ecuador, comprises stakeholders with very divergent ideologies and political views. The analysis of Ecuador's attempts to legislate coordination and cooperation mechanisms between the indigenous and ordinary jurisdictions confirms that "it is an illusion

81 J Rachelinski, 'Evidence-based Law', (2011) 96 *Cornell Law Review* 901 and G Shaffer and G Ginsburg 'The Empirical Turn in International Legal Scholarship' (2012) 106 *The American Journal of International Law* 1.

that human rights are above politics".[82] In fact, human rights, and particularly indigenous rights, are often at the centre of political power struggles to determine their scope and content. In addition, it also demonstrates that the legal construction of power relationships, in this case the constitutional recognition of the equal footing of indigenous and ordinary jurisdictions, is not necessarily reflected in the actual power relationships.[83] Regarding the dearth of knowledge about the implementation gap on indigenous peoples' rights, future research projects should focus on two areas: firstly, increasing understanding about the interaction between political power struggles and state behaviour and practices and implications for the implementation of these rights, through a combination of classical legal methods and empirical socio-legal analysis, and secondly, promoting collaborative research with state institutions to create effective monitoring tools to quantitatively and qualitatively measure advances in the fulfilment of human rights obligations regarding indigenous peoples' rights.

In recent years, Ecuador's transformational constitutional project has undergone "processes of deconstitutionalization".[84] Moreover, the intention of the political majority to use the coordination and cooperation law to limit the jurisdiction and effective application of the right to administer indigenous justice is a setback for deep societal transformations. Also, the Constitutional Court's decision in the *La Cocha 2* case is not only a missed opportunity for the effective guarantee and adequate protection of this collective right, but also for the implementation of the Pluricultural and Intercultural state project.

A question remains, however: Would a law regulating the relationship between the indigenous and ordinary jurisdictions create the necessary conditions for a state to respect and protect the exercise of indigenous justice by indigenous authorities? It has been argued that legislating human rights claims into domestic law generally creates high and unmet expectations that the state will provide effective responses to social and economic problems.[85] Moreover, a law that regulates top-down coordination might create a strict dichotomy between the ordinary legal system and indigenous justice systems, while at the grassroots level, legal pluralism is marked by inter-legality or interconnectedness between ordinary and indigenous legal practices, which makes coordinating principles fluid.[86] At the same time, the discussions about this draft law also raised demands by the indigenous movement for financial resources to strengthen indigenous justice systems. Although indigenous jurisdiction currently stands on equal footing with ordinary justice, all state resources are assigned to the ordinary justice branch.

82 M Ignatieff, *Human Rights as Politics and Idolatry* (Princeton University Press 2001).

83 Von Benda-Beckmann (n 20) 5.

84 Santos (n 50) 16–17.

85 R Wilson, 'Tyrannosaurus Lex: The Anthropology of Human Rights and Transnational Law', in M Goodale and SE Merry (eds), *The Practice of Human Rights. Tracking Law Between the Global and the Local* (Cambridge University Press 2007) 352.

86 R Sieder, 'Introducción', in R Sieder and C Flores, *Vergüenza: Autoridad, Autonomía y Derechos Indígena en la Guatemala de Posguerra* (F&G Editores 2011) 68.

In this regard and in line with the recommendations of former Special Rapporteur James Anaya, this an important opportunity for the state to act upon the rights enshrined in the constitution and assign the necessary resources, thus protecting and strengthening indigenous jurisdiction so that, in accordance with their own mechanisms, indigenous authorities can undertake the necessary changes to be aligned with international human rights standards.

Faced with the reality of political conflicts regarding respect for indigenous justice practices, the current Special Rapporteur on the Rights of Indigenous Peoples, Victoria Tauli-Corpuz, has stressed that any potential conflicts that arise between the national legal system and indigenous justice systems must be jointly resolved by the state and indigenous peoples and with full respect for indigenous peoples' rights, as recognized in international human rights instruments.[87] This will not be an easy task given the historic power asymmetry between states and indigenous peoples, but is essential for closing the gap between international and domestic legal obligations and the effective fulfilment of indigenous peoples' rights.

87 Cited in, T Howland, 'Detener a Feliciano Valencia en la Cárcel Parece una Ficción de Kafka' *La Semana* (Colombia 22 October 2015) <www.semana.com/opinion/articulo/detencion-de-feliciano-valencia-viola-los-derechos-humanos-la-jurisdiccion-indigena/446996-3> accessed 20 November 2017.

Index

For Product Safety Concerns and Information please contact our EU representative GPSR@taylorandfrancis.com
Taylor & Francis Verlag GmbH, Kaufingerstraße 24, 80331 München, Germany

www.ingramcontent.com/pod-product-compliance
Ingram Content Group UK Ltd.
Pitfield, Milton Keynes, MK11 3LW, UK
UKHW021301190926
475701UK00009B/528
9780367481353